BLACK EDELWEISS

A MEMOIR OF COMBAT AND CONSCIENCE BY A SOLDIER OF THE WAFFEN-SS

JOHANN VOSS

THE ABERJONA PRESS
BEDFORD, PENNSYLVANIA

Technical Editor: Keith E. Bonn
Production: Patricia K. Bonn
Maps: Tom Houlihan
Printer: Mercersburg Printing

The Aberjona Press is an imprint of Aegis Consulting Group, Inc.,
    Bedford, Pennsylvania 15522
© 2002 Johann Voss
All rights reserved.
Printed in the United States of America
10 09 08 07   10 9 8 7

ISBN: 0-9666389-8-0
ISBN 13: 978-0-9666389-8-1

*To the soldiers of my regiment who were
killed in action in Northern Karelia, in the
Lower Vosges, and at the borders of the Reich*

Contents

EDITOR'S INTRODUCTION

Originally written while the author was a prisoner of the United States Army in 1945–46, *Black Edelweiss* is a boon to serious historians and WWII buffs alike. In a day in which most memoirs are written at half a century's distance, the former will be gratified by the author's precise recall facilitated by the chronologically short-range (a matter of one to seven years) at which the events were captured in writing. Both will appreciate and enjoy the abundantly detailed, exceptionally accurate combat episodes.

Even more than the strictly military narrative, however, the author has given us a searingly candid view into his own mind and soul. As such, *Black Edelweiss* is much more than a "ripping yarn" or a low-level military history. It has important sociological uses as well.

Since its publication in *Public Opinion Quarterly* in the summer of 1948, "Cohesion and Disintegration in the Wehrmacht in World War II" by Edward Shils and Morris Janowitz has been the benchmark on which practically all serious inquiries into German soldiers' motivation have been based. Although subsequent scholarship has effectively disputed some relatively minor aspects of the study, former OSS interrogators (and later, University of Chicago professors) Shils and Janowitz unquestionably hit the mark with their fundamental, crucial, conclusions.

Essentially, Shils and Janowitz found that most German soldiers fought so long and so fiercely, without reasonable hope of victory, due to the continuing existence of primary groups (companies, platoons, squads) that were able to fulfill those soldier's elemental social requirements. These primary groups were preserved by leadership that was committed to their soldiers' welfare and discipline through a deeply embedded sense of soldierly honor. This sense of honor demanded that leaders be professionally fit and competent, that they share hardship with their men, and that they lead by example. Finally, even through the staggering casualties often sustained by German units, organizational integrity was maintained by what Shils and Janowitz dubbed the "hard core" of young men "who had had a gratifying adolescence in the most rewarding period of National Socialism." Such soldiers were "imbued with the ideology of *Gemeinschaft* (community solidarity)," "were enthusiasts for the military life," and "placed a very high value on 'toughness', manly comradeliness, and group solidarity." They found that, "The presence of a few such men in the group, zealous, energetic, and unsparing of themselves, provided models for weaker men and facilitated the process of identification." The authors concluded that, "The fact that the elite SS divisions and paratroop divisions had a larger "hard core" than other divisions of the army—so large as to embrace almost the entire group membership during most of the war—accounted for their greater fighting effectiveness."

There has never been a stronger anecdotal validation of Shils' and Janowitz's study than *Black Edelweiss*.

Other German soldiers' memoirs have appeared before this one, of course, and the historiography of this genre is important to understand. From the 1950s through most of the 1980s, the memoirs of higher-level commanders and staff officers predominated. These memoirs shed great light on operational and strategic issues, but were also almost invariably influenced by the need to protect reputations, explain away failure, and so on—much like some of the American military literature which appeared after the Vietnam War, and which continues to this day.

Lower level, that is, tactical and individual, memoirs appeared more slowly for a variety of reasons. First, there was a robust genre of German historical fiction that had a great following, mostly among German post-war generations. Since these were popular and commercially successful in and outside of Germany, and since real memoirs would, in many cases, conflict with their expressed *Weltanschauungen*, the latter simply did not appear. There has also long been a politico-social stigma attached to German WWII veterans throughout several important and influential sectors of post-war German society, and the vast majority of veterans simply chose to remain publicly silent about their experiences. Production of genuine memoirs for a non-German, therefore primarily English-speaking, audience was made difficult by a host of challenges, from the simple establishment of communication to the weightier commercial issues of copyright, translation, and so forth.

The explosion of interest in the Second World War in the 1990s brought about by, *inter alia*, fiftieth anniversary commemorations, the impact of the special effects of Steven Spielberg's "Saving Private Ryan," various popular history works by Stephen Ambrose, and Tom Brokaw's *The Greatest Generation* have combined to create an unprecedented burst of new literature about the war. The commercial corollaries have shattered barriers to publication of memoirs from both sides, at least in the English-speaking world. Commencing in the last decade of the twentieth century, an avalanche of personal memoirs have appeared in print, probably also due to the widespread availability of word-processing capabilities and inexpensive binding techniques.

There is great variety within these memoirs, and this is true for the German ones as well as others. With the exception of a few mid-grade officers' works (such as *From Normandy to the Ruhr*, by the now eighty-seven-year-old Heinz Günther Guderian), those appearing recently have mostly been written by lower-ranking officers and enlisted men, mainly because it is this echelon of veteran which has survived to this point. In addition to Guderian's work, over the past three years, The Aberjona Press alone has published two other German memoirs, and they are very different indeed from *Black Edelweiss*. In *Five Years, Four Fronts*, Georg Grossjohann told us about life as a "typical" wartime German Army officer who rose from the enlisted ranks to command at the platoon, company, battalion, and regimental levels in a series of regular infantry divisions that constituted the backbone of the German Armed Forces in WWII.* In *Seven Days in January*, former *Waffen-SS* officer Wolf Zoepf chose to construct a straight battle history, based on his own recollections, but also on archival sources and interviews with dozens of his own comrades, as well as with dozens of his former adversaries of the US 70th Infantry Division—of whose veterans' association he was an honorary member.

Black Edelweiss joins not only the growing body of German military memoirs, but the more select, more narrowly-focused group of personal memoirs by other *Waffen-SS* enlisted men. Beyond the microcosmic view of combat such books relate, to the extent that they are honest and candid, they are important for what they can reveal about their authors' motivations and reflections on those impulses and their consequences. To date, these works differ significantly.

One, written in the mid-late 1970s but only published in the 1990s, tells of the author's horrid, brutalized childhood and subsequent completely slavish submission to authority. It is filled with regret for having served as a *Waffen-SS* soldier and with sufficient scatological references to fascinate a psychologist of any stripe . . . in fact, the book's conclusion includes a brief psychoanalytical summary of the veteran's mental condition. That such a man fought to the end of the war certainly validates a number of Shils' and Janowitz's arguments, if perhaps from an unusual and disturbing perspective. Unfortunately, although the book was edited by accredited scholars, it lacks intrinsic proof of authenticity (photos, documentation, and so on), and may not, therefore, be accepted by some as totally reliable.

Another recently released work is a lavishly produced, privately-published affair that could easily have been written by one of the more vicious members of Goebbels' staff. Bitter, accusatory, and openly anti-Semitic, the author validates the most unfavorable possible stereotype of *Waffen-SS* soldiers. That it was privately published does not, by itself, limit its credibility—one of the most important books about the Vietnam War and its social aftermath, *Stolen Valor*, was published under the same circumstances. The latter's painstakingly researched evidence of media irresponsibility and dishonesty

---

* That Grossjohann earned the Knight's Cross along the way was certainly atypical.

on the part of numerous well-known personalities was too "hot" for any commercial publisher to touch. Similarly, the content of this particular *Waffen-SS* veteran's work was certainly too vile and incendiary for any such publisher to produce. Nevertheless, the work appears to be authentic, and is as such probably a valid part of the genre. If there is a limitation to this book's credibility, it is that the author adamantly refuses to come to terms with indisputable realities (not least, the Holocaust) and may not, therefore, have written his memoir in a completely rational frame of mind.

A third book which has only very recently appeared, also by way of private publication, provides a different perspective still. Although authenticated by documents and photos in a rather general way, the book portrays its subject's experience as a *Waffen-SS* junior enlisted man and, briefly, junior noncommissioned officer, in the last year of the Second World War as part of a narrative depicting his life overall. Thus, the book includes only a brief section about service in the *Waffen-SS*, and this precludes detailed coverage of the author's military experiences or the circumstances surrounding them. Interestingly, although the book is written in the first-person voice, credit for authorship is given to another party entirely, who was apparently very influential in the book's final form. This unusual arrangement results in the best English prose of the three, but in some ambiguities and vagaries of military subjects in general, and terminology in particular. As a result, this *Waffen-SS* veterans' story is more the biography of a human being who led an interesting, sometimes volatile, and ultimately robust spiritual life, but for whom military service was only a blurry chapter among many that appear to be more sharply focused.

As it joins the ranks of the books in this genre, *Black Edelweiss* makes a unique and very important contribution. It was conceived and, for the most part, written a long time ago, when the author was a prisoner of war in the custody of the United States Army from March 1945 to December 1946. During the ensuing decades, the idea of editing and publishing the manuscript never occurred to him; the war and what followed were closed chapters in his life. The subject surfaced only when President Ronald Reagan, Chancellor Helmut Kohl, and Generals Matthew Ridgway and Johannes Steinhoff visited the German military cemetery in Bitburg, West Germany, in 1985. This visit raised protests in many quarters because the remains of some young *Waffen-SS* enlisted men were buried there. Conducting a conciliatory ceremony in such a location was widely regarded as outrageous. Over the ensuing years, the author was moved to resurrect his journal and seek its publication because he felt that his story was probably representative of the ones that the muted voices of the roundly reviled *Waffen-SS* dead of Bitburg could not tell for themselves.

Black Edelweiss is a personal account of the author's war years, first at school and then with the *Waffen-SS*, which he joined early in 1943 at the age of seventeen. For a year and a half, the author fought as a machine gunner in SS-Mountain Infantry Regiment 11 "Reinhard Heydrich," mainly in the arctic and sub-arctic reaches of Soviet Karelia and Finland, and later at the Western frontier of the Third Reich. Although he has changed most of their names, the characters in the story are real, and the conversations and actions are recounted to the best of his ability from the short distance at which he wrote the manuscript in 1945–46.

The author is a loyal member of his unit's veterans' group, and his *bona fides* as a soldier are impeccable. Before we agreed to publish this book, to the extent possible, his accounts of action against elements of the US Army's 45th and 94th Infantry Divisions were vetted against primary source documents in the National Archives, by examination of published unit histories, and by interviews with American veterans who fought against the author's unit. Especially extensive research has been carried out by Lieutenant Colonel Hugh Foster, US Army (Retired) with hundreds of American survivors of their savage battle against the author's unit at Reipertswiller, Alsace, in January 1945. All of the author's recollections have squared with the available evidence. From every bit of archival and anecdotal information it has been possible to collect, the author's pride in his unit's wartime record and battlefield conduct is fully justified. Apart from the piercing insights into the question of why the German soldier fought as he did, the author's anguished, yet resolute examination of the dialectic between the honorable comportment of his unit and the fundamentally reprehensible conduct of other non-combat groups behind the front lines who wore the same uniform makes this book unique. His conclusions make it invaluable.

The author has officially written this book under a *nom de plume*, but not for the usual reasons. He is by no means afraid of repercussions which may eventually arise as a result of the publication of this book; the wartime photos of him, his relatives, and his comrades are all authentic, and anyone who cares enough to find out his identity will be able to do so without much effort. His surviving comrades will recognize him instantly. The real points of the author's insistence on using a pen name are more complex and unusual.

During his captivity, the author was assigned for a time as a clerk to a US Army Judge Advocate General's Corps officer, and in the performance of his administrative duties, the author had access to the mounting reams of documentation of the Holocaust. His growing recognition of *Waffen-SS* personnel involved in the monstrous crimes of that process caused him to dig deeply into his soul, to examine his most intimate and private motivations and thoughts, and to confront the most basic assumptions of his life to that point.

The author captured this process and the result in the notes that became this book, and thus metamorphosed into a different person. The book, however, still remained the account of a young man–with all his romanticism, his anger, and his search for guidance into an uncertain future. After the war, the author enjoyed a rewarding and successful professional life as a corporate lawyer with various international ties. Indeed, perhaps presaging his ultimate professional calling, this book may be seen in large part as a plea for judgment of *Waffen-SS* veterans as individuals, rather than as universally condemned members of a huge criminal cartel. Even that appeal, however, is accompanied by the realistic assessment of the future advocate; he recognizes, and even intellectually comprehends, the unlikely prospects of such a gossamer hope.

Despite wide reading of World War II history during his post-war life, the author chose not to follow the advice of some others to rewrite his prisoner's manuscript from the "enhanced" perspectives of a fully mature man of much broader learning. Such a balanced view of the past, based on so many decades of experience, travel, and reading, in particular about the crimes committed by German units behind the frontlines in the East, seemed inappropriate for the voices of those combat soldiers—such as the ones at Bitburg—who did not have the privilege to learn and grow, but rather took their limited perception of the world with them to their graves. Thus, by publishing the recollections and thoughts of the young veteran he was in 1945–46, the author feels it would be not only inappropriate, but *dishonest* to do so under the name of the much more educated, world-wise man he is today.

Honestly, forthrightly, and courageously told, *Black Edelweiss* is a precious gift to historians and other students of World War II. It not only starkly reinforces so many of Shils' and Janowitz's conclusions, but it expands on them and, in concert with other, similarly candid German WWII-era memoirs that are appearing only now, it allows us to put a more human, more comprehensible, face on the original study's impersonal and rigorous scientific construct.

Of perhaps even greater importance for soldiers and citizens today, *Black Edelweiss* vividly illuminates how well brought up, educated, thinking citizens can be manipulated into serving some very dark ends. Without explicitly addressing it, this book proves that even when some of the darkness leaks past the carefully polished and meticulously maintained veneer, skilled propagandists can still fool and exploit good people. The distance from the strident exhortations and exhilarating martial music of *Volksempfänger* during the Third Reich to today's endless barrage of spin spewed every half hour from telescreens in most every home, school, and public place may not be as great as we smugly think.

PREFACE

This book was conceived and for the most part written a long time ago. I was then a prisoner of the US Army from March 1945 to December 1946. The idea of editing and publishing the manuscript had never crossed my mind in the following decades. The war and what followed were a closed chapter. The subject surfaced only when President Reagan and Chancellor Kohl visited the German military cemetery in Bitburg, Germany, in 1985. This visit raised worldwide protests, namely because some young *Waffen-SS* soldiers were buried there. Including these soldiers in the memorial ceremony was widely regarded as an outrageous affair. Since then the indiscriminate damnation of *Waffen-SS* soldiers has become even more pervasive and intransigent. Apparently, in the sixty years since those soldiers fell in battle, the rubble, which the collapsing *Reich* heaped upon the course of their short lives, was not removed.

The book is a personal account of my war years, first at school and then with the *Waffen-SS*, which I joined early in 1943 at the age of seventeen. I saw combat with the 11th *Gebirgsjäger* (Mountain Infantry) Regiment for a year and a half, mainly in the far north and later at the western frontier of the *Reich*. For all the differences in theaters of war, troops, and personal backgrounds, however, I think that this book is also about the volunteers of my age group in general; about their thinking and feeling; about their faith and their distress; and about their endeavors to live up to their ideals, even when hope was lost.

My regiment was part of the 6th *SS-Gebirgsdivision* (Mountain Division) *Nord*, which fought from the summer of 1941 until September 1944 in the wilderness of the North Karelian front, near the Arctic Circle. The division belonged to the German 20th *Gebirgsarmee* (Mountain Army), which defended the northern half of the Finnish-German front, a line stretching some 900 miles from the Arctic Sea down to the Gulf of Finland. When Finland quit the war in September 1944 and the 20th Army had to leave the country, the *Nord* became the rear guard of the southern Corps and fought its way along the Finnish-Swedish border up to northern Norway. In the bitter cold and darkness of the Arctic winter, my regiment marched down the Norwegian coast until it reached the railway at Mo i Rana, ending a trek of some 1,000 miles. Rushed to Oslo by train, and after a few days rest in Denmark, we moved to the Western front, where the *Nord* participated in Operation *NORDWIND* in early January 1945, a bloody clash with the US Seventh Army in the snow-covered hills of the Lower Vosges. In the battles and the war of attrition that followed, the frontline units of the *Nord* were destroyed bit by bit. When the front reached the Rhine in March 1945, only remnants of the division remained. The rest was annihilated in the hills northeast of Frankfurt on 3 April, just after Easter.

I had no intention of writing military history, a field in which I am no expert. Instead, I have chronicled combat the way I saw it, from the perspective of an average soldier who, more often than not, lacked an overview of the general situation, but who was intimately familiar with life (and death) in the foxholes. What I wanted to do was to portray these young volunteers under arduous physical and mental conditions and to show how they reacted. Likewise, the characters of my story are real, to include those in my family as well as in my unit, but I have changed their names. They stand for a European youth who, at that time, saw themselves actively united in an effort to resolve a secular conflict between the Occident and Bolshevism.

Since that time I have enjoyed a rich professional life as a corporate lawyer with various international ties. My desire to understand the historical, political, and moral aspects of World War II has always been there, however, resulting in my reading of a wealth of material and then grappling with its inherent drawbacks and inconsistencies. I chose not to follow the advice of some, to rewrite the prisoner's manuscript from the perspective of a man of my age. Such a balanced view of the past, based on so many decades of experience, traveling, and reading, in particular about the crimes committed behind the frontlines in the East, seemed inappropriate for the voices of those combat soldiers who did not live to mature and grow, but instead had to die young in their limited perception of the world. The same notion applies to those who survived and found themselves, at that age, indicted and convicted as members of a criminal organization.

My generation's task was to clear away the ruins of the war and to rebuild our country. As I said before, however, there is still much rubble left. If this book would uncover a small part of that long-hidden ground, I would have done my part for my comrades.

—Johann Voss

Acknowledgments

This book wouldn't have reached the first stage of publication without "Ducker's" scholarly help; he was the first to read the manuscript, concluding with the advice to cut the original text in half. Steve, my young friend in the US Army, Ranger and writer, proved himself a constant source of encouragement during the period the manuscript was floating in the doldrums. I deem myself lucky to have found at last Kit and his wife, Patti, as empathetic publishers who not only were great editors but, by their relentless efforts, created from my text a real book. It was Wolf, my comrade of past days and my late friend, who brought us together; he wasn't to live to see this book—nor his own—appear in print. Hugh, staunch Vietnam veteran, professional soldier, and friend, walked the Reipertsweiler battle ground with me, terrain he is so much more familiar with than I; together we could clarify important points. Tom Houlihan contributed the illuminating maps; working with him via e-mail was pure fun. I very much appreciate the gracious permission of Richard Warfield of Everett Books, Gaithersburg, Maryland, for use of his privately-owned photos. I am also indebted to the management at Munin Verlag for permission to use certain photos which originally appeared in *Gebirgsjäger im Bild* by Alfred Steurich. I am especially grateful to Ken Nieman of Brookfield, Wisconsin, for his very kind permission to use the photo which appears on the cover of this book. I also very much appreciate the contribution of Ron Wolin who allowed the image of the Edelweiss badge from his truly world-class collection to be so prominently displayed on the cover of this book. All of them I want to thank very much—not least Marit for her patience with which she endured the many hours I took from our joint time of retirement.

A Guide to Tactical Unit Symbols

Types of Units

American,
Finnish,   German
or Soviet

⊠	⊠	Infantry
⊠	⊠	Mountain Infantry
⊞	⊞	Medical
☦	☦	Machine Gun Section

Example

3d Battalion,
SS-Mountain Infantry
Regiment 11

3 11

Sizes of Units

•	Squad
••	Section
•••	Platoon
I	Company/Battery/Troop
II	Battalion/Squadron
III	Regiment
X	Brigade/Group/Combat Command
XX	Division
XXX	Corps
XXXX	Army
XXXXX	Army Group

1

ROMILLY

It has been raining for the last two weeks with only a few breaks. The bituminous main road on the huge camp site is wet and shining. Inside our cage, the paths are sodden; large puddles are everywhere. Gusts of wind sweeping across the plains of Champagne make the canvas of our tents heave and jerk at their ropes. The few sunbeams during the day do not warm the heart; they shed a pale light on the rows of tents and the watchtowers that stand out sharply against the ragged sky. No, there is no joy in this autumn for us prisoners of war. It is not so much the bad weather that matters, but rather the being locked out from nature in this camp on the Seine River. There are no woods around this barren place; no leaves whirling through the air, settling on the ground like a red-brown blanket; no bonfires with their sweet smell; and, of course, no house with a fireplace to sit by and calmly wait for winter.

On this late afternoon of October 1945, on my way back to my tent, something else is on my mind, something I saw on the bulletin board outside the administration building: a public announcement of an International Military Tribunal set up by the Four Powers, where a number of war crimes will be prosecuted in a trial that is to begin at Nürnberg on 20 November.

Pete and Walther, my two companions of the last six months, lie on their cots in the clammy and cheerless atmosphere of our tent. Pete is a German medic from Hamburg; Walther a student from Vienna. Pete is explaining to Walther what he is reading in the *Stars and Stripes*. I am in no mood to join them and talk. I need to think about the announcement and its meaning for my comrades—the living and the dead. It's something I must sort out for myself.

I am just one of them, one of the thousands of soldiers who have been pouring into this camp since May, pouring out of innumerable trucks and trains, seasoned soldiers who on their campaigns with the German Army have seen France, Greece, Norway, Sicily, North, Africa, and, of course, the Russian swamps and wide plains. Younger ones like me who, after two or more years of service, are veterans, too. There are also those who managed to remain in occupied regions or in the rear, far away from combat, and others, like me, whose lot was less favorable. Even those who had no part in the fighting are stranded here. Among them boys, fifteen or sixteen years of age; old men in their forties or fifties, the last reserve who may have been caught with a uniform and a helmet on; party officials, a few still in their brown uniforms that had never won prestige except among themselves; and even some women and girls, all swept ashore on this site by the huge tide following Germany's surrender in early May.

When asked about my service record, I just tell them I'd been a machine gunner in a mountain infantry regiment. It's not the whole story. True, my regiment fought under the *Edelweiss*, the alpine flower and symbol of the mountain troops; but it fought also under the silver runes, the symbols that now stand for all the unspeakable crimes that came to light when the war ended. Since we came here in May to put up a hospital cage in this corner of the camp, reports of large-scale atrocities and mass killings kept coming in, too. There were rumors at first, then more and more newspaper articles, and, in particular, pictures of concentration camps liberated in the course of the defeat, horrible photographs gazed at in disbelief by the prisoners of war: human beings, nearly or definitely starved to death, hundreds of them. They are ghost-like skeletons, their frozen stare from their deep eye sockets one searing accusation, or just mere heaps of stiffened skins and bones with open mouths that seemed to be still wailing. In the agonizing hours, especially at night, when haunted by those pictures, I realize all these people have been held in the custody of men who wore the uniform I wore myself, and that from then on the silver runes will symbolize the guilt for what has been unearthed and still might come to light.

Now, today, I see more clearly how things will go. Aside from the political and military leadership of the *Reich*, the whole *SS*, including the combat units of the *Waffen-SS*, will be indicted as a criminal organization, charged with various war crimes. I don't fully grasp the meaning of all those accusations, but I understand that we will all be held responsible for the terrible things that have become known. The members of these organizations will be prosecuted and convicted according to the provisions of the Charter of the Tribunal. So, it is official now: we are regarded as a gang of criminals.

This news, in black and white, comes as a blow, doubling the shock already caused by the news of the crimes themselves. The men of my unit were front-line soldiers, a band of volunteers who believed in the justness of the cause and fought impeccably for our country. Can one think of a greater offense against the honor of a military unit than to be called a gang of criminals? Isn't it grotesque to see this idealism transmogrified into sheer monstrousness?

It was early in March, on our third day as prisoners, when we were first treated with loathing. For two days, we had been in the custody of American front-line infantry troops.[*] Encircled by my own regiment, our captors and the few of us who had survived were enduring round after round of our own artillery in the cellar of a farmhouse, sharing US C-rations, both sides uncertain who would be whose prisoner the next day. As soon as the Americans had forced their way through our lines, however, they carried us off at break-neck speed to the rear echelon where the frisking and interrogation began. The first thing we lost were all the outer signs of our pride: the *Edelweiss* emblems, the collar-patches, the cuff-bands embroidered with the name of our regiment.[†] They took all our watches and they took my ring with my family's coat of arms—one of their officers indifferently looking on, impassive as a stone.

Then the interrogation began. I was called into the tent first. The interrogator spoke German fluently with a slight Austrian accent. My answers were by the book: name, rank, and—since it was on my cuff title—regiment. Things got tough when I withheld further information on our whereabouts during the last weeks and months, naively relying on the Hague Convention, which protects the prisoner of war's refusal to reveal military secrets. It was an unheard of impudence; my interrogator shouted and jeered that our troops were known for all kinds of atrocities, for shooting American prisoners in particular; our rights under the Convention were totally forfeited and that they knew of ways to make us speak. I heard the name of Malmédy and gathered that US prisoners had been shot there by a combat group of the *1st SS-Panzer Division*, the *Leibstandarte Adolf Hitler*. So that was why they wanted to know where each of us had been during the months before. For the time being, I

---

[*]Many years later, I learned that these were from the US 94th Infantry Division.
[†]Our regimental title, "Reinhard Heydrich," was awarded to us in 1942 after Heydrich was assassinated by a Czech commando in Prague. Heydrich became *Reichsprotektor* in Prague in 1941. Before that, he was chief of the Security Police ("*Sicherheitsdienst*," or "*SD*") and organized the *Endlösung*, the project of exterminating the European Jews. In view of this knowledge of the post-war years, the regiment's title was nothing to be proud of—*Author.*

was pushed out, the next of my comrades pushed in, and the same procedure began all over again.

Ten of us were assembled. We were shoved into a stable and ordered to line up along a brick wall. Two guards stood in front, brandishing their rifles, fingers at the triggers. Two sharp commands rang out: hands up behind your necks, turn about, face the wall—all of which was made unmistakably clear to us. The bolts of their rifles slammed shut. I thought, "This is the way to make us speak. They'll shoot one of us and squeeze out information from the rest. But no information about our whereabouts can be that important, and they can't possibly risk of shooting one and have nine witnesses to a war crime. All of us then? No, that wouldn't make sense either."

We waited for whatever might happen. Then a sharp command by another voice, something I didn't understand. Another click of the rifle bolts. We turned around, and prodded by the high-pitched yells of the guards "C'mon, C'mon!" we were driven into a wooden shack where we spent the night like frozen sardines chilled to the bone.

One or two weeks later, we became the target of a raging mob in Luxembourg. Miserable days lay behind us, days I can only partly recollect under the veil of my own specific misery. Hungry, stiff with cold, and without anything to keep us warm, we vegetated on the tiled floors of some deserted barracks at temperatures about zero degrees Celsius.* I had contracted a really bad inflammation of the bladder, which resulted in almost total incontinence. No medical treatment was available, and the shame of wet and foul-smelling pants added humiliation to my physical pain. Then followed the transport to Luxembourg on open trucks along the winding roads of the hill country, our lunatic drivers keeping one foot on the accelerator, the other left dangling outside. Finally came the triumphal procession of the convoy of captured *Waffen-SS* soldiers through the city, the narrow streets thronged with angry people. Again and again, they threw bricks at us; we quickly retaliated with used C-ration cans, full of urine.

At the large square in front of the main station, another crowd was awaiting us. We had to cross the square to continue our journey by train. The guards opened a gap through the crowd. As more trucks arrived, the more restless the mob became. We heard threatening shouts and jeers in French and in German. People in front feasted their eyes on our humiliation and threw stones. As we marched through the crowd, the mob surged towards the center, hurling stones at us as we hurried through the gap. The shouting increased and was mixed with the now-anxious high-pitched yelling of the guards. Meanwhile, the guards had turned their backs to protect us against

*32 degrees Fahrenheit.

further assaults of the mob that kept dangerously pushing forward. Military police rushed to the scene just in time, their noisy arrival alone bringing the mass to a halt. We reached the station platform more or less unhurt.

I was still naive and would need some more explicit warning before I'd realize that however bad conditions for all of us already were, things for the soldiers of the *Waffen-SS* would get worse. The warning came from a seasoned Army *Feldwebel* one day at the former French Army post at Mailly-de-Camp, where we had been dumped from the cattle wagons of the train from Luxembourg. It was a huge camp, divided into numerous cages. Brought into one of them, we immediately dispersed ourselves among the crowd of prisoners who were milling around. Rations were so meager at Mailly-de-Camp that even the younger and healthier ones among us knew we were likely to die of starvation if things didn't improve over the next few weeks.

Once a day, at lunch-time, milk-soup was served in large cauldrons. Although thin, it contained at least some solid substance. The tent crews gathered round the various cauldrons, watching the extraordinary ritual of handing out the soup, a procedure supposed to check the wolfish, all-pervasive greed. A person thought to be trustworthy would with each helping guide the scoop through the cauldron in an artful three-dimensional figure eight, to ensure that any solid matter would be caught at random; the slightest deviation would immediately cause angry murmurs.

I was standing in the background with an Army *Feldwebel*. I liked his neat appearance and his obvious contempt for the scene before us. "Son," he said softly after a while, "If I were you I'd get rid of that uniform of yours. Soon as possible!"

"Why?" I asked, somewhat annoyed.

He shot glances at my left cuff, then at my collar, then at my right sleeve where the insignia of my unit had left faded patches on the fabric—unmistakable signs of a former member of the *Waffen-SS*. "Let me tell you," he said, "they've started to search the camp for you guys to separate you from the others. The search is already well under way in other cages. Don't make it too easy for them."

He noticed my hesitation and my dislike of the idea.

"Say, are you anxious to stand trial as a war criminal and to be sentenced to forced labor? You want ten years behind barbed wire? I wouldn't spend too much time thinking."

With that he pulled me along to his tent. "Come on, son, I'll let you have another jacket. It should fit you. Belonged to one of the boys in my tent. They took him away this morning. Didn't make it, poor guy."

From then on, I wore the blue jacket of the *Fallschirmjäger* (paratroopers). It wasn't a day I was proud of, but I had been warned, and I told Heinrich who was still with me. He followed my example. Heinrich was my comrade and companion from the beginning to the end. We would soon be separated, however. One morning another roll call was ordered. We were lined up in several blocks; the old military discipline still functioned. A German-speaking American officer called up various units of the former German Armed Forces by name and ordered us to assemble in groups by unit. When a parachute regiment was called, I quickly went over to the group belonging to that unit, pulling Heinrich with me.

It was a hot day, and the process was drawing out. So we were happy when the order came to take off our coats and shirts and line up in rows. Eventually, the segregation began. Two American sergeants went along the rows ordering with a wave of the hand each PW to lift up his left arm. Their purpose was clear enough: they were looking for blood-group tattoos in the armpit, the distinguishing marks of the members of the *Waffen-SS*. Many a sinner was selected this way. Heinrich was among them. All of them were waved over to a group assembled under an extra guard.

As luck would have it, I had never gotten that tattoo. I was on a one-day pass when our training company in the Alps underwent the procedure; my father had come for a surprise visit on his way from the Eastern Front to Italy. Later on, the matter had been forgotten.

———>●<———

Now I am in this hospital cage, serving as an interpreter. It is my duty to accompany the German doctors and their American superiors on their daily visits through the wards set up in a row of eleven tents. Sometimes I am taken out in a jeep with one of our doctors to another cage. But I have never gone to the war criminal cage, which lies at the opposite corner of the camp. I saw it only from a distance, the last time two months ago. There was shouting as on a parade ground, and we saw squads of PWs running about. The guard said it was normal routine in US Army penitentiaries to keep the convicts running all day long, and the punishment for the slightest misdemeanor was draconian. They say the inmates of that cage are members of the *Waffen-SS*, and they will have to stand trial at Nürnberg. Only rumors? Two weeks ago they cleared out, their destination unknown.

———>●<———

I keep telling myself that it would have been pointless to have reported to the camp officer and asked to be transferred to that cage. Here, in the hospital cage, I could at least be of some help, as in the case of an *Untersturmführer* of my regiment who turned up here months ago in a desperate state of health and to whom I could slip a loaf of bread as a first-aid measure. At night on my field cot, however, when reason wavers and sentiment takes over, I keep thinking of Heinrich.

A few days after the segregation, I spotted him at some distance in the cage next to mine, which was separated by a lane of barbed wire in which the Czech guards pace up and down. I cannot forget seeing him in that other cage, a forlorn figure standing apart from the crowd. I waved, I shouted, but he did not respond. Did he recognize me against the glaring sun? I do not know. I have not heard of him since.

Darkness has fallen on the camp on this chilly October day. The wind has died down. Our tent has filled with other men of our hospital staff. According to some silent understanding, my wish to be left alone is being respected. My thoughts wander from those indicted as criminals back to the dead, to those who are buried beneath crosses and life runes in our cemeteries by the Arctic Circle, and to all the others lying dispersed in the soil of the Low Vosges and the hills west of the Rhine. They, too, were members of "the troop," hence were implicitly criminals and are sharing the general indictment. Have they died in disgrace, so far in time and distance from the crimes we are hearing about? How should I know? I, an indictable criminal myself!

Again, as so many times before, I return to my memories of our past, a past which is, they say, our burden of guilt and shame. In spite of all the terrible reports connected with our name, however, I cling to my memories with affection and without regret. They are, indeed, my comfort and refuge, almost a sanctuary where I am safe: safe from drowning in the sea of hatred and accusations; safe from the loss of self-respect and pride; safe from that ultimate surrender. For there is nothing monstrous in my memories of our unit's past, no acts of crime or shameful deeds, or even knowledge of the wicked deeds. What I have seen is the commitment of youth who, in good faith, believed that Bolshevism was their common foe; a cause that in their eyes was noble, even greater than mere patriotism because it united young patriots from many countries of Europe. Their selflessness knew no bounds, not even the boundary of death, as if the fate of Europe was depending on them, on the individual volunteers as well as on their combat groups and on the unit as a whole.

Our past—it is the time when the war began and we grew up, when our country was in great distress, the time we volunteered to do our utmost, and the time of combat in the mountains and in the woods. It is a past consisting only of a few years, but in which so much happened; these few years that were the life, doom, and ruin of a battalion of mountain infantrymen who first fought in the far North and later on the Western Front; the time when loss and death pervaded our ranks and when, in spite of all the sacrifices, we came to see that what we fought for was lost.

True, there were also moments of doubt during that time, moments when I felt there was a dark, sinister side of the *Reich*: the moment of my first encounter with Russian prisoners of war on the station of my home town; certain warnings from my father; the incident with the Jews on my way to Finland. These doubts also belong to that past. They now return as the disturbing question whether I should have "seen the signs" earlier on—a question I have to face even if it is of little consequence except for my own sake.

2

THE HOUSE BY THE MOUNTAINS

Early one morning in mid-September 1938, at the age of thirteen, the first thing I sensed was the soft scraping sound of gravel being raked in the garden. The bedroom I was sharing with Nick, my elder brother, was in the attic with a view of the forest stretching uphill from across the street. We were staying in my grandmother's house for a weekend during our autumn break: my parents, my sister, my two brothers, and me. The half-timbered house was large and charming, country style. Hearing that familiar sound, I felt an exuberant joy and expectation as it evoked so many happy summer vacations at this place and made me recall that today was Mummi's (my maternal grandmother's) sixty-fifth birthday.

Bright patches of sunlight were dancing on the wall opposite the open window, promising another warm day. I jumped out of bed and in pure bliss looked down where old Brakel, Mummi's gardener, was busy with his rake on the bend leading from the gate to the house. Eager to impress with an immaculate appearance of the property on such a day, he was drawing fine parallel lines with his rake on the thick layer of yellow-brown gravel.

Stena, my mother's younger sister, leaned over the parapet of the loggia; clad in her light blue dress and a white apron, she looked up to examine the weather. "Hey, you!" she shouted when she spotted me. "Good morning! Come down. You can make yourself useful and help me set the table. I think we'll have breakfast on the loggia."

"Coming!" I shouted back. A little later I was down on the open-sided extension of the house with its checkered floor tiles and its lavish white garden furniture.

Right here, by the house, the woodland of the Harz begins, stretching over the mountains and ending eighty miles to the south. The forest—from its

mosses and ferns, its brooks and streams—exudes a strong smell of an amaz-
ing freshness, comforting and invigorating, so familiar to us whenever we
returned to the Bruckmann's house at Hardenburg.

Stena's realm was the household. Unmarried like her older sister Eda, she
lived with Mummi. Down at the loggia, the two of us were setting the table
with special care on this particular day, laying out the white-and-blue china
on white linen, flanked by ample silverware, and accompanied by an abundance of flowers. What later arrived on the table was rather modest in comparison: bread and rolls; butter; several kinds of jams and jellies, all home-
made; and, of course, hot steaming coffee with cream. Meals with the
Bruckmann's were a welcome opportunity for a pleasant setting for a simple
diet, rather than an occasion for indulging in the joys of the table. In the
absence of meat, eggs, bacon, and cheese, it was a generous silver bowl full
of criss-crossed little balls of butter, all skillfully rolled by Stena, that was typical for a breakfast with the Bruckmanns. Habits like this one were observed
rather strictly, even after there were no longer any maids in the house.

On this day, the house was full of family. Only Eda was absent. Beside my
own family—a complete set of six—there were rather unusual guests: Peter,
my father's much younger brother, and his Swedish wife, Greta, were there.
On their way from London back to Stockholm, where they lived, they had
arrived two days ago to see the family. Meanwhile, all of us were assembled
at breakfast. Mummi, calm and composed, always the unquestioned figure of
authority, presided. Stena, in her somewhat sullen way, saw to it that breakfast went smoothly. My mother, arriving a little late as usual, chatted with
Greta, her eyes resting affectionately on her sister-in-law. My father and
Peter joked about everything they came across in their conversation, and now
and again, Peter roared with laughter. At that Mummi showed subtle signs of
annoyance as she used to do as soon as the Voss family, that is, my father's,
was about to gain a certain predominance at her place.

Between breakfast and the time other well-wishers were expected, I
strolled through the garden with Nick. It was a charming piece of land, a
property of which the Bruckmanns had always been proud. With its two wide
lawns and old trees, its gravel paths bordered by neatly clipped shrubs, and
its two and a half acres, it was really more of a little park rather than a garden.
A lovely pavilion overlooked one lawn, a spacious rotunda with a dream of a
Venetian chandelier inside, a gift to my grandfather from Mr. Siemens, an
industrialist. For us children, the garden was an exciting playground. There
was the fully furnished "witch-house" my mother and her sisters used to play
in as children: an apiary; a hay-barn; a deserted pig sty; a chicken yard; a former tennis court—by then already used for bonfires at Easter; and, hidden in
a remote corner, a "*Luftbad*," or open-air-bath, which I now consider an early

and bold step of my grandparents into the modern age. Last, but not least, there were plenty of apple, pear, and cherry trees as well as a large walnut tree.

"Say," Nick asked as we sat on the steps in front of the pavilion, "what happened yesterday on your trip in the mountains? I overheard father making some remark to mother this morning, something about Uncle Peter; I couldn't make out what it was about."

I sensed Nick's curiosity about an incident that was as amusing for me as it was embarrassing for others. We had been in the mountains the day before, a party of eight: my parents, Peter, and Greta in our car; and friends of the family, Philipp von Burgdorf and his sister Nora, who had taken me with them in the Burgdorf's car. Nick had stayed behind repairing the radio to make sure that we would be able to hear the *Führer*'s speech that evening.

I wanted to hold Nick on tenterhooks for a while, so I went back a bit before coming to the point. "We had a great time," I said. "It was still rather warm, and we went bathing in the Bode brook, the three of us: Philipp, Nora, and me. The water was ice cold, but it was fun all the same. Philipp and I tried to catch trout afterwards. We could see them standing underneath the embankment, but as soon as we tried to grasp one of them, they darted off. The picnic was great, and later on, following father's old passion, we went looking for mushrooms."

Nick pressed on, saying that all that wasn't what father could have meant.

"No, that was about Uncle Peter during the *Führer*'s speech," I said, and then I told him what had happened in the village inn.

We had stopped there for a bite to eat. My father had ordered a large pan of scrambled eggs, three eggs for each of us. People were gawking when the pan, a real monster, came to the table. We hadn't finished our eggs yet when the radio was turned on for the *Führer*'s speech, and people immediately fell silent and listened. First, Hitler went to great lengths, as usual, about the Party's rise to power. Peter felt disturbed by the radio and tried to keep up our own talk. That earned him angry glances from the other people in the room—farmers, woodsmen, and a few women—all of whom were generally good-natured people. When Hitler eventually came to the Sudeten issue; his voice became louder and louder; and one could imagine him up there on the platform at Nürnberg, shaking his fists in front of the thousands of people. That was when Peter started his little joke. He blackened his upper lip with a burnt cork and pulled his hair down across his forehead. It all went very quickly, and when I looked at him he was already mimicking the *Führer*, pulling a furious face and using the people for an audience. It didn't last long, but the people hadn't failed to see him and now became really angry. Mother, too, was furious; sitting next to him, she pushed her elbow in his side. "Are you mad? Stop that nonsense," she said. "Really, you aren't in England or Sweden!" He stopped right away but one could see that he had enjoyed his little show. My father quickly asked for the check, and we took off even before the speech was over.

Nick shook his head. "Unbelievable! He really is impossible, isn't he? Now I understand father's remark, 'Quite a performance of Peter's, last night', and mother snapping back, 'Who does he think he is?' "

Peter, our tall, elegant, always cheerful uncle! For me, he was an exciting figure whenever he turned up, seldom as that was, from another world that was strange and attractive. Cheerful and somehow "different," both brothers were easy in their way with others of whatever level, background, or rank. Peter was born in Bundaberg, Australia, and my father in Sydney. Ten years the elder, my father had spent almost his whole youth there and had difficulties with German on the family's return to Germany. It was Peter who now was accustomed to travel with a British passport, a thing unthinkable for my father who had been an Army officer in the World War. After graduating from the University of Vienna in the middle of the economic crisis of the 1920s, Peter had turned his back on Germany to make a living in England. Now he was representing a British firm in Stockholm. It is hard to imagine someone more cosmopolitan and urbane. In Greta, German-born but later adopted by her stepfather, a Swedish surgeon, he had found his match. She was an attractive, sporting woman, a trained pianist, and, what counted more to me, a former tournament field hockey player. Who, indeed, was he, anyway?

Nick and I were sitting on the stairs to the pavilion, or "the Temple" as it was called by the family. Nearby, a group of thuya trees formed a semi-circle to the wall of the Temple, closely surrounding a small corner. Here, in the darkness of the niche, there was a simple wooden cross, its epigraph "Oberleutnant Günther Bruckmann, born 12.4.1895, killed in action in Volhynia 20.7.1917."*

Somehow, there were always fresh flowers at this place of remembrance. I knew well the pleasant image of Mummi's only son in his lieutenant's uniform from the photograph on my mother's bureau at home.

On that morning, I first had a faint notion of how differently members of my family were involved in past and present world affairs. Unlike my parents, Peter was not emotionally entangled in the war that had ended twenty years before nor had he, most probably, perceived the post-war order as most Germans did, that is, as nations divided between winners and losers. The war had not been the decisive experience of his youth as it had been for my parents. If Hitler addressed this post-war order as unsustainable—as he had done in his speech on the day before—his dramatic style of stirring the

---

*During WWI, Volhynia was part of western Ukraine, then a part of the Russian Empire.

masses may have been for Peter an object of amusement. Certainly this wasn't my parents' way of seeing it, however. For all his outward mocking attitude towards politics, even my father's deeper layers of consciousness were touched by the subject, layers of which the wooden cross by the Temple was a token. My father's strong dislike for any form of big talk and of displaying one's convictions had made him pass over Peter's levity; my mother, in comparison, was more outspoken.

It was Mummi's day, though. Later that morning she stood in the library, chatting and receiving congratulations from well-wishers. Her small figure was clad wholly in black, as was the custom with widows; her only concession to this special day was her white collar being a bit more generous than usual. Her posture was erect; her strikingly dense and curly hair, which was a mixture of black and silver, was cut short and brushed upwards, quite unusual among her age group. Each one of her guests was met by her energetic, attentive gaze. Now and then she would take her *lorgnon*, fixed to a long golden chain hanging down from her neck, to look more closely at some greeting card.

For me, she embodied a generation favored by the undisturbed prosperity of the decades before the wars. Active and entrepreneurial men like my grandfather had been able to acquire a comfortable amount of possessions, now prudently held on to by Mummi who exerted a gentle austerity over the family. My late grandfather, a learned figure, highly esteemed in the world of commerce and industry in Brunswick, privy councillor to the Duke, was, in a way, still nearby; from his oil portrait in the hall, he kept watching with his vivid blue eyes everyone who passed.

Meanwhile, the family and the guests had moved on to the garden and were chatting in and about the groups of white garden benches and chairs. Among the guests were the Burgdorfs, neighbors and friends of the Bruckmanns, now in the third generation since the two families had bought the grounds and built their country houses there. The Burgdorfs were owners of a Brunswick firm constructing corn mills and vegetable oil presses in various countries of the world. The Burgdorf's garden was twice as large as ours. Although I had been a frequent visitor there, I was awed by the noble interior of the house and the splendor of bygone days that both house and garden seemed to reflect; I had seen photographs from the time of my mother's girlhood, taken in their garden and portraying the Burgdorf and the Bruckmann girls. In long white gowns and wide-brimmed hats set upon flowing hair, seated under a group of birch trees against the background of a wide-open lawn, they were images which matched perfectly with the timber-framed art-nouveau architecture of the house.

Philipp von Burgdorf had come, too. He was three years older than I. Although three years matter a great deal at that age and we were living at different places—he in Brunswick—we were friends. During our vacations at Hardenburg, we had gone skiing and mountain-climbing together, and in the years before we used to strip bare the Burgdorfs' cherry trees. His sister, Nora, was frequently in on it. The year before, we had spent two weeks together at a *Jungvolk* summer camp in the Harz Mountains.* Philipp had been in charge of his "*Fähnlein*"† and I had been with the camp guard. One night, when he had finished a nightly round and I was keeping the fire burning, he sat down by me and we talked about his family; about Brunswick and the role of his ancestors in the region; and about German and Roman history, in which he was even then rather expert.

Recalling that summer camp, it occurs to me that both of us enjoyed it particularly for the responsibility it gave us for so many boys—he as a *Fähnlein*-leader and I as a camp guard. Somehow, I found satisfaction in being on guard while the others were asleep. Later on, at the front, guard duty and responsibilities for others became a burden, sometimes an intolerable one. But then, very early, it had touched a string in me that was in tune with the things to come.

Philipp's outer appearance was striking: strong and sporting and at the same time refined—"good breeding," as my mother would put it. Another reason he seemed so engaging with his boys in the *Jungvolk* as well as with adults was his way of making people feel they enjoyed his undivided attention. His open features were taut and handsome. Particularly remarkable were two small lines around the corners of his mouth, which although they seemed to betray some hidden sadness at first glance, they would suddenly burst into a dimpled and totally captivating smile.

In the afternoon, when the guests were gone and the family was scattered over the grounds, Philipp and I went off for a quick walk up the hills. We were eager for some exercise and the dogs needed some, too. Disregarding the footpaths, we took the direct route upward, scrambling, panting, and sweating on our way up until, half an hour later, we arrived at the top. Here we rested, hearing our hearts beat in the silence, listening to the wind going through the high yellow grass and relishing the spicy smell of the conifers. How I loved these hills! Far down and tiny the red-tiled roofs of Hardenburg clustered around the church, and the farmland stretched its checked pattern of the fields up to the horizon.

Did we know then how happy we were?

---

*The *Jungvolk* was the subdivision of the Hitler Youth to which boys of 10–14 years were assigned, first voluntarily, and later, when membership became mandatory. Older boys could stay with the organization as leaders; these were mostly youths attending *Gymnasium* (academic high school) and therefore available for duty in the afternoon.
†A group of a hundred.

I did not see Philipp again until two years later when he was wearing field gray, adorned with the Iron Cross.

Recalling that glorious day in September 1938, the late afternoon emerges from my memory in great clarity. The family had assembled around the grand piano in the hall for some music making. My little sister, the youngest of us, started with a little piece on the piano. I played a Pergolesi air on the violin. My father played a favorite piece of his on the cello, Tchaikovsky's Nocturne in D Minor, accompanied by my mother. It was a romantic piece, showing the most beautiful sides of the cello to advantage. Greta had put on her traditional Swedish costume for this occasion. It was something of a white blouse under a black velvet vest, a red frock, and white woolen stockings. She closed the little house concert with a nocturne by Chopin, brilliantly performed from memory. We wouldn't let her get away with that, though, wanted some more. After some coaxing, she began to sing an old Swedish folk song, *"Ack Värmeland Du Sköna"* ("Oh, Beautiful Värmland"*), accompanying herself on the piano. I was deeply moved by the melody's simple beauty that was so much in harmony with the girl and her costume.

And then, all of a sudden, Eda was there, right back from the Nürnberg Party rally. There she stood, slim and handsome, very upright in a form-fitting suit.

On her lapel was the round badge of the Party and under it her gilt-edged rhombus of the Hitler Youth, a symbol of early membership in the twenties. She glanced around with her intensely blue eagle eyes under dark brows, her dark hair tied up in a knot at the neck; raising her slightly aquiline nose—the only one in the family so endowed. She greeted us with a clear and distinct, *"Heil Hitler!"* There was nothing artificial about her addressing her own family in this way. It was her nature to wear her heart on her sleeve, and it was obvious that she wanted to display her unflinching loyalty to the *Führer*, a loyalty which had just been renewed in Nürnberg. Even knowing her, however, our family was rather startled by this unseemly greeting, given that it was Mummi's birthday and that the "Swedes" were around.

She then gave Mummi a warm hug, however, and went around to say hello. When it was Peter's turn, he met her quite earnestly with an articulated, *"Heil Hitler*, dear! How good to have you safely back." My mother, knowing the two brothers only too well, stopped my father just in time from competing with Peter in this game that might have made things awkward.

Dinner was all harmony for a long while. The family, sitting round the large table in the hall, patiently let Eda give her account of the events during the last several days at Nürnberg. She was proud of having been there, of

*Värmland is a province in southwestern Sweden.

having been a witness to the rallies, parades, and even, at the close of the rally, to a midnight *Grosse Zapfenstreich*.* It was obvious that in her view she had witnessed a historical event. The family naturally was patient with her enthusiasm, but in the end, the political controversy generated by the tense, hectic world diplomatic situation spoiled the atmosphere at our table.

Of course, at my young age, I was far from having a full grasp of the questions at hand. I remember vividly, however, the feeling of alarm when Eda forthrightly supported the *Führer*'s strong warning to the Western Powers about interfering with the Sudetenland, or the referendum Hitler was determined to bring about. What I became aware of—and what made a lasting impression on me—was that another war had become a real possibility.

"You should have been there to see the tremendous enthusiasm of the people, when the *Führer* said he would no longer tolerate the right of self-determination to be stolen from the Sudeten-Germans," Eda went on in her account. " The whole nation is behind the *Führer* on this issue."

"Well," my mother said, "I for my part have my reservations. One can only hope it's all bravado talk. Otherwise it could mean war, and let me tell you, this is not what the whole nation is after."

"I'm afraid Edith is right," Mummi said. "There is the rumor of a guarantee of support from England to France in case Czechoslovakia was attacked. It's in today's paper."

"The British and the French are well advised to stay out of this," Eda retorted, her ears getting red. "The French and the British people aren't involved in this matter. So it's none of their business."

"Yes, sure, quite so, just as the *Führer* has said," Peter butted in. He wanted to continue, but Eda interrupted, " . . . and right he is! I hope he made himself understood last night."

"Maybe he is wrong, my dear," Peter continued. "Maybe it's the other way around and that he is meddling with a business of theirs. Isn't Czechoslovakia their child, after all? Maybe they're just looking after it, just as decent parents are supposed to, and they just don't want other people telling their child how to behave."

"Obviously, my dear, you're a bit out of touch with what has been going on here in Germany in the past years," Eda snapped back with flashing eyes. "You seem to be out of touch with the new thinking. We don't believe the post-war order is sacrosanct anymore; we think it has no future. At present, the Czechs continue to oppress three-and-a-half million Germans! I can tell you, the *Führer* won't have it, and he'll put an end to it!"

---

*A "Grand Tattoo" is an elaborate and solemn military ritual with drums, bugles, and fifes recalling soldiers to quarters, dramatized by the use of torchlight.

"And what if they don't let him? What, if they don't care about what you call the *new thinking* or what is called the '*national revival*'?" Peter insisted.

"In the end they will. We believe in the justness of our cause. That's our strength. The whole nation is behind the *Führer*!"

"For heaven's sake, can't we stop talking politics!" my father growled. "There's absolutely no point in it. Do we know all the facts? Certainly not! And since we don't, does it matter what we think should be done? Please stop behaving like politicians, as if it were for us to make decisions! Really, I hate that."

But Eda, once she was at it, would not give in, "What I hate are the arch-skeptics, the nonstop grumblers who doubt the *Führer*'s good judgment as soon as a crisis is in sight. That is what has to stop!"

"If this is going on, don't count on me," my father muttered, about to leave the table.

Somehow my grandmother managed to avoid a break up of our dinner and ended the discussion. It had not been the first time that politics had intruded into our family life and had made things unpleasant.

Two weeks later, the Munich conference took place. There the problem was solved peacefully in favor of the Sudeten-Germans. For the first time, I had consciously followed an event in the world of international affairs. War had been averted. From then on, however, I felt that war, either real or imminent, would probably be part of my life, of the life of my generation, just as it had been for the earlier generations.

3

BRUNSWICK

It was late when I arrived at Brunswick to spend two days with my grand-mother Voss. My own family was staying at Hardenburg, where we had spent Christmas, our third one since the beginning of the war. As a reserve officer, my father had been called up in August 1939 and was now on the Eastern Front, somewhere near Smolensk. We knew nothing more of his where-abouts.

More snow had fallen. The land between Hardenburg and Brunswick had been wrapped in white, silent and luminous in the dark, and untroubled by the train's passage. Here at the main station people were hurrying to and fro, in the cold, dim shades with coats and turned-up collars, leaving wisps of white breath behind.

Out on the square, I was immediately struck by the city's changed charac-ter, quite different from the stimulating vitality of pre-war days. Now, in early 1942, the blackout, the snow, the muffled traffic noises and the dimmed headlights of the automobiles and streetcars added up to a theatrical unreal-ity. The strange atmosphere wasn't altogether oppressing; one could sense the system of urban life still in motion, but somehow this life seemed to flow underground rather than on the surface.

It was the war news that weighed heavily upon people. First, Pearl Harbor and the awareness that now, at last, we were at war with the United States, too. Then, at the same time but much more disturbing, the terse bulletins of the High Command of the Armed Forces, which had more or less disclosed that the Red Army's counteroffensive was shattering the center of the Eastern Front. The heroic language of the press, "gigantic battle of defense," for instance, scarcely disguised a dramatic turn for the worse. Everyone thought of our soldiers out there, first stuck in the autumn mud, and now fighting for survival while exposed without *decent* winter equipment to the cruel Russian winter, with temperatures between -20 and -30 degrees Centigrade. Looking from the train at the whiteness of the land, pictures that had earlier taken shape in my imagination while I was reading Sienkevitch's novel *1812* came back to me, scenes of an army in dissolution trying to escape the merciless blows of the Cossacks and the desolation of the wide expanses of Russia.

Then there was the dismissal of Field Marshal von Brauchitsch from his post as Supreme Commander of the Army only a week before. The *Führer* himself had taken his place. Health reasons had been put forward, but in view of the worsening situation at the Eastern Front, for some the connection between the two events was obvious. My uncle, Wolf Voss, was *aide-de-camp* to the field marshal. What secrets might Wolf know? How was he involved? Would he go with the field marshal?

Walking in the blackout made it difficult for me to find my way to my grandmother's house. One could hardly discern the different lanes and alleys in the heart of the town with its steep, timber-framed gables that looked so beautiful in daylight, but now seemed swallowed by the darkness. I loved this city for its charm, its medieval center; its Romanesque castle and cathedral, both full of exciting history; its parks; and the two arms of the Oker River encircling its center and lined by large willows whose branches dangled in the glittering water. This place had been the home town of several generations of Vosses, and my mother's family had come to live there, too. It was the town of Heinrich the Lion who, some 800 years ago, had pushed open Europe's door to the East. The bronze figure of the lion in the bailey of the castle still, in an allegorical stance, pointed east.*

*Heinrich the Lion, a European prince of the High Middle Ages, 1130–1195, scion of the dynasty of the Welfs, duke of Saxony and Bavaria, was originally the main vassal of King Friedrich (from 1155 on *Kaiser* Friedrich I "Barbarossa") during Friedrich's campaign in Upper Italy in 1154–55. At home, Heinrich founded, among others, the cities of Munich and Lübeck and, above all, followed a policy of territorial expansion into the Slavic regions east of the Elbe River. In 1179, Heinrich turned down Friedrich's request to support him in his Lombardy campaign—an act of recalcitrance as well as an expression of his engagement in the East (in contrast to the *Reich*'s imperial ambitions in Italy). He was banned in 1180, lost his lands, and went into exile to the court of his father-in-law Henry II of England. He returned and eventually died as Duke of Braunschweig-Lüneburg, the rest of his lands. All the same, his son, Otto, was chosen German king in 1198 and became *Kaiser* in 1209 (Otto IV).

In the author's school days, Heinrich the Lion was held in high esteem for his eastward-pointed territorial policy while the *Reich*'s fixation towards Italy was regarded as futile and a waste of the *Reich*'s resources. Accordingly, his fall was interpreted as the ill-fated outcome of the struggle between those two policies. Today, German historians tend to regard his fall as the result of his reckless strive for a state-like independence and of his underestimation of the *Reich*'s legal authority.

My grandmother's house was on the Wall, that is, the mound encircling the old city and overlooking the arms of the river. For whole stretches, the Wall was lined with old chestnut trees. The house was a pleasant, two-story, white villa with a neat pediment in front. From the porthole inside the pediment, my uncle Peter had told me, an Australian flag used to hang on holidays, only to be replaced by a German flag when, during World War I, my grandfather had "turned patriotic," as Peter put it.

I passed the lofty steeple of St. Andreas, climbed the stairs up to the Wall and finally reached the house. The house lay in complete darkness. Approaching the gate, I wondered about an Army car parked in front, its driver walking back and forth along the railings.

Inside the house, I was struck by the sudden change from the blackout world outside to the splendor of the brightly lit rooms. As I recall that moment, an intense feeling of that brightness comes back to me, reviving the life of the Vosses in a house that is no longer there. While the Bruckmann's house, for all its class, always had a touch of austerity, this house on the Wall had a sense of richness and refinement, a delightful atmosphere created by its lights, its furnishings, its colors, and its unmistakable scent, which I remember as a mixture of lavender and strong coffee. There were all sorts of furnishings: fine Biedermeier ash along with oil portraits of my grandfather's grandparents; Indian rattan with bright, colorful fabrics; English mahogany bookcases; Indian brass jugs with fresh flowers. One wall of the sitting room was covered with *tapa*, a brownish Polynesian cloth made from the bark of mulberry trees and printed with strong black patterns—a remnant of my grandparent's years on the Fiji Islands. Dispersed on it were spears, cudgels, arrows, and other weapons of the natives of that distant world. All of that had a stunning decorative effect, whatever its ethnological merits may have been. To me the most beautiful and precious piece was what my grandmother used to call "my Gainsborough," a beautiful, large oil painting depicting her three children right after the family's return from abroad.

I found my grandmother on the sofa right below her "Gainsborough." She looked frail, her nose more pointed since I had seen her last, but apparently in good spirits. She had a silk dress on with a black-and-white, rather lively pattern matching her white hair, which she wore in a modern style. On the table in front of her she had spread out cards, obviously just solving a bridge problem, as she often liked to do after dinner.

"Look, what I have," my grandmother said after I sat down. She reached over to a side table and handed me a small book with a hand-made *tapa* cover. "My memoirs of Australia. You can tell your mother I've done it at last!"

The text I held in my hands had been neatly typed by my aunt, Isa, and interspersed with yellowed photographs. From what I could see leafing through the first pages, it described the life and experiences of a young, adventurous women who had chosen to follow a young businessman to a distant land. That young man, who one day had shown up in his hometown in a stunning overcoat of light-brown camel hair, had been determined to choose and take a wife within the few weeks left before his return to Australia. What I remember quite clearly is that this was the first time I saw a particular photograph showing my father as a young boy. He was bent forward on splayed legs, a straw hat cocked jauntily back on his head, and happily munching a slice of a large watermelon as his aboriginal nanny looked on with a wide grin. The moment I saw that picture, I was struck by an insight, corroborated many times after, an acute sense of the transient nature of the stages of man's life. How fragile was the image of the happy boy with the straw hat, against the background of the later, no less fleeting, periods of his life: as a German artillery officer in World War I; as a father of a family between the wars with new, if humbler, expectations; and then, again, as an officer actively engaged in a life-and-death struggle deep in the Russian steppe!

What, then, is man's identity? What is my own? Only much later would I ask what the youngster playing violin in Mummi's hall had to do with the youth in combat blasting away with his machinegun only a few years later.

"Guess who is here?" Isa said coming in with a supper tray she had prepared for me. Behind her, Uncle Wolf was entering the room. I sprang up, electrified, feeling myself, young as I was, hooked to the power of history; for because of his closeness to Field Marshal von Brauchitsch, I saw him as an officer constantly involved in decisions of historic significance. For the family, however, his arrival couldn't have been that extraordinary, because he had been a frequent visitor to the house before the war.

Wolf was an imposing figure. Not very tall, his build was all the more erect and lean. He was clad in the field uniform of the General Staff with the distinctive stripes on the trousers, red, broad, and to me, awe-inspiring. His gray eyes peered out from under bushy brows. His ruddy complexion and, in particular, his quiet manner completed the image of an officer of the General Staff at its best. Although he was liked by women, he never married. In the family, it used to be said that he would have made a good actor, the result of his penchant as a youth for reciting dramatic poems in his clear, immaculate voice. Without doubt he had charm. His pre-military background had been the Youth Movement, a sign perhaps of an emotional tendency that he concealed behind a composed bearing.

On this evening, he gave no sign of the deep concern he must have felt about the developments in the East and within the High Command in particular. The conversation flowed easily and mainly dealt with the family, my grandmother's memoirs having just been finished. They caused her to recall old friendships, parties, and outdoor pleasures from her time in Australia and Polynesia—tales of a paradise lost, poignant especially in the circumstances of these somber days.

There was another surprise in store for me that evening. My grandmother had already retired when Wolf mentioned that Philipp von Burgdorf was going to see him the next morning. I was surprised; I didn't even know they had met. He explained that he knew Nora, Philipp's sister, who worked with *OKH* (*Oberkommando des Heeres*, the High Command of the Army) in Berlin and that he had happened to meet both of them a few days before. Philipp had stopped over to see Nora on his way down from Finland to Brunswick on leave before attending *SS* officer's candidate school. Wolf said that he himself still had rather close ties to Finland since the end of World War I, and had asked Philipp to let him have some direct information about the warfare in the North.

Wolf intuited that I would like to see Philipp again and suggested that I join them on their walk the next morning.

For the rest of the evening, we talked about Finland, Wolf responding with patience to all my questions about his "special relationship" with that country. I was captivated by his outline of the Finnish fight for independence, first when in 1918 the Bolsheviks tried to overthrow the new Finnish government, and then, twenty years later in the Winter War after the Russian invasion in 1939. He still had many friends among the Finnish officer corps. This unequal struggle between dwarf and giant was fascinating for the bravery and resolution of the people and soldiers of this small country. At the same time, it seemed to me to be a variation of the struggle *Between White and Red* described by Edwin Erich Dwinger in his novel of the same title. I had devoured that novel a year or two before; it had impressed me as a story of the struggle between Good and Evil and had strengthened my conviction that the arch evil in this world was Bolshevism. On that evening in Brunswick, I could not foresee that this conversation would be a prelude to an experience I was to have myself, but it was in that conversation with Wolf that the ground was laid for my sympathy and affection toward that country and its brave folk.

The next morning, the reunion with Philipp was warm and hearty. During the last few months, he had been with a mountain infantry regiment in North Karelia. He was wearing their uniform with the insignia of a corporal. In the buttonhole of his tunic there was the ribbon of the Iron Cross 2d class. He had become even leaner and more mature, a shade more grave perhaps; the two lines about his mouth had become a bit sharper. In our conversation, though, his old, winning smile still flitted over his face as it had two years ago.

Our former relationship, however, the one between the older and the younger leader of the *Jungvolk*, was gone. There was an air of remoteness about him; perhaps it was my own feeling of distance from the soldier in the front line, my own consciousness that it would still take some time until I would share his soldierly duties in this war.

The three of us, Wolf, Philipp, and I, went off for an hour's walk on the Wall. To me, Philipp's account of the fighting in North Karelia sounded like red Indian tales. The *Gebirgsjäger*, or *Jäger* for short, as the mountain infantry were called, roamed the marshy tundra and the wooded taiga wilderness, far from their bases, with their supply dependent only on endless mule trains. There were ferocious encounters with "Ivan," often man to man, relying on infantry weapons only—all of that taking place during the long summer days swarming with mosquitoes and later, as winters begin early in the far north, in the merciless cold and almost constant darkness.

I gathered that the joint German/Finnish campaign initially was directed against the railway line connecting the ice-free harbor of Murmansk to Leningrad. But it was only much later that I recalled and understood the meaning of Philipp questioning Wolf about future operational intentions with respect to that line. Wolf's response was cautious and indirect. He said something about there being no alliance between Germany and Finland and that Finland was not at war with England and the United States after all, but that this situation was likely to change if that railway line were taken. At that time, it was beyond my grasp that the two "brothers in arms," as Finland and Germany called their relationship, could have different war aims.

Philipp stayed for lunch. At the table, we talked about my uncle Peter's and his family's precarious situation in Stockholm. He had been sacked by his British employers; so much had been clear from his letters to his mother. There remained, however, some mysteries in their correspondence, which apparently were hard to explain in writing. He was considering returning to Germany because, so far, he had not succeeded in finding a suitable position elsewhere. My grandmother encouraged his return, although such a step would for him mean military service in a conflict in which we knew he had no desire to participate.

My image of Peter and my understanding of his life underwent a sobering change. Peter, the cosmopolitan, born in Australia, graduated from the university of Vienna, married in London to a Swedish girl, traveling with a British passport, had designed for himself a life without regard for political borders, or at least a regard which was more and more insignificant. Now this course of life had reached an impasse. Suddenly he found himself subjected to new regulations made for nationals rather than for cosmopolitans. Borders had become immensely important. And where did that leave him?

After lunch, Philipp stayed on, undoubtedly to get Wolf's assessment of the situation at the Eastern Front. Tacitly, I was permitted to listen in. We settled down in a corner of the sitting room. Outside dusk was falling. In the twilight of the room, the features of the two soldiers became more and more obscure in the course of Wolf's gloomy account of what was happening in the East, in Army Group Center in particular.

Anything could happen, he said. The High Command could only hope that the front line would hold. When the Russians had started their counteroffensive early in December, it had been too late for an orderly withdrawal to a more favorable line, so they had to hold on and order the troops to hold their positions wherever they were. All odds, Wolf said, were against our troops. Outnumbered by fresh Russian reserves clad in fur-lined winter clothes, our soldiers were exposed to both the attack of fresh troops and the worst Russian winter in memory. The High Command had to call for the utmost from the troops to prevent disaster, to demand that the ground be held at all costs, disregarding the soldiers' exhaustion from the autumn fighting in the mud and the lack of proper protection against the winter's cold.

Sometimes it looked as if Wolf were about to stop his gloomy appraisal, but the familiar surrounding of the house and Philipp's trustworthiness seemed to diminish his normal restraint, and he continued his account.

On his last visit out there three weeks before, he had heard reports and witnessed scenes of indescribable suffering and hardship. It made him think, he said, of Coulaincourt's description of Napoleon's campaign of 1812. "Self-Sacrifice is Duty" were the closing words of a commanding general's order of the day issued during the time Wolf had been out there. Could one think of a more blunt order? And yet, he said, it reflected precisely the situation and the needs in the Army Group Center sector. Obviously, at that time no one knew whether the thin screens of infantry, constituting the front line in the vast expanses, would hold and prevent a general collapse.

Philipp blurted, "Quite frankly, sir, it seems clear that the campaign has been a failure, stuck in the Russian winter as we are. Is this the reason why the Field Marshal has had to go?"

"We should have been finished with the campaign by the end of November; it was planned as another lightning stroke," Wolf replied. "Well, it didn't work this time. Now we know it will be a long time before it's over. Fresh Russian armies may continue to arrive on the scene, and the Americans will probably provide support via Murmansk—if our Navy and the *Luftwaffe* let them. We underestimated the Russians' strength and the endurance of their troops. And, moreover, there have been quite unnecessary delays with important decisions—certainly not the fault of the field marshal. Anyway, he's a sick man. His heart . . . the strain has been too much."

"Do you think the war can still be won?" Philipp asked in a subdued voice.

Wolf hesitated. His silence became awkward, "To be quite frank, I can't tell you because I don't know," he said at last. "As I just have said, now the odds are against us. And what is true of the Eastern Front is, in the long run, probably true for the overall situation. Seen from the view of a staff officer, our prospects are at least dubious."

He went on to muse about something he said he couldn't explain. There had been great doubts on the part of the General Staff about other campaigns in the past, very well founded in facts and figures, yet still, somehow, in the end the *Führer* had always succeeded in dispelling those doubts. His gift of reassuring his entourage and visitors to his headquarters came close to magic. He said he had seen it happen more than once and added, "What's more, until recently he's always been right! Against all odds."

We were now sitting in complete darkness. None of us had given a thought to putting on the lights. Philipp remembered that he was supposed to leave. He rose. Wolf and I got up also.

"I am most grateful, sir, for your confidence," Philipp said standing in front of Wolf, very erect, as if to suggest that this exceptional hour of frankness had now to be replaced by normal military conduct. "It may seem odd, but in the end I feel encouraged by your frankness rather than disheartened. We must believe in the things that cannot be explained. What else can we do, sir, after all!"

Wolf did not comment. He gave Philipp a warm smile instead. They shook hands. "I hope to see you again. Good luck, my boy. God bless you!"

I had suggested walking Philipp home, eager to have some words with him in private. Wolf saw us out. Before Philipp turned the corner of the house, he looked back, raising his hand to his cap. Wolf was standing in the doorway, small, lean, erect in his tight tunic, thoughtfully returning Philipp's salute.

As we trotted along the Wall, the dark lightened up only by the snow, we were in a pensive mood.

Philipp broke the silence, "Well, we have had a glimpse behind the scenes, haven't we? And what we could see was anything but encouraging."

"You said you were encouraged!"

"Well, I had to say that, but I think there is more to it than your uncle's cool military view. I like him, really. He's impressive and at the same time neither aloof nor condescending. Like many other military men, however, he appears to look at this war as a game of chess—two adversaries, one white, one black; the next game it's vice versa; it's all the same. Once you see you can't win any more, well, that's it, the game is over. In war, I'm afraid, their cool conclusion is: stop all unnecessary suffering and sacrifices, seek peace immediately."

"Now, now, Philipp, that's not what he said, " I interrupted.

"No, of course not, don't get me wrong. What I'm trying to say is that we can't look at this war in the East as a game played by the rules. It's the clash between culture and nihilism, between the values of the Occident against the negation of all values of the past. No rules are acknowledged on the other side. The only rule they acknowledge is the rule of the proletariat. Look at the innumerable crimes committed in that name: they have slain millions of *kulaks* to eradicate private property, twelve million in the Ukraine alone; they have turned churches into pigsties to get rid of God; they have trampled all values upheld before their own calendar began; then, they have started to murder their own kind; and from the beginning, they were determined to take any opportunity to impose their system on the West. First, they tried in Germany, then in Spain."

He was speaking quite dispassionately, as if talking to himself rather than to make a point against Wolf. So I let him go on and listened.

"If you think of it, it's Europe as a whole against Bolshevism; Germany is its spearhead, and for good reasons, indeed: for its most perilous position, for its will to stand up against the threat, and for its leadership. It's no game of chess, no joust between knights in shining armor, no war to be won by military strength and professionalism alone."

At heart I agreed with him, again, Dwinger's *Between White and Red* coming to my mind. I had heard similar words before, however, from quarters not held in high esteem in my family, propaganda talk from the wrong persons in their yellow-brown uniforms in their self-important, puffed-up language. So I spontaneously took on the role of the devil's advocate, "Don't you think the rules of military professionalism are paramount in times of war? I think it's dangerous to predict that *Weltanschauung* (world view) will dominate military professionalism? Would *Weltanschauung* help the soldier out there in the cold?" I asked somewhat harshly.

He was quiet, then said, "We need both! High military proficiency and a broader view than that of just another war between European nations fighting out their old rivalries, the vision of a Europe as determined as Germany is to keep out Bolshevism—a vision other young Europeans are ready to go to war for, young idealists determined to make that commitment. Your uncle may be right. Perhaps in the long run Germany alone isn't strong enough, but in the long run such, a new vision could attract hundreds of thousands of volunteers to help.

By now we had arrived at his parents' house. In the dark, he was trying to look into my eyes, grabbing me by the arm, "Do you think I'm talking propaganda? Well, I'm not! That vision is already being realized. Volunteers keep coming in from almost all parts of Europe—Norway, Sweden,

Denmark, the Netherlands, Belgium, France, Switzerland, the South Tyrol. They all have been incorporated into the *Waffen-SS*, which is about to form Germanic divisions. Soon the forces of the *Waffen-SS* will be fighting not only for our country, but for our common European heritage."

I felt carried along by his enthusiasm, anxious to hear more. He talked to me about young soldiers, all volunteers; about modern warfare of small groups of infantry operating on their own; and about their young officers he had met, their high military proficiency, picked from battle-hardened front-line troops, some of them already highly decorated. On his way back from Karelia, he had been in touch with them in Berlin. Obviously they had deeply impressed him as a new elite emerging in this war. These people, he said, are totally different from everything we knew of the general *SS*, not to speak of the Party people.

Suddenly, our old relationship was restored. Here was something new and exciting which we could share. Listening to him, I almost forgot that he was serving in the Army. When I said so, he confided to me that he had just initiated his transfer to the *Waffen-SS* and hoped to be assigned to attend their officer's candidate school before the end of his leave. His family didn't know yet, and he wasn't sure at all about their reaction. Anyway, he said he had already talked too much and really had to go now. He turned to the house and disappeared. "Good luck to you" was all I could say for a good-bye.

Walking back, I tried to form a coherent picture of the things I had learned this afternoon. I did not take the direct way back. I needed time.

First, it was the dramatic bluntness of the German General's order of the day at the Eastern Front—"Self-Sacrifice is Duty"—that rang in my ear and made my idealistic and somewhat romantic mind respond. Thrown into the turmoil of war at that age, I was no exception in my eagerness to make a contribution as soon as I was old enough. There was a good deal of daydreaming involved. It had to be something special, such as joining the paratroops and then being assigned to some daredevil jump behind the Russian lines. Against this background, Philipp's version of the *Waffen-SS* and its pan-European dimension had a new and strong attraction. Aside from the hope it offered in the gloomy atmosphere of that winter, I had the vague notion of something new coming into being, an entirely new perspective, perhaps even going beyond the war and the old rivalries of European nations. Could it be the New Reich, evoked in Stefan George's poem of which I can remember only the last lines:

Er führt durch sturm und grausige signale
Des frührots seiner treuen schar zum werk
*Des wachen tags und pflanzt das Neue Reich.**

And yet I wasn't ready for a commitment. That would come later. I only felt the need for clarity. Perhaps I could bring up the subject with Wolf if he was still awake. When I came back to the house, however, Wolf was gone. There had been a phone call requesting him to report to Berlin the next day. He had left in the car.

*He leads through storm and dreadful signals
Of pale red dawn his loyal troop unto the work
Of the awoken day, and plants the New Reich.

4

CHOICES

It's hard to explain what, in the end, made me decide to join the *Waffen-SS*. Back in 1942, I didn't ask myself that question, but now, in 1945, it has become important. What made a youth of seventeen, coming from a decent family, go astray and become a member of what the Allies had now branded as a criminal gang? How did it happen? What went wrong?

Primarily, I think, it was the unfavorable course the war had taken at that time in the fall of 1942 and the differing responses to the worsening prospects among those of my age group. On the one side, there were those who were anxious to come through the war unscathed; on the other were those who felt this was the time to redouble their efforts to win the war. In retrospect, it seems these two attitudes affected one another in a polarizing way. To explain that, however, I should go back and describe life at home in that third year of the war.

It was on an afternoon early in September when I was out in the forest with Christina. She had come up the ladder and reached the little platform of the hunter's tree stand, her face flushed with joy. Her eyes, hazel-brown, radiant and, as usual, somewhat mischievous, seemed to say, 'See? I made it! You thought I wouldn't, didn't you?' for it had not been easy to skip the two rotten rungs on her way up. We couldn't stand up under the low roof and had to crouch on the small bench.

The gap in front opened on a view of a wide glade sloping down to a creek surrounded by stands of firs. Among them a few maples and beeches glowed in the afternoon sun. There was no sound except that of the wind wafting through the tall, yellow grass, tossing gossamer in the air and sprang up to the tree tops in their slow, swinging motion. The air was rich with the pungent scent of the conifers and of the needles on the ground that had been soaking up the heat of the sun and were now exhaling.

We loved this place, our "hideaway," in the wooded hills far back of the Blessheim castle from which we had walked for almost an hour. For us, this place was the essence of home. We belonged to it and it belonged to us. It was a place of happiness and a place where we knew best that we were in love with each other.

To be here was a rare opportunity, though, and some contrivance had been necessary to enable us to sneak off together and cover up our tracks. Besides, our various duties and activities left little time for a whole afternoon with one another. School, homework, our many duties as leaders in the *Jungvolk* and the *Jungmädel*, the two youth organizations for young boys and girls, sports (various athletics in summer and gymnastics and skiing in winter), and music lessons, which in my case meant violin lessons and school orchestra. There wasn't much time left for school, either, which explains my being a rather poor pupil who maneuvered through the *Gymnasium* only by shining in some lessons I liked—German, foreign languages, history—and leaving others more or less aside, mathematics in particular. For all its importance, school was just one of the things we were engaged in at that time.

Christina's mother thought her daughter was occupied with one of these activities this afternoon. She would certainly have objected if she had known about the two of us together in the woods. Our families, however, knew of our circle of friends; they knew all the names from the time we had our first dancing class, and they certainly knew that somehow love was involved. My mother had no desire to know too much. She was, as she used to say, unable to supervise all of her four children's doings, my father having been away for three years now, and therefore had no choice but to rely on her offspring's "substance."

Christina was sixteen then, slender with a bouncing, sporting gait emphasized by her bobbing brown pony tail. Her skin was tan by nature, and her slanted, long-lashed eyes over her high cheekbones and her small nose gave her a rather striking look. We had been talking all the way up here, small things about school, teachers, our friends, and the various relationships between them—endless topics at that age. Talking and being together was about all one could expect from this gentle love affair. Except for an occasional movie, further diversions or escapades were beyond our reach in wartime. All the same, we did not think we were missing anything.

Now, up in our blind, we were silent, in harmony with our silent surroundings.

After a while, Christina looked up and said in a low voice, "Let's close our eyes and let's wish for something, one wish for each of us." With that, she

closed her eyes, and I saw her eye lashes nestling down on her cheeks as softly as a butterfly lowering its wings on a warm stone in the sun.

"Tell me your wish," she asked.

"I want to kiss you," I said.

"I knew you would say that," she replied and mischievously added, "So I
have picked a different wish for myself."

"You tell me later," I said, kissing first her eyelids and then her lips.

"We must stop now. Please!" she said, freeing herself, and after a while,
"Don't you want to know my wish ?"

"Sure! I almost forgot. Tell me."

She paused, musing and looking on the glade. When our eyes met, hers
had become dark. With a voice huskier than usual she said, "I wished that
when this war was over we would meet again, here at our place, you and me,
as soon as both of us are back."

We kissed again, knowing that for us the time for real love had not yet
come and that when it did come we would be on duty, somewhere, far from
each other. The shadow of the war that had hung over our youth from the
beginning had reached us even here. There was no sanctuary.

Yet she smiled a brave and somewhat sad smile, her eyes full of love. It was
getting dark, time to leave.

When I came home, my mother said there had been a letter from my
father in the mail. He was coming home on leave, and he had good news of
my brother, Nick, who, after passing his final exams at the *Gymnasium*, had
been drafted and was now at the Eastern Front, apparently within reach of
my father. I also got a letter from my friend, Hans, who had joined the paratroops and wrote enthusiastically about his jump training. The day before, I
had learned that my predecessor in my present function in the *Jungvolk* had
been promoted to lieutenant in the infantry. My unrest at continuing to lead
a relatively peaceful life in private was steadily increasing.

Looking forward to my father's leave, my mother had been in a talkative
mood, so after supper, we had one of the long talks we used to have in my
last year at home. To discuss current affairs—indeed everything under the
sun—was for her a vital need, just as a cat needs to sharpen its claws on bark
from time to time. I was then, next to her, the eldest member of the family
at home, so the role of partner in our discussions had fallen upon me.

My mother was understanding when we discussed once more my intention of enlisting. It must have seemed quite natural to her that young people
of my age were responding in that way to the call of duty, for this was in accor-
dance with her generation's experience in similar circumstances over twenty
years before. Her generation, however, had experienced a world war being
lost, and in the years before the current war, she never had concealed her

nagging doubts about our leadership after the "Versailles *Diktat*" and its ability to restore our national dignity with prudence . . . that is, without waging
war. Regarding the odd set of Party officials on the local and regional level
(my father used to call them the "Party Comics"), how could one possibly
believe that the political personnel as a whole were equal to the tasks with
which the nation was now confronted? After all, for most of them, their only
experience with managing violence was restricted to brawls in bars and street
riots before 1933. Now we were at war with most of the world.

The basic theme underlying almost all our talks was my parents' ambiva-
lent relationship to National Socialism. Both came from families which for
generations had been merchants, bankers, domain tenants, executives,
lawyers, and civil servants. Their characters were formed by a basically con-
servative attitude as well as by their experience of World War I and its aftermath. For all their basic convictions, it seemed to them inevitable and moral-
ly imperative that some sort of societal restructuring should follow the war.
The "*Fronterlebnis*"—the comradeship of the front, the hardships jointly
endured in the field, the joint efforts of all classes for a common cause during the four long years of the war—could not be ignored; rather, was it a matter of justice that a modern society without class barriers be formed, based on
equal opportunities and on a person's own efforts and achievements.
Bringing down class barriers acknowledging the value of any useful or cre-
ative form of work was one of my mother's favorite ideas. At the same time,
their experience with Germany's defeat and with the penalties imposed at
Versailles—perceived as unfair punitive actions—had made them open to the
idea of "national identity" and what was left of national pride.

Another important part of my parents' experience was the Bolsheviks' various attempts to usurp power in post-war Germany. My father had been with
a *Freikorps* in the Baltics for some time after the war.*

Later on, in 1920, he had witnessed the armed insurrection of Communists
in the Ruhr area and the arrival of political commissars from Russia. Then,
against this background, both had followed the brutal struggle of the
Communists for political power in Berlin. My mother used to tell about
Communist quarters in Brunswick where, after the war, people "of her kind"
were well advised to stay out lest they be stoned. For them, as for most
Germans at that time, all this experience was evidence enough of the actual
and continual danger of Germany becoming Bolshevized. I had often heard
them talk of the need to withstand the Bolshevik menace and of the importance of establishing a genuine reconciliation of the classes as a prerequisite,
an aim which National Socialism, in their view, was most likely to achieve.

---

*Autonomous military units fighting irregular troops infiltrated by the Bolsheviks trying
to destabilize and overthrow non-communist governments in post-WWI Germany.

In this connection, their thinking was also formed by the unfavorable picture of Germany's recent feeble parliamentarian governments and their incapacity for coping with our postwar problems, the Communist menace in particular. They certainly felt it was time for someone to accumulate and use political power to bring about strong joint action.

Basically well-disposed towards National Socialism for these reasons, after 1933, my mother had decided to join the "Movement," not as a mere hanger-on, but as an active member. Her interest in public affairs dated from her days when, at home in Brunswick and Hardenburg, she had listened to her parents' conversations. Her father had written his Ph.D. thesis on Marx's *Das Kapital* and was throughout his professional life involved in public affairs. Through him, she had come to like the art of dispute. She thought it her duty to make a contribution and she scorned those of the "educated class"—the intellectuals in particular—who, standing aside, thought themselves above making a commitment toward the goals of a "laborer's" party. She once said that no one was entitled to criticize unless he actually involved himself in making things better.

In our nightly discussions at home, however, she used to play the devil's advocate. She would question any official political position so I could work out my own opinions on political developments such as the ever-expanding war fronts, the boastful speeches that betrayed an underestimation of our opponents, the brutal actions against political dissenters, and other misdeeds of Party officials. I sensed, however, that she expected from our discussions some reassurance about the justness of our cause. She liked to sum up one of her more severe criticisms in the reproach that the "Nazis," even then the pejorative term for National Socialists, didn't behave much better than the Bolsheviks. Then it was my turn to set out the reasons for the justness of the Nazis's behavior, that the justness of our cause justified the means that were necessary to retaliate for the merciless brutalities of our enemy in the East. She would insist on her position, however, such as, "Evil will never be destroyed; usually it is inherited by the other side"—one of her carefully coined, sometimes astonishing, conclusions that resulted from her penchant for wrestling for days, sometimes weeks, with aspects of public affairs that worried her.

One basic idea used to prevail in our talks: that after so short a period of time—not even ten years—the Third Reich was in a state of transition that would produce a new stage in German society and its position in the world. Restoration of the Hohenzollern monarchy in any form was unthinkable, and it was evident that a new political elite was needed to replace the set that had emerged from the *Kampfzeit*.[*]

---

[*]The period before 1933 when the National Socialists struggled for political power.

The war, we hoped, would help forge that new elite; seasoned by the hardships of war service, they would return to or enter professional life and take the place of the Party people as soon as the war was over. In particular, we thought this new elite would possess a profound notion of what it really meant to serve—to serve the common good. We were quite aware, however, that the longer the war lasted, the more that idea would lose its bearing as the casualties of the war actually diminished the ranks from which that elite might grow.

All in all, this may not have been the utmost in political wisdom, but at the moment, it had at least some plausibility. It was, at any rate, entirely different from the picture of "Nazidom" that I would eventually read about in the *Stars and Stripes* according to which the evil course of the system was clearly visible from the outset. It is true that anything *could* happen under totalitarian rule, but it is also true that nothing was *bound* to happen.

The person of Hitler remained untouched in our critical talks. To think of him as an irresponsible gambler and fanatic—as I am beginning to see him now (his suicide confirming that judgment)—or even to think of him as capable of getting down to the extermination of the Jews under German control, was far beyond what we could conceive. My parents found Hitler's hate of the Jews repulsive. The *SS* paper *Der Stürmer*—with its ugly caricatures of Jews—was often cited by them as a paradigm of political vulgarity, but they saw this propaganda as but part of the revolutionary thrust of the movement and as wartime exaggerations that would recede as soon as the war was over. Besides, from what we could see, hear, or read during the Third Reich, there were no indications of any large-scale crimes one reads about now and the extent of which is still to me mind-boggling.

Certainly, in 1938 after the German diplomat had been shot in Paris by the Jewish assassin Grynszpan, there had been *Kristalnacht*, the breaking of windows of Jewish shops in our town and some other acts of violence. This incident, however, was one of those events my mother had furiously denounced in her local women's organization, postulating that those responsible for the outrages were a disgrace to the Party, just the kind of "Radikalinskis" that were no better than the Bolsheviks. In her eyes, they were the faction that must be "kept down."

I know little of any personal relations my family had with Jews. If there were any, they were not much discussed. The one of which I was aware was a high judge living across the street from my grandparents in Brunswick, a fellow of distinguished character, fond of playing in string quartets, who in the past, sometimes would ask my uncle Peter over to help out with the second violin. Outright anti-Semitism certainly wasn't part of my parents' thinking. As I recall occasional remarks, however, it becomes clear that there were certain reservations about Jews in general, certain signs of decadence my parents found disgusting in our cultural life in the twenties were associated with Jewish influence. I remember another, more significant point in their critical attitude, which was the role they assigned to Jewish intellectuals in the Russian revolution and Bolshevik ideology which the Germans, they thought, were destined to resist. It touched a string in my parents' minds when Nazi propaganda associated the evil influence of Jewish intellectuals on Bolshevism with their "rootless" existence in the Diaspora.

We knew, of course, of concentration camps. To our knowledge, they were labor camps where conditions were hard but just. Had we known the official rule of conduct in those camps "*Arbeit macht frei*" ("Work makes one free"), we readily would have consented. If, on the other hand, we had known of or suspected any willful killings in the camps, which must have begun on a large scale about the time of my political discussions with my mother, our talks would have taken a different course and our attitude would have radically changed. This thought is, I admit, a hypothesis and one of little consequence, but had the people in general known, I think that neither the killings nor the war could have continued in any meaningful way. It seems inconceivable from this distance that any authority in the Third Reich could have let the killings become public, could have taken any responsibility for them, and continued to stay in office. Inconceivable, too, that German soldiers—officers as well as plain soldiers—let alone a few fanatics, would have been ready to go on risking their lives for a cause so utterly corrupted. That kind of general knowledge would have delivered the death blow to any military morale. That, in fact, both had taken place at the same time can only be perceived under the condition that the doings inside the camps were surrounded by absolute secrecy. That the war continued is, I think, strong evidence against the assumption that the German people knew what was going on.*

I forget which subject in particular we discussed on that evening in September 1942. At that time, I felt that I personally had little part in the

---

*Of course, long after the war, various researchers have brought to light that there were soldiers, from field marshals down to entire battalions of Army field police, who were aware of the mass killings and other atrocious deeds of the *SS-Einsatzgruppen* behind the front lines in Poland and Russia. They also learned that it was a matter of governmental planning. Yet only a few of them went to engage in active or passive resistance against the regime, while the rest went right on serving. These cases don't support my opinion as a prisoner in 1945, and my thinking at that time appears overly idealistic and naïve. And yet, had front-line soldiers *in general* known of the ongoing scheme that later became known as the *Shoa*, I still hold that they wouldn't have risked their lives for that criminal regime so that military morale would have collapsed throughout the *Wehrmacht*, *Waffen-SS* included, years before the war ended.

past, that the political choices had not been for me to make, and that the only thing that mattered at present was that there was a war on that had to be won. The war had become our destiny, my destiny. I was left with the inescapable question of my age group: What are you going to do for your country? That one question became deeply engraved on our maturing minds during the war years. My response was simple enough: serve the best way I could. There was nothing specific in that except for the vague notion of belonging to a group which would have more than its normal share of duties.

It was long after midnight on that night in September 1942 when we ended our talk. I put out the light and opened the curtains, drawn closed for the blackout, to let in fresh air. Moonlight poured into the room, and I could see the outlines of two familiar objects on top of the bookcase by the window: my father's World War One steel helmet and his sword.

The next day at school, I made my decision.

On that morning, Dr. Weyrich, our headmaster and English teacher, strode briskly into the classroom. Cheerfully rubbing his hands, his rosy face in a broad smile, he said, "Good Morning, gentlemen. Please sit down. What are we going to do on this lovely morning? I think we'll write a little exercise"— all in excellent English, of course. With that, we were asked to take a dictation. I've forgotten the subject of the text and its origin, but I remember that it was, in the circumstances, a subtle piece of insinuation. He was an Anglophile. Having spent some years abroad, he felt compelled to hand down to his pupils some knowledge of British customs and character that he found worth following. He would explain that, for instance, while in German a prohibition against something was usually expressed as *Rauchen Verboten!* ("Smoking forbidden!") the English way of putting it was "Please don't smoke." With regard to the *Luftwaffe*'s offensive against targets in England he would, visibly annoyed by the loud-mouthed German propaganda, warn against the illusion that British morale would be broken by it. "You think we'll bring them to heel? No, sir!" he would say, wagging his forefinger like a metronome. "It will result in the opposite. It'll only stiffen their backbones. Believe me!"

It was not his Anglophilia, however, that endeared Weyrich to his pupils and their parents. It was generally known that he had been transferred to our school as headmaster for disciplinary reasons; in his former position as head of a department in the Brunswick Ministry of Education, he had refused to sign a letter of dismissal of a teacher who had resisted pressure to separate from his Jewish wife. My parents, associating with the Weyrichs privately, were glad to have that kind of teacher in charge of their sons' education while we, his pupils, had great respect for him.

It was during the next lesson that the two different currents in our class surfaced. There were those whose attitude toward the war was like my own, for whom the war was a personal challenge and who were eager to make a commitment. Then there were those who regarded the war as the business of others, of volunteers in particular, and who thought that no idea was worth the sacrifice of human life, at least not their own and who, therefore, were looking for a safe haven to wait for the war to end.

Of course, these two different currents were not as clear and as pure as I set them out here; there certainly were various impurities. There were varying degrees of romanticism or personal ambitions on the one hand, and personal weakness, intellectual or moral reticence, or sober calculation about the ultimate outcome of the war on the other. Nor were these currents clearly visible; they surfaced only occasionally and when they did, it was in some oblique way.

Our second lesson was German with Dr. Hinz. Handicapped by a shortened leg and a wooden arm, he had joined the Party early in the twenties when he studied German and history at the University of Munich. Endowed with a remarkable capacity for rhetoric and a sharp intellect combined with a peculiar mixture of refined and coarse language, as a sideline he assumed the responsibility of public speaker for the Party. In his lessons, he used to wander easily from matters of the German language to topics of history and from there to current politics, where he would display in passing an impressive amount of insider information. His occasional snide swipes at certain Party moguls or attitudes were especially popular, not least because they betrayed an astonishingly accurate knowledge of criticism currently circulating among the people.

On that morning, we resumed the subject of the Gothic War. For me, the Gothic War had all the elements of a drama; it was full of conflicts of characters and ideas, of love and death, of fortune and of ruin.* The events lay far back in the mist of history, some fourteen hundred years ago, the age when great myths were born: the *Nibelungen*, King Arthur, Lancelot, and, last but not least, Dietrich von Bern, the great Theoderich, king of the Ostrogoths. Altogether, it was a setting that let the contesting figures and concepts appear untainted and flawless in the way the young of any age want the world to be.

We had been reading Procopius' *Gothic War* in our history lessons and, in parallel, Felix Dahn's *A Struggle for Rome* in the German lessons, both an exercise in the critical reading of a historical novel against the background of historical sources. Hinz requested we write an essay on the novel, each of us free to choose his own specific subject. This morning, we were to indicate our different subjects and to describe a brief outline for discussion.

*The Gothic War, 535–553 AD, was between Justinian and the Ostrogoths in Italy and ended in total defeat at the battle of Vesuvius, where almost all of the Goths preferred death to slavery and only a small remainder were allowed to return to the home of their ancestors, an island in the Baltic Sea.

Various subjects came up: the question of racial superiority; the justness of the cause (what business had the Goths in Italy anyway?); the *Lebensraum* argument;* and then the characters of the last two Gothic kings, Totila and Teja, and their Roman antagonist Cethegus. All of these topics were discussed with no *explicit* reference to the present.

It was my classmate, Krug, who dashed forward with the daring thesis that basically the Gothic war was a case of poor leadership, nothing less and nothing more. Krug, a blond youth with soft features and a rather lavish hairstyle, had a sharp, analytical intellect, loved disputes, and was fond of knocking down the positions of others. Combined with this ability was a deep distrust of all convictions, even his own.

"I deny that one can call it a tragedy," he declared. "It simply was foolish for the Goths to stay in Italy after Justinianus made it clear he didn't want them in the region. They, a thin stratum of warriors, couldn't hope to conquer the whole world as it was then perceived."

"What do you think the Goths' leaders should have done instead?" Hinz asked.

"Well, it's hard to say. Perhaps they should have listened to the envoy of their relatives from the North who had urged them to return to where they came from, to Gotland," Krug replied.

"Aren't you judging from hindsight? At the time the Gothic envoy arrived, Totila, their king, was the absolute ruler of Rome, wasn't he?" Hinz objected.

"Yes, I know," Krug said, "and two years later, Totila and his people were wiped out. Prudent leadership should have seen that the reign of so few over so many was doomed from the outset."

"But it lasted for fifty years, and it had worked in other cases," Hinz insisted. "Didn't the Normans succeed and the Saxons before them?"

"Your analogy has a flaw. In the case of the Goths, barbarians tried to subject an old civilization to their rule. Not so in the case of Britain."

"Perhaps you would accept the reign of the Romans over the Greek as an example?" Hinz proposed. "But I shouldn't do all the talking. What's your opinion, Voss?" he asked, looking at me.

"I think Krug's view is rather superficial," I began. "The crucial question is what the Gothic kings and their advisors thought they could compromise on and what they thought was inalienable. Obviously, the Goths perceived Italy as their home country, as their *Lebensraum* (living space) after their

---

*A nation's living space, the soil a nation is entitled to "by the might of its victorious sword." Although the term's origin lies in the nineteenth century, it gained political momentum when it was adopted by National Socialism to justify Germany's territorial expansion to the East (see Adolf Hitler, *Mein Kampf*, Engl. ed. by Houghton Mifflin. Sentry Edition, 1971, p. 652 ff.).

ancestors had left Gotland and later had been expelled from the Black Sea. And how can you give up your home?"

"I see. Next he'll say, 'Just like ourselves, fighting for *Lebensraum* in the East'," Krug audibly murmured from the background.

"Certainly not!" I said looking at him. "That wouldn't support my point; the Germans are a nation with a country of their own, after all. I leave the issue of *Lebensraum* to others to defend. If you want me to name something inalienable in the present, I should say it's the values of European culture that can't be compromised in our fight with Bolshevism. Prudence is irrelevant when it comes to basic convictions. Must I elaborate on that?"

"Certainly you should do so in your essay, though very briefly," Hinz said.

Krug resumed his point, "You can't deny that the last battle the Goths fought at Vesuvius was a useless sacrifice. A classic example of poor leadership!"

"Did you consider that the alternative would have been slavery, women and children included ?" Hinz asked.

"I considered that lives would have been saved, lives that were vital for the survival of the Goths as such. Hasn't the *Führer* said that the survival of the species is the ultimate goal?" Krug sneered.

"Life is only one of the values I mentioned," I cut in. "There are others like freedom, honor, and duty. I need not explain that it may be necessary to sacrifice one for the other, do I? And it was for the king to weigh and to decide; that's what he was elected for."

"He was not free to decide," Krug insisted. "He was bound by his loyalty to his people. Teja, the last king, acted disloyally when he sent his men to their deaths. He led his people into ruin; the Goths were physically destroyed. After the Vesuvius battle, the Goths vanished from history. That is the reality we have to acknowledge."

Now all of us felt the tension that had arisen in the classroom; by now, the historical analogy was unmistakable. Krug had spoken as if he was the only realist in the room while the others were pursuing insubstantial metaphysics.

"Reality?" Hinz took up the argument. "What, actually, *is* reality? I shall tell you: reality is anything that is efficacious. If we are observing something that in some way has an effect on something else, we are facing reality. In this sense, aren't the Goths still present? Don't they affect our minds and, perhaps, even our actions? Don't they still influence our consciousness? Have they really vanished from history? Has Christ vanished from history? Have King Arthur or Dietrich von Bern? Have Mozart or Beethoven?"

"I beg your pardon, sir, but how on earth can the Goths be named in one breath with Christ?" another classmate of ours interjected on his authority as a pastor's son.

"Don't you see?" Hinz continued. "Christ lived and died to hand down a message that has lasted for nearly two thousand years; Beethoven lived to give to mankind such music as his string quartet Opus 131 as an everlasting present. The Goths may have come into existence and perished to give us a precedent of a people's will of self-assertion, of collective courage, of honor, and of group loyalty to basic convictions."

He paused and then added as an afterthought, "Of course, it always needs some sort of receptiveness on the side of later generations to make these forces efficacious, some open-mindedness, however naive or refined. Beethoven's string quartet doesn't have an impact on everybody; it needs some musical maturity to be effective." He smiled. "People are different, aren't they?"

Outside in front of our school, the park lay in the sun. Its sweeping lawns, chestnut-lined paths, flowerbeds, and white benches made a beautiful sight, and our school building with its classical façade provided a pleasant counterpoint. The inscription under the pediment above the portal of our school read *Humanitati Sapientiae* ["Wisdom (is to serve) mankind"]. Standing on the steps in front of the portal, I looked upon a scene of serene peace. Pupils of all ages between ten and eighteen were chatting, romping, playing, and munching bread on the square under the chestnuts.

My classmates stood divided in two clusters, apparently continuing our discussion. After so many years, I knew most of them well, their backgrounds and their way of thinking. I knew Krug would volunteer for a career as a medical doctor with the *Luftwaffe*, something which would guarantee him studies at the university safe from front service for the next several years. Two clusters, two factions, I thought: idealists and pragmatists—those ready to make commitments and sacrifices for a cause reaching beyond themselves and those who, for whatever reasons, were not. The epigraph under the pediment didn't say which one had the wisdom to serve humanity best.

This wasn't the time for philosophy, however, I thought. It was the time for a firm commitment. I felt a sudden urge to demonstrate where I stood, and I wanted the difference between me and the other group to be great.

As I was passing by the Krug group, I could overhear arguments in support of Krug, which had not occurred to his cronies earlier. When Krug noticed me, I congratulated him, "Good show, Krug. I was impressed."

"I hope I have convinced you."

"Certainly not; you wouldn't expect that, would you ?"

"Of course not. How could I?" he laughed. "I guess you found that idealistic stuff of Hinz's very exciting. How can you expect a prominent leader of the *Jungvolk* to be anything else than an idealist, praising honor, loyalty, duty and all that?"

"Why so sarcastic? Do I detect an urge to justify your special choice for a military career?"

"I need not justify anything. In case you're hinting at my volunteering for the *Luftwaffe*, try this, I'll volunteer for a doctor's career because there must be doctors to stitch together people like you who can't wait for their dreams of glory to come true."

"Let's be honest, we haven't noticed your medical vocation or any other humanitarian conviction before, have we? Why hide the true reason? It's so obvious."

"Speaking of honesty, what kind of contribution are you going to make anyway?" he snapped back.

I hesitated for a moment, looking at him and the others of his group as they watched me. But my answer had been on my mind for a long time, Philipp's example, my talks with him, my intent to do something beyond the average, and now this sudden urge to make the difference between us evident. Why not abandon my last reservations now? Wasn't everything clear? It was a matter of self respect, and it was the right moment to make my decision.

"Me?" I said. "Why, I'll join the *Waffen-SS*."

5

REVELATIONS

"So you are determined to volunteer? All right then. But why the *Waffen-SS?*"
"It's hard to explain," I said. "I just think that's where I belong."

My father and I were sitting across from one another at a table in the large waiting room of the Hallstadt station, sipping hot ersatz coffee among a throng of other people, mostly servicemen. We had arrived by train on a small, private railway line that served the Harz Mountains and linked Blessheim to the *Reichsbahn* net. He was on his way back to the front. He wore his artillery major's uniform, looked rested and his old self: tall, handsome, trustworthy, and self-confident in his own way.

"Now listen, Johann. I have talked to a regimental comrade of mine. He can manage to bring you into my old regiment at Hannover if you would volunteer there. It's a distinguished regiment with a distinguished name, Scharnhorst, as you know. There you could do your duty just as well. To me, it would be a great relief to know there were people higher up who would keep an eye on you."

With all his usually good spirits, he now seemed worried. His hopes for a short war and for his sons to be spared his own experience as a frontline soldier had not been realized. He had seen his eldest son sent to the front lines of the notorious center sector in Russia as an artillery forward observer—hardly a safe assignment—and now his second was striving for perhaps even riskier ventures. Also, he had first hand experience of the last winter at Smolensk, where he was in charge of keeping the fleets of motor vehicles of the center sector rolling, and always faced the possibility of a total collapse of the front. Rather taciturn on serious matters, during his leave he made some remarks from which I gathered that in these dark months things had been on a razor's edge and that he had his doubts about the outcome of the war.

I suddenly felt sorry for him. He used to be such a devoted father when the four of us were still children. On weekends, he would often take the family out in the car for picnics or searching for mushrooms in the mountains. At our insistence, in the evenings he would play his guitar and sing, mostly English and Australian songs from of his boyhood. We were enchanted and used to know all the melodies and the words, except for their meaning. There were merry songs and some that were sad, but my father was never sad in those days. Now I was not sure of that anymore, in spite of what he allowed others to see.

"You know," I said, hoping to get through with this matter as quickly as possible, "I so much wanted to serve with a mountain division and this is my chance. Can you understand?"

"Are you sure you will get what you want? You might get neither the mountains nor any other adventures you may think of. Believe me, war for the infantryman in the front line is nasty. And in the rear there are assignments for the SS of a kind I want you even less to get mixed up with. Why not join a nice, decent, traditional regiment?"

Now that I remember our talk, I wonder what my father had in mind when he referred to the assignments with the SS "in the rear." At that time, however, I did not pursue the point. "Certainly, it would be a privilege to serve with your regiment. I can see that. But I think that this war is different. It is not a war between Prussia and Napoleon as in Scharnhorst's day. It's even no longer between Germany and her adversaries as it was in your time. It is between European civilization and Bolshevism. It's time for beginning a new tradition, one built by European youth. That is what I want to take part in.

I probably used some more arguments and talked somewhat more gently and certainly more clumsily. In my father's ears, what I said might have even sounded like propaganda but I did say that I was going my own way and why. He must have understood, for he dropped the matter without further comment. Perhaps it was also because of his strong dislike for discussing abstract subjects, all "isms" in particular. He often covered what was going on inside himself with a quick change to cheerfulness. He looked at his watch and briskly put on his gloves.

"Well, before we part let's have a drink, soldier," he said smiling, while he rose and moved me to the bar.

I saw him off on the platform. Both of us were experiencing another one of those gloomy goodbyes on a railway station in wartime. We did our best to get through it. When the train pulled out, my father remained standing behind the window of the door of his coach, lifting his hand in a military salute.

As the last coach slid by, it cleared the view of another train, a goods train as it appeared, slowly passing by on the track behind the one next to the platform. Lost in thought, I noticed at first only the freshly-painted propaganda slogans across the wagons: WHEELS ARE ROLLING FOR VICTORY. Then, looking more closely at the wall of a wagon opposite me, however, I became conscious, with a sudden chill, of what seemed to be fingers, yellowish human fingers clinging to a few square holes in the side wall; behind strings of barbed wire, I saw human eyes, dark and wide open, trying to catch a glimpse of the outside world. Stunned, I gazed upon the long row of wagons. Now and then one of those little holes with fingers and eyes slowly shunted out of sight.

Strong as it was, the sight left me with mixed feelings: *Vae victis!* Woe to the Vanquished! Scum of the earth! Poor devils! I hope they will be put to some decent work in the field. This thought, however, also occurred to me: Never must the "dictatorship of the proletariat" prevail in Europe.

6

WILD GEESE

My memory of my last fall at home is marked by two different episodes at different places: in Brunswick, another encounter with Uncle Peter, revealing his predicament as a neutral; and in Hardenberg, with Philipp, watching the flight of wild geese, giving wings to a romanticism which cannot go unmentioned in a true account of my war years.

The wind was blowing down the first leaves from the chestnut trees on the Wall in Brunswick. The large yellow-fingered remnants of summer were glued to the ground, soaked with the rain. On this day in October 1942, my grandparents' house was still there, its charming white facade defying the turn of the season. From there, across the pond through the thinning foliage of the chestnut trees, one could see the manor on the island, where some years ago the *SS* had set up their local headquarters.

I was on my way home from a pre-military training camp in the *Westerwald*, stopping over for a short visit to my aunt Isa. I also hoped to see Philipp, whom I knew to be home waiting for his next assignment. Three weeks of hard training behind me, I was glad to be back in "civilization." My grandmother had died from heart failure earlier that year. Afterwards, things had changed rapidly in the house. Approaching the entrance, I was bluntly reminded of the new situation when I bumped into an *SS* officer coming out of the house—not in the field-gray uniform I was used to from the weeks in the camp, but in the black and silver of the Allgemeine (General, or political) *SS*. He was wearing riding breeches and immaculately polished riding boots, an attire which I never could help finding somewhat silly in the absence of a horse. The ground floor and the first floor of the house were leased to the *SS* as a convenient annex to their headquarters.

Isa was now living in her new apartment in the attic. She used to call it her *"Himmelreich"* ("Elysium"). It was an entirely new, enchanting place with the finest and most precious pieces of furniture, paintings, and books of the old household. Climbing up the stairs, I even sensed the same old fragrance of lavender, now mixed with a faint smell of fresh paint. The flat had turned out to be an exquisite place for Isa to live indeed.

It was on this occasion that I saw "the Swedes" again. My Uncle Peter was there with Greta.

Peter and his family had come to Germany in May after his prospects in Stockholm had rapidly dwindled. I knew he had lost his position with a British firm by the end of 1939, and they had since been living off their savings and odd jobs. Somehow, he seemed to have lost his British passport, too, which must have meant a radical change in his status. Moreover, as he had indicated in one of his letters, with the German Army entering the Soviet Union, it had become clear to him that now the war would drag on for a long time and that he couldn't hope simply to wait out his uncomfortable situation. Eventually, he was offered a position in Brunswick by an old friend of his. They had taken the opportunity, packed up their belongings, now in storage, and moved into a furnished apartment right in the neighborhood of Isa's place on the Wall.

There was a great hullaballoo when I found the three of them in Isa's sitting room. We had not seen each other since our last meeting at Hardenburg four years earlier. They still looked as I had remembered them: attractive, elegant, cosmopolitan; Peter's fancy shoes made it obvious that he had been living abroad. Greta was smoking a small black cigar–most unusual, too. Altogether, they were a bright spot in our bleak wartime surroundings.

Yet, for all the familiarity between us, it was an odd situation. I was wearing my navy-blue uniform of the *Jungvolk*, and in those days, I was used to seeing men of Peter's age in field-gray uniforms. The Swedes, in contrast, were utterly civilian. There was another thing, too. Somehow I felt I had just intruded into a situation of which I had no knowledge.

They watched with curiosity while I gave a brief account of my trip from the *Westerwald* and of my pre-military training. They may have been comparing what I, a young German, was doing at this stage in life, with the activities of my Swedish contemporaries, namely more peaceful diversions like sailing, tennis, and traveling abroad.

"How did you like it up there, you and your comrades?" Peter asked. "It can't have been fun."

I tried a bit of irony and quoted, casually, "We left 'proudly conscious of having gladly done our duty'."*

---

*"*Im stolzen Bewusstsein freudig erfüllter Pflicht.*"

He roared with laughter (as he was able to do at any moment), "... proudly conscious of having ... What? ... gladly! ... done our duty! That's wonderful! That's simply wonderful. Where did you get that?" His eyes were watering.

"It's a quotation," I explained, when he had calmed down. "It's from the Army Regulation Book. Nicely put, after all, isn't it?"

"All the same, I'm afraid it is above my head," Peter said, now chuckling good-naturedly. "Did you really enjoy your training?"

"You've become thin, Johann," Isa said, "it looks as if they've let you starve."

"It was a bit tough, yes. No fun and games."

"Not even some little war games?" Peter teased.

"Not exactly, rather a lot of field training, topography, cross-country marches, that kind of stuff. No military drill, if you mean that, not in the usual sense at least. Much different."

"Well, it sounds as if something new is going on," Peter continued bantering. "Perhaps it's the new secret weapon everyone is talking about, a secret weapon in the making up there in the hills of the *Westerwald*—German youth, vintage 1925, best quality, 'tough as leather, hard as Krupp steel, quick as greyhounds'. Wasn't this what the *Führer* used to say of the Hitler Youth? It should have occurred to us earlier."

"Peter! Please! Don't be at it again!" Greta interrupted. "Next time they won't let you off so easily." She seemed disturbed.

"Did I say anything wrong?" he protested with an air of innocence. "Or is somebody listening?" Facetiously, he looked around and under the table.

I found him amusing as ever, and to humor him I said, "Don't mind me! Besides, in a certain sense you could even be right. In the camp, the *Waffen-SS* is picking the best of the livestock as volunteers for a new division. Rumor has it that it'll be called '*Hitlerjugend*'."

"Won't you tell Johann what brought us here at this hour?" Greta now asked Peter.

"Why, yes, of course," he began, unfolding an extraordinary story. It had started a few days before. Late one afternoon, he and his colleagues had a little chat at the office, a friend of his to whom he owed his present job among them. They were quite at ease. One of them, an agreeable chap for all Peter knew of him, got rather boastful about the latest achievements of the German Army in Russia and, in consequence, about the general prospects for the war. After a while, Peter couldn't help butting in, "You fellows don't believe in earnest we can win the war, do you?" This had stopped the boasting immediately, but at the same moment, the room had fallen into dead silence. Afterward, Peter's friend had given him to understand that the group had been a little too large for such loose talk.

Three days later, Peter got a summons from the *Gestapo*.[*] First he didn't know what to think of it; it could be a matter of routine. Gradually, however, Greta and he had become upset. On that day, on that very morning, he had been there and had returned only some hours before. Arriving at the room indicated in the summons, he was told that the chief himself wanted to see him. "That's either good or very bad," he thought. When he was let in to the chief's office, however, he saw to his greatest surprise his old pal and school-mate, Manni, now in charge of the local Gestapo section. As soon as the door closed behind him, Manni immediately fell into their old relationship.

"Man alive! Peter! It's really you! I couldn't believe it at first. Have a seat. How did it go since we left school? You must tell me. First of all, though, you're lucky I got hold of that silly report on your talk in the office. For heaven's sake, Peter, stop talking that sort of nonsense! You can get yourself into real trouble by that. Please, do me a favor and hold your tongue next time. Promise?"

And with that, the whole matter was dropped. Afterwards, they had a long chat that had lasted almost until noon. Now, here he was, back again, counting himself lucky.

Isa brought in some snacks she had been preparing in the kitchen, where she had overheard Peter's account anew. "You forgot to mention, my dear," she said to Peter, "that I, too, was scared to death. I didn't have a wink of sleep last night. I thought, even if they didn't lock you up, they surely could make you regret you returned to Germany altogether."

I well remember how at that point Peter's mood changed from his usual bantering to deadly earnest.

"Germany or elsewhere, does it really matter? I think people like us can always be sure of the attention of the police anywhere else, one way or the other," Peter replied. "Do I regret being back in Germany? I don't think that's the question. There is no room for regret, nor for delight for that matter, because you are forced to take sides, no matter how much you feel that it's none of your business."

"Well," Isa remarked, "you're not the only one in that condition. There are a lot of other people who hate to make choices in that way, no matter where they may live, here or abroad."

"Certainly, I can even imagine many Germans thinking this war is none of their business. It's pretty obvious. But with me it's different. There's nothing I owe to Germany, as little as I owe to any other country. Neither have I been a dissident in any way. So where is the justification for forcing me into this situation? Can you explain that to me? Real citizens of a state owe loyalty

---

[*]An acronym which stood for *Geheime Staats Polizei*, or the Secret State Police.

because of certain advantages they've been enjoying and hope to enjoy later: security, education, opportunities in life, public welfare, and what have you. With me, it's different. I didn't even study here. And afterwards? No opportunities at all. I had to go abroad. In England, I arrived penniless. And why is that? Because my home country was unable to protect my father's property against confiscation by the British; securities, in fact, he earned through life-long hard work. So, after the first war there was nothing left but this house. On the other hand, I haven't worked against this state, either. So I ask you, Who has the right to force me to take sides? To whom do I owe loyalty?"

He paused. Our talk had taken a serious turn. And then he added more calmly, "I have tried to stay out of this, out of this chauvinistic contest between European countries, but it didn't work. Europe is still too immature. Can you imagine anything more immature than countries waging this war?"

Interesting as I found his view, at that time it didn't sink in. I was already too committed. Besides, many questions were left open, but I thought it would be better to leave it at that. Otherwise, it would lead to an endless, perhaps unpleasant, discussion.

Greta was keen to get going, "We shouldn't keep the child waiting too long," she said. They had left their little daughter at home with their landlord. Peter, too, seemed to be glad to end our talk and say goodbye.

"Are we going to see you again tomorrow?" Peter asked me.

"I'm afraid not. I'll be leaving this evening for a stopover at Hardenberg. Philipp will be with me on the train, Philipp von Burgdorf; you met him four years ago, remember ?"

"Yes, I remember!" Greta exclaimed. "Wasn't he the lad living next door?"

"How is he doing?" Greta asked.

"He's doing fine. He just finished his course at officer's candidate school here at Brunswick. Just now he's on leave, waiting for his new assignment."

"Officer's candidate school here in Brunswick? Are you saying he is with the *Waffen-SS*?" Peter asked, quite startled, knowing that there was no other officer's candidate school at Brunswick.

"That's right. He was transferred to the *Waffen-SS* early this year," I replied.

"You mean he was forced to? I can't imagine anyone of his family wanting to mix up with that bunch."

"Whatever you think, he has volunteered."

Shaking his head, he muttered, "I really think I need some more education to understand what is going on over here."

I saw them out. On my way up to Isa's flat, I kept wondering about what I had heard. What did Peter mean by being forced to take sides? Had there been some pressure other than his economic situation?

Isa was a bit surprised when she found me uninformed about the circum-stances of Peter's return to Germany. It had been late in 1940 when he had applied for the extension of his passport's validity, not knowing what lay ahead for him. At first, the people at the British embassy had been very nice. It was only months later that Peter realized they were stalling. Then, one day, he was given to understand that his case could easily be solved by some sort of cooperation on his part. Eventually, they came up with an idea which must have been their intention from the beginning: they suggested that he should sign up with the British intelligence in the UK. They said for him, because of his German origin and his command of several languages, there were var-ious opportunities to make himself useful during the war. They offered to move his family to the UK at their expense. Unfortunately, however, they said, apologizing for the inconvenience, Greta and her daughter were to be taken care of in an internment camp, "for security reasons," whatever that meant. Peter refused, but as a result, he deprived himself of all chances to get his passport renewed. He then applied for a German passport. The people at the German embassy were eager to help, happy about the prodigal son, but they, too, had their conditions. He got his passport by the end of the year, but only on the condition that he return to Germany as soon as possible.

I felt sorry for Peter and Greta. All of this must have been very distressing for them. "They must feel as though they're wandering about in no-man's land," I said. "Why didn't our own people make use of him in Sweden, the country being neutral? One should think that there were enough opportuni-ties for someone like Peter. Aren't we getting most of our iron-ore from there, for instance?"

"He has tried that, of course. But I understand they preferred their own people, Party liners or people of similar reliability," Isa said.

"It's too bad. He can't be too happy with his German passport. How is Greta taking it?"

"For Greta, it seems quite natural to stand by his side. Both have come to terms with the situation as it is. That is my impression. Think of the alterna-tive! And then, she's the daughter of a German Navy captain, after all. Mother was grateful for the opportunity to start a new life when she married father after the war, but the old ties still hold. I know in a way it's also true of Greta."

At the station, Philipp was in uniform. I had not seen him in his *Waffen-SS* uniform before, and from the distance I didn't recognize him for a moment. Looking back to that morning, I still have the sight clearly in my mind. It is a strange thing with uniforms; to a certain degree, they seem to lend a new identity to a person. In most cases, of course, people just appear to change from civilians to soldiers. In so doing, however, some gain in stature, others change from vulgar to pompous (as in the case of most Party officials) and some again change from sensible to ridiculous figures. With Philipp, it was different altogether. The gray, high-buttoned tunic with the ribbon of the Iron Cross emphasized certain qualities of his that could be observed even before: his modest nobility, his serene commitment to serve, a trace of askesis. The uniform let him look still young and seemed to preserve much of the image of the popular *Jungvolk* leader I had known in the summer camp. That and his youthful intrepidity were stressed by the peaked cap of gray cloth with the black band and the Death's Head badge in front. He was wearing it a bit askew and had removed the stiffener from inside to make the cap look worn and unpretentious. So much was he a personality of his own that the two silver runes on the black collar patches and the silvery belt buckle with the epigraph *Meine Ehre Heisst Treue* ("My Honor Is My Loyalty") seemed to be symbols of his very own loyalty to the values he had imparted to me early that year.

Our compartment was empty so that our talk flowed easily from the start. Philipp's wish to be posted to the *Wiking*, where most of the non-German European volunteers were serving, had come true as he had learned only on the day before.* He was all enthusiasm, looking forward to his new assignment. In a few days, he would be on his way down to the south of Russia, he would take command of a rifle platoon and before long, he would be promoted to *Untersturmführer*.† At that time, we, that is, my age group, still being at school, were rather well informed about where the front lines ran, especially in the East. At home, many of us used to follow our armies' positions by sticking little brightly-colored pins on large wall maps in our rooms, indicating the towns, rivers, or territories that were the topics of the daily news. It was a habit taken up during the early years of the war and gladly resumed at the next *Sondermeldung* announcing further advances of our forces.‡ So I was aware of the German summer offensive in southern Russia, the powerful thrust toward the oilfields behind the Caucasus Mountains by the Caspian Sea. I also knew that the *Wiking* was somewhere in that region. Although he did not have much to say about the actual operations, I listened all the more to what Philipp said about the strategic design behind it all. He said it wasn't only that control of the oil wells was an absolute necessity for winning the war, but that reaching the Volga River was equally important. Only then would the way north be open to envelop the Russian armies around Moscow.

---

*5th SS-Panzer-Division "*Wiking*," or "Viking."
†Rank taken from the general *SS*-organization, equivalent to Second Lieutenant.
‡Special radio news reporting important events on the war theaters, each time dramatically announced by a blast of trumpets and followed by the playing of military marches.

Naturally, I was impressed. This was, I think, the first time I got a vague notion of the economic meaning of the war, its opportunities, and its limits. I was confident, though, that the limits of our oil supply would be stretched by the far-sighted leadership of the *Führer*. At that time in October 1942, however, it was known that our troops had become mixed up in ferocious battles in the Caucasus as well as on their way farther up to the Volga, and even from our radio news, it appeared that our advance was making only little progress or, as in the mountains, had virtually come to a halt. Therefore, Philipp's optimism was an invitation for raising doubts from my side about the successful outcome of the operation. He was confident all the same. As our success was an absolute must for winning the war, he said, all our strength was being concentrated in that region; didn't I know that some advance units of ours had already reached the Caspian shore? Moreover, he said, the stream of young volunteers from Europe into the divisions of the *Waffen-SS* had even become stronger during the last year; it was bound to grow further the more it became evident for the public outside Germany that she needed help to crush the Bolshevik menace. For me, all that made this train ride memorable. At the same time, I was proud to join the organization that would allow me to make my own contribution.

Meanwhile, the compartment had filled with country people. An elderly lady seemed to take an interest in the bits she could pick up from our talk. So we let our conversation take a more general course.

On our arrival at Hardenburg, Philipp took the occasion to pay a call on my grandmother. We found the house, at first sight, unaffected by the war. Against the setting of the garden and the forest, both in full color, it looked as beautiful as ever. The lawns, however, had turned into wild meadows with high grass. On the old tennis court, potatoes were being grown, hens were picking in the chicken yard, and the hedges badly needed a trimming. Inside we found my Mummi, now doing much of the housework herself. Eda was fully occupied with her function as head of the local women's organization, boosting people's morale at the "home front." At present, she was organizing a collection of warm clothes for the soldiers at the front. Stena had become a nurse again, and was serving with the Red Cross somewhere in southern Russia. Although the last days had been chilly, the central heating system of the house was not in operation. Only in the sitting room and in the adjoining library the green-tiled stove radiated a comfortable heat.

The library had become Mummi's favorite room in recent years, where she was near Schopenhauer, Nietzsche, and Spengler, the philosophers she used to read quite thoroughly as appeared from her annotations in the margins that I had found some time ago. She was pleased to see us and seemed to relish

the vivid conversation now going on between her and the younger generation. She dignified the occasion by offering us some of her sherry which she
asked me to fetch from downstairs. Given her critical mind, I think that
Philipp's sober account of his duties and experiences must have been a relief
to her in comparison to Eda's way of amplifying the party line at home.

Eda came in just when Philipp was about to leave. Obviously, she was
impressed by his appearance in uniform, and when she heard that he was
going back to the front, she seized him by his shoulders focusing her blue
eagle-eyes on him as if bidding farewell to a warrior marching to the battlefield the next minute.

Outside it was dark, the sky brilliant with stars. As we were standing at the
gate, there were strange sounds high up in the air, very faintly at first, but
gradually becoming more distinct, a jumble of shrill cries growing louder and
louder. And suddenly we saw them coming, quite discernible now, two, three
huge wedge-like flights of geese high up, steadily beating their wings, their
long necks stretched forward, coming from the far north and flying southward
across the mountains. We looked up in awe, our hearts moving along with the
graceful birds that took no heed of the turmoil on the earth, that knew no borders and no war, only following the peaceful call of their nature. Both of us
had Walter Flex's verses in mind, *Wildgänse rauschen durch die Nacht,* verses
widely known among us and full of foreboding.* We watched and listened
until the last sound had faded away. I felt the sudden appearance of the geese
held a deeper meaning. It was sign, a call for duty.

We didn't know then that disaster was imminent in the East. Soon after,
the retreat from the Caucasus began and the catastrophe of Stalingrad was on
the way. I was not to see Philipp again.

---

*Wildgänse rauschen durch die Nacht, "Wild geese rushing through the night. . . ."

7

JÄGER TRAINING

February 1943. Our platoon had ascended the steep slope on skis in combat gear with full equipment. We assembled on the saddle of the *Torrener Joch*, some 1,800 meters above the *Königssee* on one side and the valley of the Salzach on the other.

Panting and leaning on our ski poles, we enjoyed the short break. Clad in snow shirts with hoods drawn over our mountain caps, we were discernible only by the machineguns, the rifles, and our other military equipment against the general whiteness of our surroundings, a whiteness that dazzled in the intense midday sun. Some had removed their caps and revealed sharp contrasts between the white skin of their hairlines and the dark tan of their faces. Our lips were covered with a thick layer of cream, our eyes protected by blue-tinted glasses with gleaming aluminum frames.

We had received our tans during field training over the last few weeks. The time had proved extremely demanding, making up for the absence of the military drill that regular recruits must endure on the parade ground. Accommodations were of Spartan simplicity. Put up in two lodges, one of them on top, the other huddled to the side of the saddle, the company rose at dawn, washed outside in the snow, performed calisthenics, ate breakfast, and then began ski instruction and other high-mountain training such as traversing ice fields, building igloos, and so on.

The snow on the ridge was hard and iced over as the wind up here gave no rest to anything loose, and the sun melted what was left of the fresh snow. Less than ten kilometers away, the white massif of the *Watzmann* stood out against the dark blue sky. Here, on our side of the lake, the *Hohe Göll* and the *Schneibstein* towered north and south of the saddle.

The spectacular tableau was a grand sight indeed. Looking around, in the midst of my comrades, I thought that this was what I had wanted.

Before we finished the morning's exercise, we would have one more downhill run. At the moment, we were practicing gun displacement. Our machine guns were mounted on *akjas*, small, boat-like sleds, that were guided by three men harnessed to each, two in front and the machinegunner in the back. The first gun got ready. Rifles tightly slung across the back and ammunition cases strapped to the body, the three men with the *akja* formed their triangle and off they went. The leader went ahead, the machinegun unit behind, the other *Jäger* following, all of them rushing down in wide swinging turns, moving in full harmony. The last week's ski training was paying off. Soon they would disappear behind a rock and then it was our turn.

Fresh snow fell in the afternoon. We returned to the lodge early. After supper, I stood guard duty for the first two hours of the night. Gusts of wind drove snow over the ridge and around the house, piling up drifts in the lee. Inside, in the light shining through the curtains, my comrades were singing. Our repertoire then had a distinct South Tyrolian touch, for the majority of our company came from that region. Their "national anthem," a song of gladness and praise of South Tyrol, had become the battalion's main song:

> *Wie ist die Welt so groß und weit und voller Sonnenschein,*
> *Das allerschönste Stück davon ist doch die Heimat mein . . .**

In the cramped room with the large, tiled stove, the men sat tightly packed around ash tables scrubbed white. The NCOs were among them, and the company commander, *Hauptsturmführer* von Hartmann, dropped in regularly. We recruits respected him greatly, and he seemed to have a soft spot in his heart for us. His training program was tough, but he always ensured that we found pleasure in the performance of our duty. He was a handsome man, and he had style; dark haired, cultivated, of Bavarian nobility, his mother allegedly came from Hungary. In his features, however, there were also distinct marks of toughness and willpower. A wounded leg forced him to walk with a stick, which he did with grace. The Iron Cross on the left side of his tunic added to the overall image of a seasoned veteran whom we could admire and be inspired to emulate. Often on those evenings at the lodge, he would play his guitar and teach us new songs.

When I was relieved from the guard post, a welcome surprise was waiting for me: our platoon leader ordered me and three others to go down to the

---

*Roughly,
  "The world's so great and wide, and full of bright sunshine,
   But the most beautiful part of all is still that home of mine."

village of Königssee the next morning for provisions. To receive that duty was a privilege, almost as good as being on leave. Normally, our supplies would come up with the mules, but when there was heavy snowfall, more than one-meter deep, the pack animals, with their large wicker baskets strapped to their sides, would get stuck before they reached our station. Living the life of monks, every one of us used to look forward to a few hours of village life, no matter how innocent the diversions offered.

There was another, very special reason for my anticipation: if I was lucky I would find Christina there. As I learned from her last letter, as a leader of the *Jungmädel*, she was assigned to one of the hotels at Königssee that had been turned into a camp of the *Kinder-Landverschickung (KLV).** She should have arrived there by now. Unfortunately, though, I didn't know at which hotel she would be staying.

The snow stopped falling on the next morning. Our squad fell in. In our winter outfits, we made a smart-looking group. We wore stretch trousers and white anoraks with black epaulets and the emblem of the *Gebirgsjäger* on the right sleeve. This distinctive insignia was an *Edelweiss* on a black, oval badge. We had slung furs around our waists, which we would need under the skis on our way back up.

Despite the deep snow, we were at once engaged in a wild race toward the *Jenner Alm*, an alpine pasture where the mules were stationed and which was about halfway down. The first to arrive was Stricker, who, later on, was to be my faithful, reliable number two machine gunner. He was a sturdy farmer's son from the South Tyrol with a shock of hair as yellow-white as the mane of a *Haflinger* pony from his home pastures. He was by far the wildest of us on skis and the most experienced. From the *Jenner Alm* the way was less steep, and we arrived safely at the lake. There were two hours to go before we would meet at our base in the village to pick up the provisions and start back to our station.

We found the village deep in fresh snow. Going along the lake, we were already passing hotels now serving as *KLV* camps, for we could see the children and their leaders in *Jungmädel* uniform. I left the others and inquired about Christina. I had been in and out of almost all the places without success when I suddenly stood before her, face to face, on the village street. I had to say "Hello, Christina" before she recognized me. Amazed, her face lit up with joy. When we kissed she said, quite exasperated, "What on earth are you doing here?" I told her and she said she had arrived here only one week

---

Jungmädel is the young girls' youth organization, equivalent to the *Jungvolk*. The *Kinder-Landverschickung* are accomodations in remote regions of Germany for children from bombed-out cities.

ago and now was on duty. So there was nothing I could do but walk her back to her hotel where I met two of her teammates and her superior, a girl of eighteen. There was no time left for the two of us except for a cup of coffee in the kitchen. Children ran about noisily as in an elementary school. I was able to watch her handle the gang of little girls, which she did with firm ease, a new and endearing side of her that beguiled my heart even more.

Walking back to our base in the village, I was not disappointed with the brevity of our meeting. What else could we expect in these days? Was it not a lucky coincidence to have met at all in this remote corner of Germany? At the base, we stuffed our rucksacks full of fresh food (among others, a special Bavarian sausage that was part of the high-altitude ration). And when we began our ascent back to the station, I kept thinking of all the girls who were on duty so far away from home. For all their cheerfulness and charm, there was little girlishness about them, but instead a self-confident, matter-of-fact way in their manner, reflecting the unusual responsibility with which they were entrusted at an early age.

That was the last time I saw Christina. Two months later, she wrote that she was assigned to another camp, far away in Austria, in the province of Styria.

Up on the ridge, our training program continued for several more weeks. Looking back, my impression is that we and our instructors were a team. They wanted us to become highly proficient soldiers, acting with others in small groups on our own; knowing how to survive, not only in combat, but also in a hostile wilderness; and moving about in difficult terrain with vigor, circumspection, and, in particular, speed. Our exercises, therefore, had a distinctly athletic touch, a training for winners in regions where heavy weapons and armored vehicles were of no use.

The notion of the *Waffen-SS* as politically or racially indoctrinated fanatics, driven by Party ideology and hate, was, in my experience, far from reality. Our training was focused on preparation for victory in modern warfare, and all of us were volunteers who wanted just that kind of preparation. Yes, we did feel a bit different from other parts of the armed forces, but this fact was true of many other units, too, such as the panzer and panzer-grenadier divisions and the *Fallschirmjäger,* or paratroops.

In the *Waffen-SS*, the officers did not belong to a different class, they were picked from among the best seasoned soldiers who had shown leadership qualities in combat. Officers were not to be addressed as "Sir," but with their rank only; it was the same with the NCOs. There was the special military salute of ours: not the right hand to the cap, but the right arm raised at eye level. In practice, however, the arm wasn't quite stretched but rather casually raised as to avoid conformity with the Party salute. Some regulations were in sharp contrast to those of the Army such as those regarding rations which were equal for officers and men, or regarding lockers in the barracks. In the Army, an unlocked locker meant three days in the guardhouse; in the *Waffen-SS*, it was the opposite way around. The very thought of a soldier stealing or touching his comrade's belongings was completely incompatible with our code of honor.

The company returned to the barracks in the valley by the middle of April. Descending the other side of the ridge, opposite the *Königssee*, we experienced the sudden transition from winter to spring so common in the mountains. As the long single file of men and mules walked down the narrow path to the valley, suddenly, halfway down, the snow cover ended abruptly, melted away by the alpine sun. From under the snow's fringe, green meadows with hundreds of primulas, gentian, and other spring flowers had already come to full blossom.

During our time down in the barracks, the company would march to the firing range once a week—quite a distance. We would depart at dawn and walk over the hills between the *Salzach* and Berchtesgaden. We would arrive just in time to wake up the residents of the narrow streets with our battalion's song:

Wie ist die Welt so groß und weit und voller Sonnenschein . . ."

Many a face, ugly from sleep or lovely as the morning, would appear from behind the green shutters that opened as we marched through the little town. Our commander, on horseback, politely responded to the salutes and salutations from some of the windows.

In the afternoon, on our way back, we crossed Berchtesgaden once more, singing, yodeling, and showing off our cheerful, disciplined unit. Upon entering the hills east of the town, however, we would form a single file again, take off our caps, roll up the sleeves of our tunics, and slowly climb the winding, steep ascent. This march always was, once more, part of our physical conditioning, especially in summer when the sun heated up the hillside all afternoon. Then the unique beauty of the surrounding area would soon become irrelevant, and grinding uphill, our eyes would be fixed on our hobnail boots as they ground step by step into the trail's white limestone. Tired from the day's strain, we would think of a decent meal and of stretching out on our bunks.

Passing the *Berghof* on the *Obersalzberg*, our attention would be diverted for a short while from the monotonous pace. We hoped to catch a glimpse of something important, appropriate to the importance of the place, although the *Führer's* residence was bypassed in a wide arc and could be seen only from afar. What we actually could see were the *SS* guards, outposts in black uniforms, black helmets, polished boots, submachine guns, and so forth. They were strangely different, this Old Guard, with their sinister, awe-inspiring look. Here was the seat of ultimate power, of ultimate responsibility for our country's course through this war. It was the place where the highest representatives of the European powers had come to parlay, the place where the *Führer* sought to relax from his ascetic and focused life; to know all that amounted to the atmosphere of awe that surrounded the *Berghof*.

There were exercises far more demanding than our homeward trek, such as ascending the *Untersberg*, the massif towering over the city of Salzburg. We took off at dawn toward a hamlet south of the city. We carried no heavy gear, just rifles. At the hamlet, however, our rucksacks were filled with potatoes, supply for the station on the mountain peak—35 pounds for each of us, which was quite something given that 1,300 meters of altitude had to be conquered along a horizontal distance of only two kilometers. The first quarter of our way up was normal strain, the potatoes on our backs seeming heavier and heavier. The second quarter became steeper as we turned toward a huge wall above us, yet we carried on with long steps at a steady pace. Some of us experienced difficulty on this part of the way. Our company commander, coming up from the rear and guiding his horse by the rein, noticed a man behind me panting and barely keeping pace. He approached him as a coach would do, "Come on, soldier! You can do it! Let me take your rifle for a while. I'll be back soon to see how you are doing." With that he slung the rifle over his shoulder and passed on at a quicker pace than ours, nimbly using his stick and guiding his horse at the same time.

Halfway up we paused. The commander's orderly was to return from here with the horse and take those with him who seemed unfit to make it up the wall. Pride forbade any of us to report sick, but the commander singled out a few whom he considered to be not in adequate shape for the climb.

We then started for the wall, first crossing scree that seemed to bleed away the strength we had left with each stride of poor foothold on the loose gravel. Then, before assailing the rock, we paused again to build up strength for the last and most difficult stretch. The rock was fairly well prepared for climbing. The path was, at some stretches, hewn into the stone itself. Higher up, though, an irregular flight of steps began—huge steps, impossible for us to master, carrying 35 pounds of potatoes and our gear on our backs, without pulling ourselves up by the ropes fastened along the steps. This last part of the climb turned out to be the ultimate athletic performance of our training course. We were sweating, panting, cursing and yet doggedly pulling ourselves up the steps, one by one. Eventually the men ahead and above me, one after another, disappeared over the edge. Only a few more steps, a last effort and it would be done!

Then, standing there on the flat, slightly sloped roof, seeing the lodge only a hundred meters away, I fainted. My knees began to give, the sky started to whirl, and I collapsed. The spell lasted only a short moment, a fit of altitude sickness that did not spoil the unequalled joy of the mountaineer who made it to the top. The landlady, grateful for the potato supply, rewarded us with a hearty meal.

The descent two hours later followed an easier route. As soon as we reached the forest, we took the most direct way down. Rifles slung around the neck and resting across the breast, firmly gripped by both hands, we cut all corners of the winding, serpentine path in wide downward leaps and eventually assembled at the hamlet within less than half an hour. Down there we laughed at each other's uncontrollably shaking knees.

That event marked the end of our training course. The tempo slowed. There was time and strength left for trips to Salzburg. Exploring this city and going to concerts added much to the wonderful time of my military training around Salzburg and Berchtesgaden.

At that time, however, our training company received an assignment that was quite apart from our training program, namely one week's guard duty at a labor camp with about fifty inmates. Our duty was limited to guarding the enclosure. Two guards had to walk around the outside of the perimeter fence for two hour reliefs. It was a dull, tiresome duty which we performed with less than full enthusiasm, as we felt it was beneath our dignity. Within the camp were a few huts, wooden structures with bunks. The military discipline with which the camp was run corresponded, as far as we could see, to the tidiness with which the whole place was kept. Except for the sick, the inmates used to leave for work early in the morning and return for supper.

The camp kitchen, a small shack with a field stove under an awning, was in a corner of the compound, immediately adjacent to the fence. The cook stayed in during the day. He was a huge, middle-aged man, bull-necked with thick muscles on his arms and chest, which he kept bare on warm days and which was, like his bald head, deeply tanned. I watched him working with deft motions, cleaning, maintaining the fire under the kettle, each day preparing different stews, often cutting thick slabs of meat into it, a remarkable thing at that time of general rationing. Apparently, he took no notice of me. Likewise, I avoided showing him that I found him a figure of some interest, but on my last day of duty there, in the afternoon, he approached me without turning from his work, "It's your last day with us, isn't it?"

"Well, yes, that's right. How did you know?" I replied, stopping slightly startled.

He ignored my question and continued, "You didn't like your duty here, did you? I know none of you boys do. Can't wait to go up front. But believe me, it's better here than out there. One day you'll be longing to be back."

I was in no mood to comment on that remark, but I could not help asking what had been on my mind the whole time, "By the way, why are you here?"

He shot a glance at me that expressed self-esteem, mockery, and total frankness, "I'm a Communist, a *Volksfeind*.* They picked me up the day the war began, and they won't let me loose before it ends. Won't be for long anymore, I guess."

I felt some respect for his frankness, "It's a pity. You might have made a good soldier."

He chuckled. Both his hands gripped a large wooden spoon that he continued to stir in the stew, which by now should have been ready. "Want a plateful?" he suddenly asked. "You're hungry, aren't you?"

"No, not really," I lied.

"Don't deny it. You boys are always hungry," he insisted. And then, without waiting for me to reply, he put some stew on a dish and passed it to me through the fence. "You may at least have a try. It's not too bad."

I instinctively took the dish. His was a simple gesture of friendliness, however undeserved, without a trace of calculation. How could I reject it? I wasn't that narrow minded. Still, it was an awkward situation. I did my best to cover up my confusion. The stew, by the way, was good, quite a decent meal.

Soon after, the men of our training company left for Finland. I was picked for additional training as an NCO, which meant another stay up at the *Torrener Joch*. I was taught to lead a heavy machine-gun squad in action. Apart from that, the training was a rather advanced course in alpine techniques.

When we were back in the valley, it was autumn. A small, silver braid on my epaulets marked the end of the course. Soon I would be in combat. I wondered which division I would join. There was an *SS*-mountain division, the 7th, operating in the Balkans. Most likely, though, my assignment would be to the outfit operating near the Arctic Circle. This area had remained strange for me, cold and very far away. What I had heard of Wolf and Philipp, however, had stirred some warm feelings in me about the land and its people.

I again took up my visits to Salzburg, indulging in concerts and operas. But upon returning one Sunday night, Puccini's powerful music of *Madame Butterfly* still ringing in my ears and realizing that on this night I had once more been in the very center of Europe's cultural life, I learned that my training time was coming to an abrupt end. When I passed the guard room about midnight, the NCO on duty called me in and said, "Voss, you're on the transport leaving for Finland tomorrow morning at six."

---

*"Public Enemy."

8

A Glimpse into an Abyss

The train had been slowing down for a while and now came to a halt. The dim light of dawn peeked through the little openings in the walls of our box car, but was too weak to reveal the soldiers who stretched out under their blankets on the straw-covered floor. Dozing and still half asleep, pictures of our journey to the north came back to mind. We had reached Vienna at dusk on our first day. I had never been there before, but the name had inspired images of magnificent edifices, wide boulevards, and parks—all symbols of the city's splendor. Instead, we saw only the backyards, infinitely depressing in their shabbiness and obscurity. From there, delayed by endless stops on forlorn sidings, our progress on this journey was slow. The train had wound through the hillsides of Bohemia and Moravia (occupied Czechoslovakia), and then had entered the industrial areas of Upper Silesia. Now, on the morning of our third day, we were perhaps somewhere in the plains of the *Wartheland*, the western part of occupied Poland.

I knew only three or four of the men in the car from the course of the last three months. The others belonged to the recruits' training course that had followed ours. I was very glad to hear that von Hartmann was on the train though. They said he had asked for a transfer back to his division. He was still using his stick.

I rose and cautiously stepped over the bodies toward the door, which I opened just a bit to climb outside. The train had stopped between stations. The locomotive rhythmically hissed, puffed, and clanked, emitting white plumes of steam which quickly dissolved in the drizzling rain. The scene was somber. Far ahead, dark shadows moved around the track, a repair gang apparently already at work at this early hour.

No sooner had I relieved myself than the train again began to move. The few of us still outside jumped on the cars. I remained at the door, joined by a few others, curious to see the cause of our delay. Slowly, the shadows I had seen from afar took shape. They were ragged figures, twenty or thirty of them, in civilian clothes, dark and skimpy, guarded by men who wore the greatcoats of the *Waffen-SS* and who were armed with rifles loosely held in the crooks of their right arms.

As the train crawled over the stretch under repair, I saw the faces of the gang, who had stepped back from the rails as we passed by. Horror struck me. Large black eyes in deep eye sockets, imploring and frightened, stared from pale, emaciated faces under woolen peaked caps that looked ridiculously large. Most of them wore the yellow, six-pointed Star of David on their jackets. I shivered as I watched them lift their hands to us and timidly shout, *"Herr Soldat, bitte ein Stück Brot!"* ("Mr. Soldier sir, a piece of bread, please!"), their spindly arms sticking out of the sleeves so that their hands appeared much too large, emphasizing their imploring gestures. These were humans at their lowest level of debasement.

As the train moved slowly on, we who stood by the door wanted to give them something, but there weren't any provisions left as we were living from hand to mouth. I saw half a loaf of bread handed down from the wagon next to us, snatched up by a youngster who immediately hid it under his jacket.

The train stopped again, and we could see from afar what was happening now. The youngster with the half loaf was dragged by one of his mates toward the guard next to him. As it seemed, he was ordered to hand over the bread, but refused to obey. The guard ripped the bread from him and violently flung it away. At once the youngster darted after it. He had thrown himself over his prey before he could be stopped by the sharp command, *"Halt! Stehen bleiben!"* which is the ultimate order before a guard shoots. The guard stepped up to him, first gesturing with his rifle to make him stand up, and then kicked him as he lay on the ground. The guard beat him with the butt of his rifle. The sight was intolerable. There were angry shouts of "Hey! Hey! Hey!" from our wagons, even threats from those who were near. Then the rest happened quickly. From the passenger coach of our train, two of our officers resolutely went to the scene. The first was von Hartmann; the second one, unknown to me and much younger, followed. Approaching the guard from the side, von Hartmann shouted a command that could be heard clearly by all, "Stop that immediately! That's an order!"

The guard spun, his rifle now pointed at the two officers. The younger officer, standing one step behind his senior, drew his pistol and pointed it at the guard. The confrontation lasted only seconds. The guard set down his rifle, and the pistol went back into the holster. Von Hartmann gave an order which we could not understand, but without further delay, the young prisoner went over to the two officers. He appeared to be taken into our officers' custody.

The officers turned to the train and waved the youngster to march ahead. To watch von Hartmann walking from the scene at a measured pace and with his graceful limp was deeply impressive. They stopped in front of the boxcar next to the officers' coach, handed the prisoner over to the NCO in the car, and mounted the train, which soon jerked into motion and slowly picked up speed.

We closed the door and started tidying up our quarters. Those who had watched from the door told the others what had happened. All of us were glad of the interference of our officers. One of my mates said he hoped the youngster would get double rations at the next station where we would have breakfast. The incident had disturbed me deeply. Certainly, in this case and for the time being, order had been restored, but a strong feeling of uneasiness continued all the same.

We reached the port of Danzig in the evening. On the train, I had been thinking of this city with growing anticipation. I had been there before, six years ago in 1937, together with Nick at the end of a four-week *Jungvolk* hike through East Prussia. An independent German city lying in the middle of the otherwise Polish-controlled corridor artificially created by the Allies at Versailles, Danzig had long been a symbol of the humiliation inflicted on Germany after the armistice of 1918. During that summer of 1937, there had been many *Jungvolk* hiking groups in this region, and at the end, we all had met at Danzig for a torchlight rally with fanfares and drums—a stirring experience. Since then, for me Danzig was a town full of bright memories, of ancient houses in beautiful streets and sunlight on glittering water.

Now the town was lying in the dark, and we were at war. The large ship was moored at the quay, her bow towering above our heads as we waited to embark. We would spend the night on the ship. As we stood around, von Hartmann came out of the dark, accompanied by the NCO who was in charge of the forced laborer. Seeing us he turned to our group and greeted us quite casually, "How are our young heroes feeling? Looking forward to a cruise on the Baltic Sea?"

As it happened I was standing face to face with him, "We're feeling great," I said. "May I add, with your permission, that we were relieved when you intervened in the incident this morning."

His face grew stern; only his eyes showed that he appreciated what was implied. "It was a severe offense against discipline," he said. "In a case like this, it's the duty of everyone to see that discipline is restored on the spot."

He went on to have a few words with the next group.

We were curious and asked the NCO what had happened to the Jewish youngster. "All went well," he said. "The chief made a report and personally handed him over to the local authority. They were understanding. He made sure that the boy will not be sent back to his former labor unit."

This incident was my first encounter with the dark side of the Third Reich, cruel and inhumane. I had seen a concrete example of what the persecution of the Jews was like, what was being done to subjects who were regarded as public enemies or as scum of the earth. At that time, however, I played down my feelings. Yes, we were aware of certain things that we thought must be changed right after the war ended, but first we must win this war. I remember recalling then an incident my mother was teased about in the family, amusing and encouraging as well. She, as a young girl, under the eyes of people in a street at Hardenburg, furiously beat up a coachman with her umbrella to stop him from cruelly whipping his horse, which had fallen on the ground and tried in vain to stand up. "That's the right spirit," I told myself when it came back to my mind on that transport, the same spirit von Hartmann had just shown and which was shared by all who had watched. I was convinced that, in the end, this spirit would prevail.

What had only been a vague feeling at that time, however, seems now established—that I had had only a glimpse into an abyss of evil.

9

IN NO-MAN'S LAND

While writing down my account of the past, I am still confined to the PW camp at Romilly. By day, my companions and I are occupied with various jobs: Pete is an assistant to an American dentist; Walther, a store-keeper; I interpret in the hospital cage and, recently, sometimes even in the Military Police station downtown, helping out the GIs with French. My life involves talking to all kinds of doctors, American soldiers, and German prisoners, reading the *Stars and Stripes,* and, to some extent, watching the way of life in the US Army.

This character of the world in which I live during the day is determined by fundamental truths that have resulted from the outcome of the war and are uncontested, as a whole, even among my German fellow prisoners. The basic truth here is that the war against Germany was a crusade against the arch evil, embodied by "Hitler and his henchmen," the *SS* in particular.

At night, however, when I return to my writing I enter a different world, a world with truths of its own that resulted from a period when the outcome of the war was still undecided and wherein the arch evil was the Communist enemy in the East. Some fortitude is required to change from one world to the other, and I can never wholly escape the doubt about whether the past ought best be forgotten, since it ended in such singular catastrophe—above all, for the people some thought to be inferior, but also for ourselves. Is there a more convincing proof of the falseness of all our former truths?

There is another nagging doubt: Am I giving up my own self in the course of concealing my true identity as a volunteer of the *Waffen-SS*? Am I leaving behind the person I was (together with the dead and the outlaws) and trying to reach the other side, the land of the righteous? Am I already wandering about in a moral No-Man's Land?

How I wish there was someone to discuss these doubts with, someone my own age who shared the same ideas, with whom I could speak in confidence. Regarding my past and my predicament, however, I am by myself in these surroundings, unable to reveal myself in the hostile atmosphere of these days. So, sometimes I take to soliloquies with my *alter ego*, something rather intricate:

Here you are, on your own now, out in the open, groping in an unknown environment for an idea of a decent future life. If you aren't prepared to defect to the land of the righteous, where, then, are you going and who is your guide?

It's hard for me to find my way in this new condition, where facts and values are surrounded by uncertainties and doubts, but I hope my orientation won't fail. I must rely on the old spirit.

And what, my dear Voss, actually is 'the old spirit,' and what is it telling you now? Hold fast to the old values? Despite all those horrible revelations? Or feel sorry for yourself for the rest of your life? Aren't you too young for that?

No, neither way; not blind loyalty, but not total abjuration either, not of the basic values at least . . . and don't give in to self pity. What is still valid, I think, is loyalty to one's country. So one must continue to serve one's country. I'll do my best under the circumstances. Do I abandon my old self by proceeding as such?

No, certainly not. It sounds convincing, as a general rule, but remember where your service has gotten you and your country. Who would dare say today that you and the Old Spirit served your country well?

Don't get me confused now with our former leadership!

All right, your service didn't cause the catastrophe, but it was instrumental to it, wasn't it?

That doesn't say much; it's true of any military service if you agree that the war itself was a catastrophe from the outset.

All the same, you said "continue to serve." First of all, there won't be any continuation. If at all, we must start from zero.

Whatever it is, it's we who continue to be, the ones who are left. And the land that is left and from which we'll have to continue to wring a living—our country.

Alright. But how do you think it could work in practice? Your country will be— has to be—some sort of organized community, and most probably the rules of that community will be inconsistent with our old self, maybe a country you won't even want to serve. Don't forget, you are an outlaw, and, judging from the newspapers, it seems likely that the new country, too, will regard you as such. Still bound by the old loyalty to the Old Spirit? No need for crossing the line?

We'll see what can be rescued of the Old Spirit. At least it won't be inconsistent with the responsibility our country must take on for what has been done to the 'inferiors.' I am quite confident there will be new causes that are worth the effort. I'll have to make my choice when the time is there. We had to make choices before, hadn't we? Besides, I rather thought of a modest, inconspicuous way to serve, the way we did before.

Well, let's leave it at that for the time being.

Discussions with my companions are different. They are more abstract, more philosophical (normally, at our age, the three of us would be at university now), and, of course, they start from the new verities. Nevertheless, they are helping me to find my way. Only last Sunday afternoon, Pete, Walther, and I had another one of these discussions, when Pete and I we returned from our Greek lessons with the Protestant chaplain.

Walther is Austrian, or to be more precise, a Viennese—tall, haggard, with a distinct aquiline nose between deep-set, almost black eyes that made me think of Paganini when I first met him. He was called up for service straight after leaving school. Walther is the intellectual among us. He has a piercing analytical mind, is well-read, and, in my opinion, a cynic. Pete is different in almost every way. Coming from a Hamburg family, he is sturdy, strong, blond with blue eyes, a believer rather than an intellectual, optimistic compared to Walther, who always leans toward the gloomy side.

When Pete and I entered our tent, back from our lesson, we were received by Walther with one of his typical sarcasms, "Ah, our disciples of Greek are back. Are our educational aspirations satisfied for today? I hope our distinguished teacher has brought us safely through the Greek alphabet."

Walther was lying on his field cot, hands clasped behind his neck, meditating as usual. Without turning his head towards us, he continued, "I wonder what you think you'll gain from Greek. Believe me, it's of no use. At least it's been of no use to me. On the contrary, my education kept me from learning English. Do I owe my steep career climb in this cage from store man to storekeeper to Greek? Not that I know of. Was it of any use to me in the Army? No sir, on the contrary again; I learned very quickly never to mention my knowledge of Greek, not even that I had been a student at the *Gymnasium*."

"As for me, there's a simple practical reason," Pete took up Walther's skepticism. "I want to know the roots of so many medical terms derived from Greek. I'm certain it'll help me a lot at university."

"Maybe yes. And what about you, Johann? Also interested in etymology? It's not as obvious as with Pete."

"Well, no, you're right, although it's obvious that you need something to occupy your mind with," I replied rather lamely I had no desire to let myself be drawn into another one of our discussions that often turned acid.

"What?" Walther exploded. "Need to occupy your mind? My dear Johann, I don't know how to unload my mind from the heap of problems that keep troubling me. Can you explain to me, for instance, how it could happen that I am stuck in this goddamned cage although I did everything to stay out of the mess? How did all of this come about? What were the mechanisms at work? Those are only *some* of the questions my mind is occupied with day and night."

"Don't think, Walther, you're the only one troubled with these questions," I replied. "Privileged as you are with knowing Greek, however, I'd think the philosophers would make it easy for you to solve your problems."

"Are you thinking of someone in particular?"

"Plato's *State* just crossed my mind—the chaplain and I talked about it the other day. Little as I know of him, I would think that you could find some answers there. Wasn't he born into a war as we were? And didn't he know from experience that an individual cannot exist except within a community and that, in turn, the individual owes certain obligations to the state so that both will survive? I think that's an answer to your question, isn't it? It's a wisdom as old as philosophy. It's a strong argument for Greek, by the way."

"Old and rotten," Walther retorted passionately, rising from his cot. "The idea of the individual as a subordinate of the state is the root of all evil in the history of man. It's the same with the church. It always ended with the oppression of man by the ruling class in the name of some higher entity. The Enlightenment put reason in the place of the authority of the church; the French revolution restored the natural freedom of the individual, his freedom from state authorities. All in vain! Somehow the old institutions and patronage returned or prevailed. Incredible but true. If the state would only ensure that everybody can look after his own interests, all would be fine. Harmony would be the result, brought about by the Invisible Hand of Reason. You ever heard about the Invisible Hand of Reason? That's the wisdom of the modern age. Plato's *State*, my dear Johann, is dead."

Walther sat down on Pete's field cot opposite mine, ready for a new round of discussion.

"I'm no expert in this. I don't know whether Plato's ideas are dead in the world of philosophy," I said. "But I do know they are alive in the real world. Aren't we constantly dealing with national states and their endless rivalries and, in the last decades, also with aggressive organizations like the Comintern? The question is: How to prevail in this world where insoluble issues are fought out in wars? Individual freedom is fine, as long as there is peace. You can't prevail, though, can't fight or prepare for a war on the basis of individualism. If everybody only looks after his own personal interests, a state cannot exist nor can a nation; both will perish in the world of reality, and with them the rest of your personal freedom you can only enjoy within an organized community. Thank goodness there are people who feel there are values that reach beyond one's own self and that are worth sacrificing some of one's precious individuality."

"You just won't learn," Walther replied. "If it weren't for people like you, always eager to make sacrifices for the so-called common good, people like Hitler or Stalin would never succeed. 'You are nothing; your people are all that matter'! That's what you were taught in the *Reich*. It's the philosophy of all totalitarian systems; they depend on people like you. The evil lies with the idealists. God save us from the faithful, the patriots, the do-gooders!"

It was not Walther's first challenge, but this time, it was unmistakably serious. He was glaring at me with flashing eyes, waiting for me to reply.

"Now you are talking nonsense, Walther. It's not the philosophy of totalitarian systems; it's true of all states. Neither Churchill nor Roosevelt could have waged war without suspending individual freedom and relying on the idealists to whom I gladly profess allegiance. With individualists, both would have lost their war long since, which, I'm afraid, is not quite what you had in mind," I added, accusingly. "I can see no virtue in individualism nor reason. In the world we are living in, it comes down to egoism, selfishness."

"What is the opinion of a medic on that?" I added, seeing that the discussion with Walther wouldn't get us anywhere.

"Well, coming from a practicing Protestant family, I must raise objections against both of your attitudes," Pete began. "I don't know what to do with the state, the common good, the Invisible Hand of Reason, liberalism, and all that. A Christian simply wants to help his fellow human beings. 'Love Thy Neighbor' is the guiding principle. Doing that you have to make sacrifices, to give away much of your personal interests and freedom. It's quite natural. Yes, there will always be sacrifices for goals that reach beyond your own self, but in the name of God rather than in the name of the people, which is a questionable authority. And then, yes, there must be freedom of the individual—freedom to act as a Christian. As long as you are aware of that—I mean of serving God—you are secure from sacrifices in the name of evil and from egoism and selfishness. It's all quite simple." He smiled at us.

"It's too simple," Walther said. "Must I enumerate all the evil done in the world in the name of Christianity? There is no security against abuse as long as man will continue to act in the name of some higher authority. First subordination; then devotion and slavish obedience, fanaticism, inquisition, security police; and in the end, slavery and death for all who want to resist. It's so obvious after all we have been through. No more altruism, Christian or national, no more idealists, for these are the elements of collectivism which is the arch-enemy of individual freedom and is the reason why I am here."

"Sophism, Walther! Pure sophism!" Pete protested. "With that, you won't overthrow basic principles of Christian religion. It's so obvious to me that it is a natural virtue of man to want to serve a cause that reaches beyond his own self. Of course, it must be safeguarded against abuse, namely by the conscience, sharpened by the principles of our religion. The safeguard of conscience may fail with the weak, but it is there; it's the true and natural authority within ourselves."

"I have severe reservations, too, Walther," I said. "Nothing of your chain of events was bound to happen, nor were there events linked together by altruism and idealism. There always were so many factors and vectors involved, each oscillating continuously from weak to strong, that any outcome, the obvious as well as the inconceivable, is possible. I simply can't accept the view that with National Socialism, it was clear from the outset where it would end. Anything could have happened, even peace after the 'Anschluss' and perhaps even after our campaign in Poland and France. All the same, one lesson is clear: never again must there be any public authority without active popular control."

In writing down the details of this discussion, it becomes quite clear there is much truth in Pete's view. There must be some reasonable combination of altruism and individualism to combat both egoism and collectivism. The core of individual freedom must be preserved under all circumstances, even in war. And there must be no such thing as unconditional commitment! I think that is the lesson we learned from our experience.

Perhaps partly out of an intellectual thirst and partly from a desire for more congenial surroundings, I suddenly wished I were at Hardenburg in my grandmother's library to have a closer look into Plato's *State* and into the philosophers of the Enlightenment. . . .

10

THE 66TH PARALLEL

The messenger stood before us. We hadn't noticed him in the twilight that enveloped the snow-covered woodland. The motionless, white figure seemed a mere part of the frozen environment, leaning against a fir, helmet and parka covered with a hooded snow shirt, his right arm resting on the black barrel of the machine pi-stol that hung horizontally under his shoulder. Even now, pushing himself off the trunk and coming closer, his face could barely be seen; only his eyes were visible under the brim of his helmet as he watched our small group.

We were assembled on the path leading to the front line. I started to report: name, rank, and assignment. The messenger made a motion of his hand to indicate that I should lower my voice. He spoke softly when he greeted us and shook hands with me and the other four replacements. I was to go with him to the *Hauptkampflinie* (*HKL*), the main combat line, but first we had to take the other four to the *mungo* emplacement, which was nearby. He pointed to the right where the path disappeared between the birch trees and the firs around the foot of the little hill. It was the first time I heard mortars called "*mungos.*"

As we were taking up our gear, one of our group let his rifle butt clank against his metal gas mask container. The messenger quickly stepped up to the man, took his rifle off his back, arranged it under his right shoulder so that the barrel pointed down, and gently laid the man's hand on top. I understood that the Russians were within earshot. And now, for the first time on this day, I noticed how still everything was around us, a frozen stillness that seemed to be the very nature of this strange terrain.

The messenger motioned the group to the path, and we set off in single file for the *mungo* emplacement. He pointed up the hill. "Right over there,

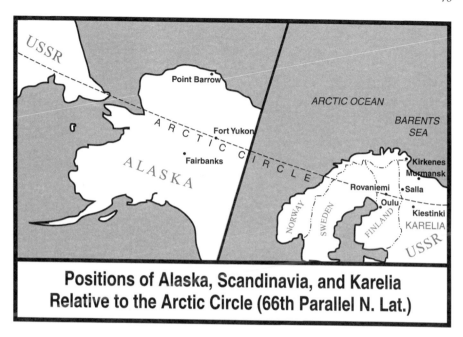

**Positions of Alaska, Scandinavia, and Karelia
Relative to the Arctic Circle (66th Parallel N. Lat.)**

behind it, is the *HKL*," he said. On the hill, the thin stand of firs and birches stood out, still and black, from the snow and the semi-darkness of the sky.

The mortar platoon emplacement was almost invisible; only when standing in front of a ditch leading to an entrance did I realize that the flat mound on top of the burrow was the top of a snow-covered bunker. The messenger and my four companions disappeared in the first bunker, leaving me waiting outside for a while.

We had come with the mules. From the rear echelon up to here it had been a march of about two hours, trudging along the supply trail in single file. The mules accompanied us with their warm smell, their soft snorts, and the creaking of the wicker baskets that swung at their sides in the rhythm of their steady pace. After a while, I was lulled into a semi-hypnotic state, strangely possessed by a monotonous song I had heard at Oulu, the seaport, trivially romantic stuff:

> "*In Oulu da sind wir gelandet,*
> *uns're Träume versanken im Meer . . .*"*

It expressed the sentiments of those who saw themselves, against all their zealous expectations, banished to the "ass of the earth," as this remote arctic

*"We have landed there at Oulu,
  Our dreams sank into the sea . . ."

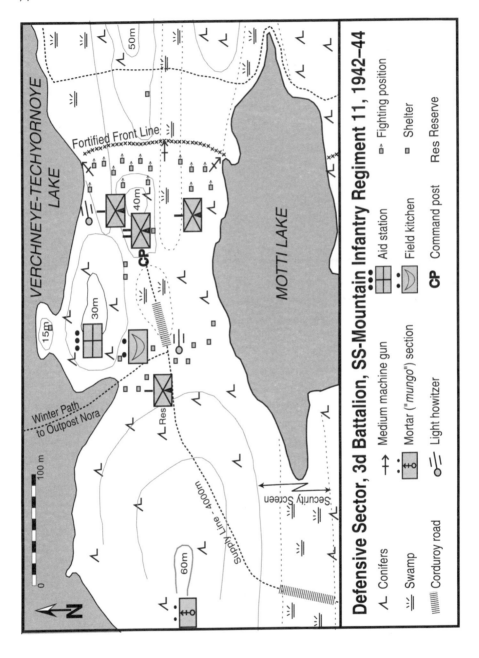

Defensive Sector, 3d Battalion, SS-Mountain Infantry Regiment 11, 1942–44

VERCHNEYE-TECHYORNOYE LAKE

MOTTI LAKE

Fortified Front Line

Winter Path to Outpost Nora

Security Screen

Supply Line – 4000m

Res Reserve

⋏ Conifers

≋ Swamp

▥ Corduroy road

→ Medium machine gun

⊡ Mortar ("*mungo*") section

⚲ Light howitzer

▦ Aid station

◗ Field kitchen

CP Command post

▭ Fighting position

□ Shelter

CP Command post

region generally was regarded. For the last kilometer, we had been on our own. The mule drivers had stayed back and described the way to the spot where we would meet the messenger.

And yet, standing here in the darkness at this strange place, I felt I hadn't arrived yet. I was still somewhere in between a former and a future existence. I had seen the contrast of both when, more than a week ago, we were putting out to sea and were watching the coast of East Prussia disappear in the night. I had been there, at that coast, six years ago, in the sun on the beach of Palmnicken with Nick and the other boys of our hiking group. I was diving for amber then, in the surf again and again, and I would throw the pieces I had found on the hot sand, proud and full of joy. Now, leaving the coast on a troopship, I understood that now it wasn't time for fun on the beach; it was a time to serve, a time of duty. It was as if I was leaving somebody back on that coast, an old acquaintance of mine whom I hadn't seen for quite a while.

There were other strange moments on the way to the front. When our ship was maneuvering through the marvels of the archipelago off Turku and we were looking over the railing down on the numerous green islands adorned with little red painted huts and boats; when we were amused at the toy-like, wood-fired locomotive that was to take our train to the North; and when, eventually, after our arrival at the port of Oulu, we were sitting in our huts together with our comrades. All were but fleeting phrases in the prelude to my new life.

There, at our base at Oulu, we had received our new equipment, winter uniform items in particular. The camp was in a grove at the outskirts of the little town. The camp was comprised of dispersed huts, and the aromatic smell of wood smoke filled the air; the first snow of the early winter decked the ground throughout the camp. In the few evenings while waiting for our transport, we sat in the canteen, drinking and singing, sometimes being joined by some of the veterans of our division's motorized infantry battalion, *SS-Schützen Bataillon* 6, located in reserve there.* On the third morning, I had seen off the first batch of replacements to the front. They were a resolute pack of young volunteers sitting in the rear of the trucks, with eager faces under their helmets, framed by the fur-lined hoods of their parkas, rifles upright between their knees. The chance of running into one of them or someone of my former training company out there was small. Another farewell then, some brave smiles, some waving, and the transport quickly vanished into the whirling snow.

---

*Unlike Army mountain divisions—or the other *Waffen-SS* mountain divisions, for that matter—*SS-Nord* retained this "extra" infantry battalion, a remnant of the Division's motorized infantry origins, throughout the war. By late 1944, it was redesignated "SS-Panzer-Grenadier Battalion 506."

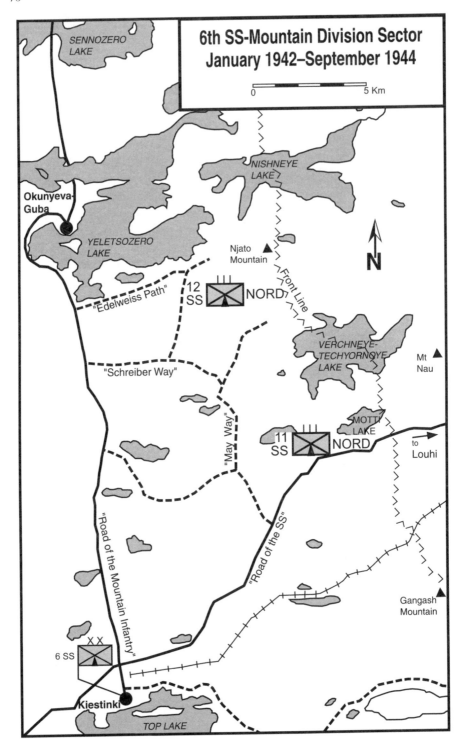

6th SS-Mountain Division Sector
January 1942–September 1944

0   5 Km

SENNOZERO
LAKE

NISHNEYE
LAKE

Okunyeva-
Guba

YELETSOZERO
LAKE

Njato
Mountain

N

"Edelweiss Path"

12
SS   NORD

Front Line

VERCHNEYE-
TECHYORNOYE
LAKE

Mt
Nau

"Schreiber Way"

MOTTI
LAKE

11
SS   NORD

to
Louhi

"May Way"

"Road of the SS"

"Road of the Mountain Infantry"

Gangash
Mountain

6 SS

Kiestinki

TOP LAKE

"Cigarette?" I spun around, facing the messenger, who silently had returned from the bunker. My reverie was over.

"Thanks!" I lighted a match for him, cupping the flame. For the first time I could see his features more closely. He had a pleasant, clean-shaven, young face and light hair. He was only two or three years older than I but looked seasoned. Under his half-opened parka, I could see the ribbon of the Iron Cross.

"Welcome again," he said in his soft way of speaking that I'd become accustomed to. "You know it's the heavy machine-gun company of our battalion you're going to, the 14th. The gun I'll bring you to is integrated in the sector of the other mountain infantry regiment in our division; pretty near the Ivan, hardly 150 meters distant. Over there is our company command post," he continued, pointing in the direction opposite the *mungo* emplacement. "The chief wants to see you in the morning; I'll take you there." Turning ahead he pointed to the left, "Over there is a lake; that's where the sector of our regiment ends towards the north. On the other side of the lake the positions of our sister regiment begin, stretching farther up to the north and ending nowhere, in the swamps and lakes with only some strongpoints; that's the North Flank (which was a common expression with us). "And over there, to the right, runs the road to Loukhi, 'The Road' as we call it. That's where other parts of our regiment are positioned, on both sides of it."

I nodded to all he had said, but I must have looked somewhat perplexed. I had understood nothing. All I could perceive was that the division's positions were concealed somewhere in this snow-covered, thinly-wooded environment.

"You'll figure it out for yourself before long," he said. We put out our cigarettes. "Let's go. And be quiet! There are snipers over there, even when it's dark." He went ahead, along the path up the hill.

Suddenly, I heard a pistol shot. A flare hissed skyward, quivering high above the ground and casting a tremulous, white magnesium light over the sparse birch trees and conifers. Black stripes shaded the snow. Both of us stood frozen on the flat top of the hill, he from experience and I from awe. Now I could see that the slope ended in a depression, which extended toward a hill opposite ours. I tried in vain to discover the enemy positions the messenger said were only 150 meters away.

The flare went out, and another soared up. At that moment, further down on our side, a machine pistol opened up, firing two short bursts, then the sustained fire of a machine gun followed. Immediately, all hell broke loose. From the opposite hill, two machine guns opened fire. To the left, another one of our machine guns joined in. I remained standing upright in the shade of a tree, just as if I were a bystander, uninvolved in what was happening in front of us, only that there were strange sounds all around me, "*peeeuuh - peeeuuh - patch oiinng - oiing - patch - peeeuuh.*"

"Take cover! Hit the ground, man!" the messenger shouted. He was lying flat in a small hollow. I came down the same second, suddenly realizing that we were amidst the scattered fire of a Russian machine gun that was raking the surface of the hill and hitting the trunks with sharp smacks. It dawned on me that I had just escaped an early death, a stupid and entirely useless one.

"Over here!" the messenger shouted. With a few jumps, I was at his side. Down in front, short burps of submachine guns mixed with the other small arms fire. The messenger cursed. He pointed down the slope, "Over there, the ditch! We must be in there before they start off with their *mungos*! I'll jump first. You follow me right away," he hissed. When the messenger dart-ed off, I heard the mortar discharges on the other side, "*pop - pop - pop - pop.*" I waited. Then the bursts of the first round came hurrying up the slope, "*wham - wham - wham - wham,*" in rapid succession. "Now! Quick!" the mes-senger yelled, and up I jumped and landed beside him in the ditch. The real-ity of the *HKL* was tougher and crueler than I had imagined, reminding me of the surprise in my boxing lesssons in the *Jungvolk* camp when I got hit full in the face for the first time.

More mortar fire followed, with shells bursting all over the hill, and there were more firings on both sides in between, "*pop - pop - pop - pop.*" But the messenger, disregarding the turmoil, rushed forward along the system of ditches we were in now, ducking and running, while I kept stumbling and panting behind. Suddenly, hearing the swish of another shell, quite close, we took cover on the floor of the ditch. Instantly, I was shocked by the blast of the shell bursting right on the parapet. When I came to, the messenger was kneeling beside me.

"You all right?"

"Yes, quite all right, I think."

"It's over," he said.

I got up and looked over the parapet where the impact had torn a dirty gap, but the woodland around us was dark and still as before. I felt a sharp pain behind my left ear and realized that when I had thrown myself down on the floor I had been hit hard by the butt of my rifle.

The bunker was right behind the next corner.

A curved ditch led down to the entrance. A few steps and we stopped short in front of the crude door. We could hear a tune being played on a harmoni-ca coming from within. The messenger grinned and pushed the door open. Nobody was there except for a fire guard slowly emerging from the dark background and casually knocking out his instrument in his palm.

"You're a fine one! Playing your harmonica while hell is breaking loose outside!" the messenger said and shook hands with the black-haired, sturdy man.

"It's just because of the noise," he said with a broad grin. "Gets on my nerves. And whom do we have here? Our replacement I guess."

"Right. It's Johann Voss. And this is Heinz Bäumer, rifleman three on this gun."

We shook hands. I had a look around. It was a dugout built for seven, warmed by a small stove and lit by a carbide lamp that gave off a blue-white light and a pungent smell. In the back, squeezed under the low ceiling of thick logs, were some bunk beds, crudely joined together by spruce sticks and sprigs. The side walls were also solid blocks of logs. There was a neat gun rack, a little table, and two benches around it. On the walls all sorts of equipment were stashed: ammunition, clothes, felt boots and, among others, two expended artillery shell casings connected with the outside by a string.

The others returned in a moment. First in was a group of three with white-covered helmets, their faces flushed with excitement, and all armed to the teeth. They squeezed themselves through the narrow entrance with easy, practiced movements. The silver runes on their right collar patches glinted in the light of the carbide lamp. They were all talking at the same time, animated by the short fight. I gathered that a Russian patrol must have been lying for hours in the snow not far in front of our positions to wait for its chance to jump into our ditch.

One of the three who had just come in, a blond one called Schmidtchen, recounted in a strong Köln accent how he had been on guard, had fired the flares, and then was lucky enough to kill the first one of the patrol.* The Russian had jumped up right in front of him, but entangled his submachine gun in his own snow shirt, and enabled Schmidtchen to get the better of him. The other Russians had been caught by our machine-gun fire and, with their attack stalled, the rest had taken flight, probably with some casualties.

The three of them removed their helmets and stashed their rifles into the rack. Two others were still out in the ditch, one they called *"Der Alte"* ("the Old One") and their first gunner, named Heinrich. I was standing in the background by a bunk. They hadn't noticed me.

Then I saw *"Der Alte"* coming in. A submachine gun hung across his lean figure; a pair of deep-set eyes peered out under the brim of his steel helmet, and a wide mouth formed two strong parallel lines above a square jaw—it was a face like a woodcut.

*In English, Köln is the city of Cologne.

"Attention!" he called while he slowly filled his two pouches with new magazines for his machine pistol. "Order of the chief: You stay as you are, all of you. No taking off your boots, no sleeping, absolutely no schnapps! The Ivan might try again before long." He had spoken in a calm, commanding voice salted by a very strong Upper Silesian dialect, his protrusive Adam's apple bobbing up and down his long throat. He was the leader of this gun section, about twenty-five years old, one of the old guard who had joined up before the war.

Just as I was going to report to him, he spotted me, "Hey soldier, who are you?"

The others, too, then noticed me. The messenger had already left. I went forward, saluted, and reported for duty. His salute was casual. A thin smile went over his face. Perhaps my report had turned out a bit too snappily for these wizened combat veterans.[*]

He sized me up. Both of us were feeling the certain difference between the old and the young volunteers. His manner was neither cold nor warm. His nickname, though, appeared quite appropriate to me as he obviously was the oldest and the most seasoned of the squad. His stern, nutcracker face also matched with the name. He seemed to enjoy a considerable natural respect among the men of his squad.

"Put your things on the bunk in the upper left. In case of an alarm, don't come out. Under any circumstances!" And turning to the others, "Take care of him."

I shook hands with the others and answered their questions about my personal and military backgrounds.

Such was my first encounter with the front line. I arrived in a still forest, experienced an explosion of violence, and had a friendly reception in the bunker. The vague notions about my new assignment now had found their form: the land, the front, and the faces of my new comrades. Here, in this setting of icy marshes and swamps, of snow-covered woodland, of brooks and lakes, of a front line clutching at a forlorn slope and ribs of land at the 66th degree north latitude (the Arctic Circle), I had met what would from now on be my home, my life, and my fate: the 3d Battalion.

---

[*]Military discipline required a soldier to salute anyone in command, in this case the leader of the gun section, even though he was a noncommissioned, not a commissioned, officer.

11

ST. NICHOLAS DAY

A terrible bang jolted me from a deep sleep. I was on the upper bunk in our dugout. It was the sixth day of December in 1943. Feeling a piercing pain, I realized I had bumped my forehead against the log ceiling. Above the bunk next to me, the roof had been ripped open; a big hole let in the dim light of a sub-arctic noon. A Russian antitank gun was blasting away on our position and had torn apart the thick layers of logs, stones, and dirt on the top of our bunker. The gun's reports were fast, dry, and hard, instantly followed by the impacts of the shells. Inside our bunker, the expended shell casings, jerked by the string from our MG emplacement, jangled their maddening alarm. Still numb, I jumped into my felt boots, getting ready to rush outside. The alarm stopped, and at the same moment, I heard our own machine gun opening fire. Then the *mungos* on the other side began firing, "*pop - pop - pop - pop*," sending over shell after shell that plastered the ground around us.

The "*Alte,*" already in his parka and with his helmet on, was grabbing his submachine gun; with quick, measured movements he stuffed his pockets full of hand grenades.

"Folks, it's getting serious. C'mon out, quick!" he shouted and dashed outside.

Heinrich was right behind him, both on their way to the machine gun emplacement. I followed with the others, running along the ditch, always ducking from the mortar fire. Orders were unnecessary in a situation like this. Each knew his place. Mine was next to Heinrich as number two gunner.

At our machine gun bunker, Bäumer was blasting away in short bursts, swiveling the gun on its tripod mounting. The antitank gun was silent. It had disappeared behind its camouflage. The Russian *mungos* went on firing. Ours had joined in, too; we could see their rounds impact on the enemy's position. The roof of our emplacement had been hit by the Russian antitank gun, but neither Bäumer nor our machine gun were harmed. Together with one of the 12th Company's machine guns, he had repelled an assault of a Russian patrol to the left of our gun position. When Heinrich and I took over, we could see some white-clad figures withdrawing, every other second jumping up, running, and quickly taking cover again in a deep trail they had flattened in the snow while stealthily creeping forward all night. Three bundles remained lying in the snow, indistinct, not far from our barbed wire entanglement.

The firing stopped for a while; the white patrol disappeared into a stand of spruce and birches. Quickly, we changed the hot barrel; I took another belt from the ammunition box and loaded it into the breech of the gun.

"Everyone alright here?" a voice behind us asked.

I turned around. The officer on duty had entered our bunker.

With him was *Oberscharführer* Schaper, our platoon leader. The two were in full gear, submachine guns across their chests, white-covered helmets on. They couldn't have been more different in appearance, though. The officer, *Untersturmführer* Mannhard, was a platoon leader in the 12th Company of our regiment. I had never really spoken to him. He was a handsome man, lean and young, about Philipp's age. When he walked through the trenches, it was with a markedly springy gait. Now, in the narrowness of the bunker I saw his face close up and noticed under the rim of his helmet eyes that were full of willpower and resolution, as they peered out through the embrasure. Schaper, on the other hand, was sturdily built, ruddy faced, a man from a village in Lower Saxony; he clearly was another one of the Old Guard. He also had a remarkable gait that always reminded me of a farmer trudging in rubber boots across a rain-soaked field of sugar beets.

"Yes, so far, *Untersturmführer*," the *Alte* said.

Mannhard was in a hurry, pressing on with questions: how many we had seen? How many casualties left in the field? What sort of equipment were they carrying? Most importantly, where was the antitank gun?

The *Alte* pointed to a spot directly across the hollow. "Right over there, just beside their machine-gun bunker. I've never seen that son of a bitch around here before. Can't be much of an emplacement. Guess they've done it overnight. It happened all of a sudden. Bäumer here had them right in his telescopic sight when they tore down the camouflage from the gun and started banging away."

Mannhard stepped up to the rabbit-ear trench scope and searched the opposite hill for the gun. "They tried the same stunt with the 1st Battalion a few weeks ago," he said.

"What do you think they're up to?" the *Alte* asked.

"Don't know yet; a probe I guess. Whatever, I think they'll try again before long and then, I'm afraid, your emplacement will be their first target. Listen, at this distance they'll blow the whole bunker away with that gun if you let them. Make sure they don't get another chance. You *must* silence that gun before it starts doing real harm! Don't let them out of your sight! I'll request special fire support from our *mungos*." With that he departed.

We were waiting while the *Alte* remained glued to the scope, now and again traversing it slowly to the right and to the left. Heinrich peered over his sight. More than an hour passed in silence, tense and threatening. The three bundles in front of the wire remained still. Noon was over and it was getting dark again, as dark as it gets at this snow-covered latitude. The cold slowly crept up from the ground to my knees, despite my thick boots and the brushwood underneath.

Heinrich took a break, leaving the gun to me. No sooner had he left that I saw their gun right across from us as it slowly appeared from behind a screen being torn down and then loomed over the parapet, aimed at our firing position.

"There it is!" the *Alte* and I yelled at the same time.

"*Fire!*" the *Alte* yelled. The first burst of tracers arced over. I had the Russian piece firmly in my sight and kept the trigger handle tightly pressed. I could imagine the bullets cracking against the shield of their gun and rattling the nerves of the gunners, but penetrate their armor they did not, not even at the range of only 150 meters. Then came their response. The first round slammed into the roof of our emplacement, tearing away another part of it. The second round was too short. If the next one went through the embrasure, we'd have had it. Heinrich was back and took over, keeping the Russian gunners pinned down by long bursts of fire. Their third shot also missed, but the duel of life and death wasn't over yet.

Then, finally, our mortars started firing. I saw a rapid sequence of impacts around our target, four at a time. Another round and then more. The *Alte* kept watching through his telescope, getting more and more excited about our well-placed *mungo* fire. "Cease fire, Heinrich!" he called suddenly. "Don't see the gun anymore. I think it's busted."

We had a break. We had no sooner changed the barrel, though, when Heinrich had discovered a second Russian patrol, quite distant yet, but coming from the same direction. He swung his gun around, aiming at the white shadows working their way forward in the twilight.

"Hold it!" the *Alte* said. "We'll get them at closer range."

Suddenly he yelled, "Watch out!" At the same time, the burp of a Russian submachine gun sounded right in front of us, followed by the *Alte* emptying a whole magazine of his submachine gun right above my head. One of the three Russians lying in front of our wire had crept forward, waited for his chance and, trying to accomplish what had gone wrong before, had leapt to his feet. The *Alte* had spotted him almost too late, but shot him just in time. The Russian soldier collapsed, his body twisting as one arm became caught in the barbed wire. Then he lay still, his arm remaining raised as if in remonstration against his own, useless act of bravery.

At the same time, our defensive fire broke loose. Heinrich blasted away with his gun and our mortars plastered the No-Man's Land. The Ivans had advanced pretty far, but for all their bravery, their patrol had to fall back.

All of a sudden, our mortars stopped firing. "Hey, look!" the *Alte* shouted. "I think the 12th is going after them. Can't believe it! These devils!"

I jumped up and, looking through the embrasure, I could see the shadows of our men dashing over the white treeless expanse at the left of our hill and in an oblique direction toward the patrol. They had come rather close and were already about to cut the Russian patrol in two. I heard Mannhard's command, loud and clear, ordering the men on his left flank to wheel around and block the Russians' withdrawal. All went very quickly then. Shooting and storming, they broke through the patrol in no time, herded the last of the Ivans together, and were already well on their way back with them before the Russian *mungos* opened fire.

Afterwards, the forest was as still and as dark as it had been in the morning. It was late afternoon, and I remained on guard for the next hour. The *Alte* came by to tell us there were no casualties on our side. As I inhaled deeply on my first cigarette, the tension gave way to the feeling that this was the place where I wanted to be in this time of war.

Upon my return to the bunker, the men were in high spirits. Mail had arrived. Under the circumstances of our crowded dwelling, it was inevitable that mail, to a certain extent, was a public affair rather than a retreat into privacy. A bottle of cognac, part of the monthly ration for each of us, was standing next to the carbide lamp. Letters and photographs were passed around. Some of the men were still cleaning their weapons. I was met with a special welcome since I had received a parcel from home, and everybody knew they would somehow participate. When I opened it, I could hardly believe my eyes. It was a St. Nicholas parcel from home with everything in it that used to be in our shoes on the morning of the 6th of December when we were children: biscuits, nuts, chocolate, twigs of spruce with red bows and some little gift—a knife, a notebook or what have you; this time it was a small book: *Hamsun, Under Autumn Stars*. To think that this parcel had reached me over the distance of 4,000 kilometers, by ship, by train, by truck and on the backs of mules, and that it had arrived in time on the very day—all that was a near miracle.

Outside the frost had increased. The little stove roared, its top red hot. Our spirits escalated after another bottle of cognac had come to the table. At first, the *Alte* dominated the scene by starting the songs to be sung, telling jokes, ordering others to tell jokes, and showing approval or contempt depending on the degree of filthiness.

"Know the story of the two fleas?" he started once more. "No? You don't? Well, here it is: Two fleas meet in the beard of a motorcyclist. 'Like it here?' says the one. 'Well, one gets around; but every time he rides, there's this awful dreadful draft! Drives me crazy.' 'Well, if you want my advice, find a young woman and nestle in her bosom as soon as possible. It's a fine life there, I can tell you, calm and warm.' And that's what the other flea actually did; one day it was gone. But a few weeks later it was back again. 'How did you fare, my dear friend? You followed my advice?' 'Yes, indeed! I crawled into the bosom of a young beauty and I had a wonderful time there, just as you said. But one day I discovered an even better place not far away, one that was bushy, warm, and cozy. Absolutely splendid! Magnificent!' 'Good to hear. But tell me, why didn't you stay?' 'Well, I don't know. One day, some-how, I found myself back in the beard'"

There was a roar of laughter. Heinrich and I were somewhat more sub-dued; in general, filthy jokes were not so much in favor among us younger ones. All the more reason for another round of cognac and another song. Bäumer on his harmonica started a doleful melody, a favorite of Schmidt-chen's, the song of a poacher, his daughter and his master who, after a couple of verses, eventually all died. Schmidtchen loved that kind of song. And so it went on; the sadder the better. Bäumer used to be a master at the art of draw-ing elegiac melodies out of his simple instrument. Those of us who did not know the words kept humming the melodies, except for the *Alte* whose mood had changed and who was leaning back with a deeply troubled look on his face. All of a sudden he got up and quietly said, "Stop it now, I won't have more of it."

"Hey, *Alte*, don't be a bore. Let's have some more songs!" Schmidtchen shouted, intoning another melody.

"I said stop it!" the *Alte* roared, banging the flat of his hand down on the table. "Curfew now! Tomorrow we'll have our hands full of repair work on the roof. Time to turn in."

With that, he left and prepared for his round in the trenches. Before Schmidtchen could further object, Heinrich quickly grabbed his arm, forcing him to understand that it was better not to insist. Our little party was over.

The *Alte* was gone. Heinrich was due for the next guard tour and sat by the fire. I was curious about the *Alte*'s strange behavior and asked Heinrich what he knew of it.

"Well," he said, "seems he can't stand these kitchen songs; they get him down." And then he told me the story of Salla and the *Alte*'s role in it. He said sooner or later I would hear of it anyway, at least hints or indications which would make me wonder; so it was just as well if he told me now. The *Alte* was with the combat group that had been the predecessor of our division. Pulled out of the south of Norway, they were thrown to the new front in North Karelia in June 1941 when the campaign up here started. As a motorized unit, entirely unprepared for combat in the woods, their first mission was to take some hills in the wilderness between the Finnish-Russian border and the hamlet of Salla.

It was terrain that should have been identified as the stronghold it actually was, if there had been proper reconnaissance, but to safeguard the operation's surprise, none had been allowed. So hardly had they advanced to the foot of the hills when they were cut down by the Russian *mungos* and machine guns blasting away from their bunkers on high ground. Our men were pinned down under the enemy's fire. In no time, the dry forest began to burn. Heinrich wasn't with the unit then, but he was told it was dreadful. Roaring fire and smoke filled the area, mortar shells exploded and scattered machine gun fire caused more and more casualties among men and officers. Communications had collapsed. Before long, they panicked and retreated. The *Alte*, aware he might burn to death himself, left his comrades behind, either wounded or dead. After Salla had been taken, the dead were recovered, hundreds of them. The *Alte* was still haunted by his buddies' cries for help in the burning wood.*

Heinrich finished the story and put some more wood on. His profile was silhouetted by the fire. The account of the grim truth of the division's baptism of fire added to the somber expression that used to mark his pale, narrow face with the dark eyes. We had talked before and had become kind of close. Born in Königsberg in East Prussia, he had volunteered right after leaving the *Gymnasium*. But for all his idealism, he was a skeptic who took some satisfaction in telling me, the new replacement, that the division's combat record wasn't entirely glorious.

After a while, he continued, "The division fought with distinction thereafter, and was reorganized as a mountain division in 1942. The *Alte* got the Iron Cross. He isn't over it, though, and I doubt he'll ever be."

I was to relieve Heinrich on guard at midnight, so it was time to get some sleep. I climbed up into my bunk and fixed the twigs and the bows from the parcel to the logs of the wall. The roof had been patched up for the time

---

*For more information about *SS-Kampfgruppe Nord*'s unpreparedness for its first action and how the unit recovered to become an elite formation, see *Seven Days in January* by Wolf T. Zoepf, Aberjona Press, 2001.

being. In the morning, we would begin with the repair behind a camouflage screen that had to be put up before daybreak.

It must have been around that time that I became acquainted with *Untersturmführer* Mannhard.

I was on guard waiting for my relief to come. More snow had fallen. The sky had cleared and it became bitterly cold. We had slipped into that season when nature goes numb with cold, and when the men on both sides fight the frost as their common enemy. Even minor negligence could cause frostbite on the extremities, ears, and noses. On guard, standing on layers of twigs of spruce, we were clad in felt boots, padded trousers, fur-lined anoraks, snow shirts, huge mittens, our heads protected by a woolen mask with holes only for the eyes and mouth, looking like fat market women rather than young soldiers.

Beyond such hardships, though, there were winter days and nights when this strange land presented itself in great glamor. I had already seen northern lights of immaculate beauty—a huge gleaming, dancing, wavering, and flickering of marvelous forms and colors—captivating us earthbound dwarfs and belittling our belligerent doings. At noon on that day, the sun had, for a short time, risen above the horizon and made the snow glitter and sparkle, even around the dead Russian's upright arm by the wire entanglement.

On his round through the trench, Schaper was about to leave our gun emplacement when he told me I was to see Mannhard in his bunker on my return from duty. "Seems to be personal," he said. I wondered what it could possibly be.

As it turned out, he and Schaper had been in our bunker before to talk to the *Alte*. There he had spotted my *Hamsun* book left on the table and inquired to whom it belonged.

"I'm very glad to have someone in the neighborhood who reads *Hamsun*," he said with a handshake after I had reported to him. I saw him the first time without his helmet or cap. Immediately I thought of Philipp, different face, same type. On his tunic, he wore the EK I and the *Verwundetenabzeichen*, which was very unusual.*

"Have you read more of him?"

"*Growth of the Soil*," I replied, "I'm very fond of it."

"So we've something in common," he said. "Sit down and tell me about yourself."

I briefly told him about my background and learned he was from Münster/Westphalia. He asked me to lend him my *Hamsun* saying that there was a special reason for his interest: he was going to be assuming command

---

*EK I is the *Eisernes Kreuz* (Iron Cross) 1st class, worn on the left side of tunic; the *Verwundetenabzeichen* is the equivalent of the Purple Heart.

of a company of the division reconnaissance battalion up on the North Flank where they would be operating together with the Norwegian volunteers. I wasn't aware of Norwegians in our division and my curiosity was aroused. He explained they had volunteered for the cause of Finland, first forming a company and then having grown to a full battalion, *SS-Skijäger Battalion "Norge"* (Norway). They were experts on skis and fully mastered that inhospitable terrain. The North Flank was about thirty kilometers north of our location, Mannhard said, with no coherent front line but merely a few outposts and strongpoints of various sizes. These were built for all-around defense with lots of ammunition and rations, all spread out over a vast terrain of swamps, lakes, woodland, and some forlorn huts. Warfare in that region primarily meant patrolling the No-Man's Land. He had been stationed there before he went to the officers' candidate school and was familiar with the terrain.

All that fired my imagination. Noticing my interest, Mannhard casually remarked, "Sounds you are interested in joining one of those patrols." "Sure, why not?" I said idly, not knowing that this was to have important consequences.

12

PATROL ON THE NORTH FLANK

In the course of March 1944, with the sun steadily climbing up the meridian each day, the reconnaissance activities in the division's sector increased. Twelve hours of daylight, frozen lakes, and the snowbound terrain were ideal conditions for *Gebirgsjäger* (mountain infantry) ski patrols. It was particularly crucial on the North Flank for the survival of the outposts and of the division as a whole to track down the enemy, concealed somewhere in the wilderness, and to find and destroy his bases.

The winter had not been as hard as the last few had been. In our bunker, we had survived quite safely. And yet, looking back, it seems impossible that a front line could be maintained in such extremely hostile climatic conditions. However, the bunkers were much improved dugouts with several layers of logs on top, proof even against heavy artillery fire, and thus provided relatively comfortable shelter as well. The adverse effects on morale of constant darkness from November until February were eased by the "battalion schnapps," a clear, white booze issued quite lavishly once a week. The long hours inside were spent with "Seventeen and Four," a poker-like game with heaps of rubles involved, the currency of our pay with which we could do absolutely nothing else.

I think what enabled us to get through the winter fairly well was our youth and a certain spirit of bravado. Of course, as youths, we were always hungry and our hunger was beyond the capacity of any rationing system to satisfy. No doubt the constant nervous strain added to our hunger. Most of us were so keen on sweets that when we got our weekly ration of mixed fruit jam, we devoured it at full tilt.

Early that month, I was called to the company command post where I was informed that I was going to be transferred to SS-Reconnaissance Battalion 6 *Nord* deployed on the North Flank. Whether Mannhard had pulled some strings with the Division staff, I never found out. My feelings about it were mixed. On one hand, I would miss the comrades in the *Alte*'s squad, Heinrich in particular; on the other hand, I was trained especially for ski patrols and felt I was more at home in the open, even in this inhospitable region, than in the trenches and bunkers. At any rate, it is not least for another encounter with the wild geese that I think the long-range ski raid in that season belongs to my portrait of the volunteers. The flight of the geese followed the call of nature as we thought we were destined to follow our mission in the near-arctic north.

A few days later, I was on a truck rumbling along the road to the north. This road had been cut out by our engineer battalion across the hills and swamps of the wilderness, some ten kilometers distant from, and parallel to, the front line, a massive corduroy road of tree-trunks and planks. It was the counterpart of the railway on the Russian side, and the difference between them symbolized the gross disadvantages with which our own logisticians had to cope.

The road ended at a lakeside that was still and frozen, sporting a few sheds and two overturned boats—a place of infinite loneliness. A sleigh brought us eastward across the lake. On the other edge, a small settlement of log cabins emerged from the white surroundings. It served as the base of the reconnaissance battalion's front line, which blocked the passage between two other lakes some kilometers further east.

When I reported to the command post, I learned that I was assigned to Mannhard's company. As it turned out, three ski patrols were to start in parallel in a few days; they were to operate independently and were led by three officers: Mannhard, a Norwegian officer and, to my great surprise, von Hartmann.

With a three-squad total of 32 men, two NCOs, and one officer, our group was the smallest, one squad consisting of Norwegian volunteers. We were assigned to search for the enemy in the Russian rear echelon, take prisoners, and return immediately, while the others would be out for two days reconnoitering north and south. Our preparations were already well under way. I got skis and Finnish ski boots but kept my own rifle; about half of the group was armed with submachine guns. Several *akjas* were being loaded with ammunition, rations (among others, as a specialty for reconnaissance parties, a mixture of nuts, almonds and raisins), tents, and spare skis for the prisoners we were to take.

We were to depart shortly after dusk, and we hoped to hunt down the enemy behind their lines by the next morning. We assembled at 0700.

Mannhard had a Russian submachine gun with several round magazines—an indestructible, never failing, most coveted weapon. We wore no helmets, our mountain caps being more expedient on a mission like this.

It took us another half hour to reach our positions for departure. We conducted a short pause, and then slipped in single file through the safe lane in the minefield out into the No-Man's Land that lay in semi-darkness under a clear, night sky.

The Russians, we supposed, were operating in an area between two lakes that were about ten and twelve kilometers east of our *HKL*. Our route was planned as a wide arc around that area, leading into their rear. The patrol was not unfamiliar with the terrain. We had maps that showed the lakes (they were numbered), the rivers and the flat hills, and they gave us a general idea of the marshes. Experience from previous patrols added to our sense of familiarity. Some spots, I learned, were marked to indicate where comrades had been killed in an earlier action and had had to be left behind. Later, in the huge vastness and desolation of the region, though, I never quite lost the feeling that no human being had ever before trodden on the ground we were crossing.

We traversed thin woodland and open expanses, worked through thick undergrowth, and had to get over ditches and frozen water; rocks and fallen trees had to be bypassed, and sometimes we would go smoothly along our track. The *akjas* were drawn in turns. The tour was laborious, and we sweated in spite of the cold. After months in the trenches, I was out of shape. Now and again, the patrol would come to a halt when the terrain in front had to be secured in preparation for our passage. At such times, there was an utter stillness, a stillness so absolute you could hear your own heartbeat and feel the rush of the blood in your ears.

We paused around midnight. We assembled by a small glade in a mixed stand of birches and spruce. Here we were relatively secure so that each squad could kindle a small fire for tea, the way the Finns had taught us. We used cylindrical cans with holes poked through the sides just above the bottom; strips of bark from birch trees were thrown in and kindled while chips of birchwood kept the fire burning, steadily and almost smokeless; it was sufficient to provide us with a warm drink. The men stood around, talking in low voices. Above, the sky formed a huge, glittering vault, and I reflected that we didn't have that sort of sky at home.

I was talking to Herweg, the squad leader of the Norwegians, who had been with Mannhard on missions before and seemed to be particularly devoted to him. Suddenly, Mannhard was standing by us pointing overhead. "Listen! Hear that?" he asked, listening raptly. "Be quiet for a moment!" he said to the men. Then I heard the trumpet-like cries of geese, high up, still far off, but coming nearer. All of us were listening now and looking up. A wide, triangular formation of the birds appeared against the sky, rushing from the south to the north and singing their shrill, plaintive, endless song. We watched the birds until they vanished in the dark. Again, I could not help thinking of the song we had sung so often in the *Jungvolk*:

Wildgänse rauschen durch die Nacht,
mit schrillem Schrei nach Norden.
Unstete Fahrt; hab'acht, hab'acht!
Was ist aus uns geworden?

Fahr zu, fahr zu, du graues Heer,
Fahr zu, fahr zu, nach Norden!
Und fahren wir ohne Wiederkehr,
rauscht uns im Herbst ein Amen.*

Trying to express my feelings in that moment, I think it was then that I began to regard the wild geese as an image of our own mission, of our fight against Bolshevism in this forlorn region, as natural and inevitable a thing as the flight of the birds. No doubt, the song was also in the minds of many of us, much as we were focused on our task to operate out there on our own in the enemy's rear. We did not then see, however, the prophesy in the lines of the song, the prophesy of things that had happened but were unknown to us, and of things to come.

We went on to cross the land in an easterly direction. In the dark, there was no sign of the enemy. In single file, we laid our track without disturbing the silence of the woods; there was only the soft noise of the gliding skis and the rhythmic clicks of the poles muffled by the snow. As the hours went by, the strain increased; there seemed to be no beginning and no end of the white vastness. Only sparse trees filled the void, trunks standing upright in defiance of their hostile habitat.

Before dawn, we took another rest. Mannhard consulted with the two squad leaders over a map lit by a flashlight. Turning southwest, we were bound to cut across the Russian lines of communication sooner or later. With first light, all our movements grew more cautious: there were more stops at

---

*Wild geese are rushing through the night,
  with shrill cries, on to the north.
  Unsteady journey; look out, look out!
  What has become of us?

  Sail on, sail on, you grayish host.
  Sail on, sail on. On to the north!
  And were we to sail without return,
  In fall your rush will be for us an Amen.

the front, more surveying the terrain with binoculars, and more security measures.

At about 1000 hours, we approached Lake No. 20, some six kilometers south of our night's route. At a signal from Mannhard, we took cover in the snow. In front of us, the lake formed a smooth, white expanse amid the woodland. Mannhard and the squad leaders swept again over the terrain with their binoculars. Suddenly, at last, they spotted the enemy. We heard distant voices. We moved forward and then I saw them: a Russian detachment going eastward across the lake while from its eastern edge a detail with two horse-drawn sleighs and several men came out of the wood to meet them.

Mannhard motioned us further back into the forest where we took a turn toward the northwestern corner of the lake, paralleling the lakeshore and the Russian line of communications. Meanwhile, the two Russian groups met in the middle of the lake and proceeded westward together. We arrived early enough at the western edge for Herweg's Norwegians to slip unnoticed across Ivan's track and to move into a concealed position in the woods while Mannhard's squad took an opposite position. The third squad remained in reserve. Slowly and quite at ease, the Russians approached. Mannhard let them come on up to a distance of 50 meters and then shouted at them in Russian, "Hands up! Throw away all weapons!"

They chose to not comply!

After some confusion, their answer was a hail of small arms fire in our direction, meant for an enemy they did not see. They had taken cover behind their sleighs and kept firing. We had gotten rid of our skis, dispersed on the edge of the lake, and held our fire as we prepared to attack. Then Mannhard, kneeling by a trunk and observing the Russian group through his binoculars, gave his orders, loudly and clearly. Under his lead and under covering fire of our riflemen, the men with the submachine guns stormed forward, forming a cordon. The snow prevented them from running, so they took their time and rushed ahead in short jumps, taking cover in the snow between jumps, while we held down the Ivans with our rifle fire. The poor devils had no chance. Soon their fire became weaker, although some of them kept bravely defending themselves. Our men were so near now that we had to stop our fire. Mannhard's squad had already made it to the last sleigh and appeared behind the Russians. A few more burps from sub-machine guns and it was over.

We stood up. One of the Norwegians was leading one Russian, hands raised, back to our position. As it turned out he was the only one who survived. There were no casualties on our side. Slowly, our men returned. Among the dead Russians was the commander of a ski-battalion, which well explained their stiff resistance. After securing the papers and documents he had on him, we found the sleighs loaded with rations.

There was no time to be lost. Although the fight had lasted no more than 20 minutes, it must have alarmed the whole Russian rear echelon. We took off, heading toward Lake No. 17 to the northwest where we were expected by von Hartmann's group. Unfortunately, our brave prisoner turned out to be a hopeless failure on skis, so we did not make too much progress. Once in a while, however, we left a few land mines underneath our track, a wise precautionary measure as we noticed with satisfaction when we heard an explosion behind us about an hour after we started.

We reached von Hartmann's position early in the afternoon. Although by then we had been on our way for almost 20 hours, we had another three hours to go. A detail of von Hartmann's group joined us on our way back. On two *akjas* they were drawing a sad load: three *Jäger* killed in a previous battle were found the way they had been left early that winter. Now, enveloped in canvas, they were returning for burial in our cemetery.

The main force of von Hartmann's group stayed behind to intercept a Russian combat unit they assumed was operating in the area. For us, having performed the main part of our mission, the tension eased off, but almost 24 hours of skiing, interrupted only by the fight at Lake No. 20, left us physically exhausted. About one hour had passed when we heard intense small arms fire from behind. Von Hartmann must have met the enemy somewhere around Lake No. 17. After a while, the noise ceased. We wondered if that had been all there was. Indeed, late in the afternoon, we heard the noise of another clash. This time it sounded more serious and didn't stop as quickly. We heard discharges and impacts of heavy mortars. Now we knew von Hartmann's group was in real trouble.

We reached our lines safely.

Von Hartmann's group returned late the next day. Of the 30 men, five had been killed and 15 wounded. They bedded their dead, covered with canvas, in a row of *akjas* in front of the cabin where I arrived a few days before. Among them was von Hartmann. The news spread like wildfire; he was killed by a direct mortar shell hit.

The two days of rest we were granted afterwards were clouded by von Hartmann's death. Certainly, the casualties of the Russians had been by far heavier, but it was the general opinion that we had paid a high price. For me, von Hartmann's death was a personal loss. I had lost the very model of what I thought a modern officer should be. I had watched him inspecting his group on the day before our departure, his easy, affable way with the men; he had lost his limp but was still using his stick. From that moment, the North Flank had seemed to me brighter and somehow familiar. I had hoped there would be an opportunity to speak to him, and when I heard the news of his death I felt, for a moment, forsaken. It was another step in the process of becoming a seasoned soldier.

On one of these days, Mannhard asked me to come by the cabin he stayed in; he still had my book and wanted to give it back. We sat down on two stools and made ourselves comfortable in front of a fire in the crude, whitewashed fireplace that formed the center of the cabin. The rest of the furniture was of the simplest kind. Earlier in this house of roughly hewn logs, people had lived their lives, a whole family most likely, now gone, evacuated together with their small herd of livestock. What was left still was a pastoral setting of utter simplicity and innocence.

"This is straight from *Hamsun*'s world," Mannhard said, "the world of *Blessing of the Earth*. Isak's and Inger's first house at Sellanraa must have been like this."

His remark did not require confirmation. For a while we let the fire do the talking, our thoughts lingering around the strangeness of the situation. The war had placed both of us into this environment so different from our own, and yet so familiar to us through that Nordic novelist's work.

Mannhard was in a somber mood, however, and needed someone with whom he could talk. It wasn't only von Hartmann's death he had to get over. He also grieved about the recent bombing of his hometown in Westphalia, which was almost totally destroyed, including his family's home. He said the war was no longer only about destroying the enemy's military power but also of annihilating their cities and the people living there. And it wasn't even two different cultures doing that to one another; it was old Europe bombing itself to pieces. If that would go on, he said, Europe would be easy prey for the Red Army.

Asked about my own family I told him that the house on the Wall in Brunswick had recently been destroyed, too, its beautiful façade, Isa's Elysium—burned to the ground, all rubble now. I spoke of my mother's last letter writing about my little brother Peter now being a *Luftwaffenhelfer** and staying at a *Flak*-emplacement near Brunswick. He became the fourth soldier in the family with my father serving in Italy and my elder brother, Nick, at the Army officers' candidate school in Soissons, France. It wasn't much consolation.

At that time, the Allies already had adopted the "Unconditional Sur-render" formula which, we realized in our talk, left us no choice. Now it was either destruction for us or for them. Our mission up there, we found, was all the more clear: hold the ground against the Bolsheviks as long as possible. Mannhard thought our cause wasn't yet lost. His hope was founded on what he called "a new European spirit coming into being," shared by our brothers in arms, the Finns, our Norwegian comrades, and by all the other volunteers serving in our ranks from France, Denmark, Belgium, the Netherlands and

*Pupils of sixteen serving as helpers with anti-aircraft units (*Flak*).

even Switzerland.* I told him how much I agreed and that this vision had brought me to join the "troop" with Philipp's help. My casual remark that Philipp now was serving with the *Wiking* Division alerted him instantly.

"Why," he said, "I came from the *Wiking* to the *Nord* after I was released from the hospital; I was still a NCO then."

We talked a while about that division, and then I said I was curious whether he had earned his Iron Cross 1st class there and what for.

"That's right," he said, "I got it from the *Wiking* in the hospital. I had destroyed five Russian tanks. It was pure chance. No one else was there to do it. The tanks stood in a row obliquely to my anti-tank gun and couldn't turn against me, at least not as quickly as they got busted, one after another." He played it down.

We watched the flames and put some more wood on the fire. Despite the difference in rank and my great respect for him, we had become closer in mutual interests and shared beliefs.

---

*There were nearly 2,000 Swiss volunteers in WW II on the German side, most of them serving in the *Waffen-SS*, from summer 1942 in general they were posted to the 6th *SS-Gebirgs-Division Nord* (see Vincenz Oertle, *Schweizer Freiwillige an deutscher Seite*, Zürich, 1997, 561, 638).

13

COMBAT PATROL

I was back with my battalion before Easter. The regiment had requested my return when the leader of another heavy machine-gun crew in our platoon had been killed by a sniper. I was to replace him. It meant a different position, a different squad, and a different bunker, even different equipment. Now I had a submachine gun and a pistol instead of a rifle.

The new machine-gun emplacement, north of my former position, had as its field of fire a wide expanse with a few thin stands of trees. The Russian positions were rather far off, their front line receding northward to meet the eastern inlet of Lake No. 70. Here the ground was flat and, in summer, swampy, with only a few small elevations, or "ribs," as we used to call them. The lower stretches of the trenches, connecting my former position with the new one, were no more than shallow ditches, providing only the most inadequate protection. Here, in the sharp light of a sunny morning, my predecessor had met his sudden death.

I looked forward to my new assignment not least because I knew I would find Stricker there, my South Tyrolean comrade from the training camp. Thanks to him, I had a warm reception in the new bunker when Schaper, our platoon leader, introduced me to the men. Stricker was the number two gunner in the squad. Number one was Bing, an Alsatian, another one of the old guard, a veteran of Salla. In the course of time, he turned out to be a gunner of unfailing calm and cold-bloodedness in the most precarious situations, no matter whether he had been drinking or not. One of the riflemen was Otto Berger, a Bavarian worker's son; he cherished an ardent devotion to the *Führer* and regarded him as the savior of his family. As he told me some time later, in tears after quite a few glasses of booze, his family had been saved from misery, despair and humiliation when his father's long-term unemployment ended in the course of Hitler's first job-creation program.

It was early in April. The ground was still covered with snow, but as it was past the vernal equinox, dawn came at an almost normal hour of the day. I was on guard duty in the machine-gun bunker. Above the still-frozen land, the sky arched into a huge vault. From the horizon in the southeast, an array of separate, flat cloudbanks, broadening in perspective, extended up to the zenith in peaceful immobility. Dawn was waning and, in a subtle change, was giving way to daylight. First, a pale pink appeared between the dark firs in the east, and then it gradually changed into a deep orange, which slowly spread over the sky. Against this glow, the cloudbanks turned dark violet first, then lavender and green, and eventually a serene saffron.

I peered across our sector, now lying in full daylight. Sweeping the rabbit-eared trench scope slowly across the enemy's position, I stopped at the Russian machine-gun emplacement opposite from us. There I saw two fur-capped figures moving about. I could only see their heads, first popping up from behind the parapet and then dimly behind the embrasure. The two Russians were practicing on their gun, rather carelessly, in fact. The sight of them, so much enlarged in my sight reticule, was something of a sudden confrontation, the more so as the clear weather allowed me to get a distinct impression of their features.

I mused, so here were two of the "Red hordes" sent by the Bolsheviks to overrun our occidental culture; people who had turned churches into pig stalls. Seeing them at close range, they looked strange, foreign, uncivilized, and, yes, frightening, but then, they belonged to a Soviet Ski Brigade that was one of their best units, as far as we knew. Hadn't these people—or at least their older brothers or parents—filled their magnificent churches with their wonderful voices not too long ago? Hadn't their powerful and deeply moving anthems, never heard in German church choirs, been sent as praise to the same God to whom we prayed at home? And didn't Tchaikovsky's symphonies, which I loved so much, have their roots in these peoples' souls?

I was torn from my thoughts when two officers, accompanied by Schaper, entered my emplacement. One of the two was Mannhard's successor with the 12th Company down from the *Junkerschule* (*Waffen-SS* officer candidate school) only recently; the other one I recognized by the three silver pips and the two braids on his left collar. It was *Hauptsturmführer* Hansen, our battalion commander, whom I faced then for the first time. "The battalioner," as we used to call him, was, from all I had heard of him, a highly respected, very popular commander. He was respected for his vigorous leadership and proven bravery, and popular for his friendly way with the men. Now I thought his appearance and manner met all the qualities I had heard of, but he struck me as young, much younger than I had thought. He accepted my report, saluted, and immediately stepped up to the telescope where he began searching the enemy's positions. From time to time, he talked to the officer of the 12th, pointing to some of the positions. Then, straightening up, he seemed to have confirmed his decision about a mission they apparently had discussed in detail before. The mission was to be started across the No-Man's Land in front of us that same night.

It was a combat patrol. Later, Schaper turned up to ask me to go out with the patrol and secure their left flank with my gun.

Outside it was dark, early in the morning of the day of our patrol. The air in the bunker was hot and loaded with the pungent smell of burning wood and glowing cigarettes, of leather and wet things. The men were standing close around the carbide lamp so that the room was darkened by their shadows. Tightly packed under the low ceiling in the cramped room they wore white-covered helmets and had stowed away their equipment with belts and straps on the white anoraks. The men of the assault team carried as many hand grenades and as much ammunition for their automatic weapons as they could manage. The three of us, Bing, Stricker, and I, had slung ammunition belts over our shoulders. I was holding our MG 34 pressed to my body; I was my own number one gunner this time.

Silence had fallen on the room. All was set. The mission was clear: an assault group would breach the Russian positions opposite us, penetrate their bunker system, and return with prisoners before dawn. Now everyone was more or less occupied with keeping his uneasy feelings under control. I, for one, kept telling myself, *we are an excellent team, we have excellent leadership; it can be done if we are smart enough; don't worry, and for heaven's sake stay cool!* I watched the stern, inscrutable faces of the men which were occasionally illuminated by the glow of a cigarette.

A group of four were standing by the exit, strangely separated, the hoods of their anoraks drawn over their helmets. They carried no weapons, but each had fastened to his chest several kilograms of explosives. They were a detachment from the Regiment's penal platoon and were given the opportunity to redeem themselves in combat. These were men who had committed some infraction of military discipline, such as laxity while on guard duty, drunkenness, insubordination, or some offense in the rear, such as the misappropriation of government property or harassment of a girl. Their mission was to pick up the mines to make a path across our own mine belt and to clear the way for the demolition team in front of the enemy bunker line. At that moment, I found their presence, their mission, and their unarmed status deeply disturbing, as one could sense the grim enforcement of military discipline. Their presence added to the gloom in the bunker. At a sign from their leader, a combat engineer sergeant, they left the bunker to begin their work. We stayed behind for what seemed to us another eternity.

Our patrol leader looked at his watch. "It's time. Let's go."

Relieved, we took up our gear and pushed to the exit, first the assault team, then us, the support element. Passing the stove, we flung our cigarettes into the fire and made for the trench. At the exit to the cleared path through the minefield stood the battalioner, making a remark now and then to a man he knew by name or just briefly lifting his hand in an informal salute. When I came by he gave me a smile, remembering perhaps our encounter that morning in our emplacement.

The three of us reached our position unnoticed, and I fixed the gun in firing position behind a fallen trunk. To the left lay the bare expanse; in front, at a distance of about 70 meters, was the Russian main combat position. I could dimly recognize the dark rectangle of the embrasure of their machine gun emplacement in the snowbound bunker line I had had in my sight that morning. I adjusted my gun over the foresight.

"*Wham! Wham!*" There were two flashes ahead to our right, directly in front of the enemy position. "*Wham!*" The third charge went off. The assault team was jumping ahead toward the Russian ditch. A flare went up. Seconds later, the Russian machine gun burst into life. The same moment, I sent half a belt with some tracers directly through the embrasure. The recoil of my gun hammered into my shoulder and the bipod rattled from the force of the bursts. Our fire silenced the Russian gun just in time for our engineers to dash through its field of fire. More Russian flares soared up. Now the Russian machine gun fired again. After another burst from our gun, though, our demolition team managed to throw a three-kilo charge into the embrasure. A muffled detonation lifted the wooden structure. Our men jumped over the parapet, and rolled up the trenches to the left and to the right; submachine guns blazed and hand grenades blasted as they knocked out the two emplacements.

Everything had happened in a few minutes, but the fighting continued in the Russian position. We constantly heard brief bursts of automatic weapons fire, and imagined the hand-to-hand combat which was probably going on in the Russian position. Their mortars were sure to open up soon. Suddenly, the burps and explosions in the Russian position stopped. The scene was still again. I saw our team coming back, dim figures running back from the Russian bunker line and heading directly towards our position. They immediately came under fire from another machine gun the Ivans somehow had managed to mount to the left of the demolished bunker. I threw myself around and aimed at the muzzle flash of the gun. The Russian gun had to be neutralized. Bing, lying beside me, fed another belt into the MG34. Stricker rushed up with more tracer ammunition. We fired a few more bursts and the Russian gun stopped. Now it was high time to change our position after that most conspicuous show of our gun.

Then we heard the first discharges of the Russian heavy mortars, a sequence of "*pop - pop - pop - pop.*" Instinctively, we counted each of them. "*Wham - wham - wham - wham.*" After the first sheaf hit, we jumped up and took cover in two of the craters. The next discharges went off and more of their shells crashed down around us. Then there were even more mortar rounds fired, and they began to merge into into an indistinct thunder. We were lying stiff among the blasts. This barrage was the worst I had experienced until then. Round after round came down. I don't know how long it lasted. It seemed impossible that we would escape this inferno alive or at least unhurt. And yet, lying there under the concentrated fire, our bodies pressed into the shallow craters, there was this desperate, irrepressible hope to be spared this time. For whatever we felt or hoped, we had to stay on to cover the retreat of our comrades. Last out, last in! Eventually our 10.5 centimeter mountain howitzers made their entry and sent their rounds over to the Russian *mungo* firing positions. Lifting our heads as the fire died down, we saw that, so far, the three of us were unhurt.

In the silence that followed, another Russian flare went up. All was quiet. The assault group must be at home by now. Why didn't they give us the signal for our return? Since our departure, about half an hour had passed. Before long it would be dawn. Suddenly, from behind, the messenger appeared and threw himself down beside me. The order was to stay on for another assault. We had lost our only prisoner through enemy fire on the way back; the battalioner was determined to get the mission accomplished nevertheless; he sent them back again, promising massive fire support.

The messenger had just left when the fire of our howitzers and *mungos* opened up. We saw their flashing impacts on the Russian bunker line. Our assault team made for the gap in the minefield with quick, wide jumps. Our fire stopped as suddenly as it began. Then came the clatter of small arms fire in the Russian position, but not as much as before. Could we have caught the Ivans again by surprise? It wasn't long before we saw them return, alternately jumping, taking cover, firing back, and jumping again. The machine gun opposite us remained silent this time. Our gun on the right flank blazed away towards the bunker line. Our artillery had shifted their fire to the mortar emplacements. All the same, there they were again, the dreaded discharges of the Russian *mungos*, "*pop - pop - pop - pop,*" the terrifying swish and blast of their shells that sent us down again on our bellies. This time, however, their fire went to the rear where they assumed the rest of our patrol was.

It was dawn when the signal came for us to return. Still out on the expanse of wide open terrain, we were all fairly visible by now. We had to cross quite a stretch to get back to the safety of our ditch. I forget how we finally made it, I only remember that the *mungo* fire lasted as long as we were out in the open and that our howitzers did their best to hold down the enemy fire.

Back in the ditch and inhaling deeply on our first cigarettes, the three of us triumphed out of a sense of sheer survival rather than because of the mission's outcome—which we didn't know at that moment anyway. There was that surge of intense happiness, a temporary and an utterly false feeling of physical integrity; all of this was the reverse of that fear of death we had been through during the last two hours.

I entered the bunker to give my report. The battalioner hadn't left for his CP, but was still sitting with the patrol leader and some other men from our patrol. Among them was a Russian prisoner, rather good looking, smoking a cigarette as he was questioned by an interpreter. They tried to extract from him fresh intelligence about an offensive our people were expecting around Easter. Here in the forward combat zone, he almost seemed to be one of us, a soldier among other soldiers and being treated as such. Our mission, I concluded, had been successful. We had two casualties: the messenger, who had been killed by shrapnel, and one man of the penal platoon, whose honor had been considered restored in the process of dying in the Russian wire entanglement. Both bodies were recovered.

When I emerged from the bunker, the setting of clouds still hung unchanged in the sky in that peaceful immobility. The play of colors had begun anew.

It was only in the afternoon of that day that I felt the death of the messenger sink in. Stricker and I were on our way to Schaper. The sun was falling obliquely through the sparse trees, throwing black stripes across our quiet, wintry position. In front of the medics' bunker there was an *akja* left on the snow with a human shape concealed under a canvas. We stepped up to it. I knew what we would see. Stricker lifted the sheet, and now we had a full look at the waxen face of the messenger; he had a deadly wound at his neck, and his anorak was covered with frozen blood. I was deeply shocked by the sight of the comrade I had known quite well.

At this instant, I fully realized that death would always be close to us, as close as our comrades next to us and as long as we were with this unit. Now I had a full grasp of the dark side of the duty I had been so anxious to take up, and it was as if, for a short moment, my former self was standing beside me asking, "See that? How do you like it now?" From then on, deep inside, the knowledge of the imminence of death was to be my sullen companion until the end.

Stricker softly put the sheet back over the messenger's face. We turned away from our dead comrade and went on, the snow crunching under our boots. Dusk would fall soon. The bark of the trees had darkened. The first trace of spring was in the air.

The "House by the Mountains" in the Harz region (above), the location of some of the author's happiest days—and first inklings of foreboding—before the war. (Author's Collection)

The "House by the Wall" in Brunswick (left), where the idea of becoming an *SS-Gebirgsjäger* first enthralled the author. (Author's Collection)

The lodge on the ridge above the Königssee, home to the author and other *SS-Gebirgsjäger* during their training. (Author's Collection)

The author while in
Gebirgsjäger training,
Bavaria, early 1943.
(Author's Collection)

Enroute between assignments on
the Eastern Front and in Italy, the
author's father visits with his son
during a rare one-day pass during
Gebirgsjäger training in Bavaria.
The author's absence during this
single day of training had a profound effect on his future.
(Author's Collection)

The author (left) and some of his comrades prepare for alpine training outside the lodge. (Author's Collection)

An *SS-Nord* patrol prepares for a raid—such as that on the Soviet lines in which the author participated in April 1944. (Steurich/Munin)

SS-Nord Gebirgsjäger accepting the surrender of Soviet troops (above) (Author's Collection)

SS-Nord Gebirgsjäger (right) on outpost duty peer through the frozen taiga. (Author's Collection)

An *SS-Nord* patrol negotiates the dense taiga of northern Karelia on skis with white camouflage coats. This closely resembers the author's patrol on the North Flank in March 1944. (Steurich/Munin)

The author's own patrol on the North Flank in March 1944 looked quite similar to this one. (Steurich/Munin)

The strain of combat—in the far
north, against a tenacious and unre-
lenting foe—is mapped on the race
of this *SS-Nord Gebirgsjäger* (left)
(Warfield collection)

An *SS-Nord Unter-*
sturmführer (right) questions Soviet prisoners in
the snow of a bitter
Karelian winter
(Warfield Collection)

One of *SS*-Mountain
Artillery Regiment 6's
105mm howitzers (*leFH*
18) (below) and part of
its crew are silhouetted
against the sub-arctic sky
(Warfield Collection)

Element of SS-*Gebirgsjäger* Regiment 11 (above) man defensive positions south of Sennozero. (Author's Collection)

This photo (below) could have been taken on the way back from the raid at Sennozero. (Author's Collection)

Taking advantage of smoke to mask their movement, *SS-Nord Gebirgsjäger* advance through the sub-arctic forest (Warfield collection)

The commanders of the Sennozero Pocket, both wounded in hand-to-hand combat. *Hauptsturmführer* Renz (Commander, SS-Motorized Infantry Battalion 6), third from left, was wounded in the thigh; *Hauptmann* Lapp (Commander, Army Ski-Battalion 82) suffered a fractured arm. Our "battalioner," *Haupsturmführer* Hansen is on the far left, with binoculars around his neck. (Author's Collection)

This command car parked on the side of a road thorugh the taiga clearly displays the *SS-Nord Hagalrune* insignia, as well as the wear and tear of protracted operations in the sub-arctic (Warfield collection)

Anticipation
(Warfield collection)

With the "garbage gang," the detail to which the author was assigned as punishment for being insubordinate to an American officer. The author is on the far left, standing. (Author's Collection)

In American captivity at Romilly-sûr-Seine. The two arrows show the author (left) and Pete (right). (Author's Collection)

At Romilly, the author (far left) with Walther (far right) (Author's Collection)

14

SUMMERTIME

On the first of June 1944, my nineteenth birthday, in the land northeast of Kiestinki, winter had changed to summer. For the last two weeks, the weather had been warm and clear, with the sun describing its low arc above the horizon for more than twenty hours a day and bringing about the extravagant phenomena of light and the play of color. The snow had disappeared and given way to the wilderness in all its greenness. The earth had begun to breathe again and was exhaling the fresh and rich smell of pine resin, humus, and moss. The ground was still moisture laden, the swamps marshier than ever—breeding grounds for myriads of mosquitoes. Under the stunted birches and conifers flared a luxuriant variety of flowers and berries, tufts of grass, and lichens.

With the change of season, we had changed our uniforms. The thick, mostly white winter garments were replaced by speckled-pattern camouflaged shirts, the warm mountain caps by the light camouflaged ones, and our helmets were worn with covers made from the same material, a special type of military gear that had become the characteristic feature of our combat units. Together with the green mosquito veils covering our faces, we had become an almost invisible part of the green wilderness.

The expected Russian offensive at the end of the winter had not taken place. Now, in the swampy terrain, it was impossible to carry out any major operations. The front was quiet on the whole length of the division's sector. It was time for a respite, particularly for the squads in the bunkers whose nerves were thinned out from the long months of guard duty, from their intense watching and listening in the dark. There was time for an escape from the anxiety of combat as well as from the monotony that filled the gaps in between.

We made the most of the sun that warmed the hollow behind our bunker. Sometimes, when the wind chased the mosquitoes away, we would sit there, bare to the waist in our free hours, ravenously absorbing the sunbeams and feeling some of our natural exuberance return when we closed our eyes. With our eyes open, we only had the sight of pale-skinned youths plucking lice from their shirts and tunics.

That I was still among them was a near wonder. In the spring during the thaw, I had been on my way to our old bunker to see Heinrich. It was a bright day. Instead of taking the turn around the hill, I took the direct way through the trench that had, as I have mentioned before, a dangerously shallow stretch. As I ran through the trench, only slightly stooped for cover, I suddenly felt the hiss of an bullet smacking right beside me into the dirt of the trench wall. Instantly flat on my stomach in the mud, I crawled over to the deeper stretch of the trench. When I reached my old bunker, Heinrich was horrified by my sight, "Oh, my God! Are you sick? You're as pale as a tablecloth!"

"Never mind," I said, "I'm fine. I just stumbled in the trench."

Heinrich immediately got the picture; he'd heard the single rifle shot on this quiet morning. "I think I could do with a schnapps now," I said a bit lamely, "a big one, if you don't mind!"

Now, on the morning of my birthday it was Heinrich's turn to come and see me. He brought a fine bottle of his monthly ration. We were sitting in the sun behind our bunker, drinking what was left of his bottle after it had gone around my squad. I was on leave for twenty-four hours. Schaper had suggested a visit to the *Soldatenheim*, the division's recreation lodge. According to Heinrich, it was quite an impressive wooden structure built by our engineers. He warned me, though,"Maybe it's not what you'd expect. Go and find out for yourself."

Half an hour later I was on my way. I don't know whether it was the drink or the glorious weather or both, but I marched along our supply trail with a bounce in my step. The path wound through the woodland, up and down the hills, across swampy hollows and brooks over corduroy paths and little bridges. Again I was amazed by the Nordic sky, an immense blue arch, decorated with white cumulus clouds. I had left the artillery emplacements far behind me. More and more the tension, which had constantly racked and worn down our nerves in the front line, was evaporating and giving way to a feeling of utter release.

Here, in the communications zone, the land had remained almost untouched and empty. I had been alone for the last hour or so when I met a train of pack animals on their way to the front accompanied by two grooms, one trotting ahead and the other behind. Stepping aside, I let them pass, the pack animals with their relentless nodding and dainty pace, and the grooms with their round, good-natured faces that seemed to belong much more to the mules than to the combat troops. As I watched them pass, I had my submachine gun casually slung over my shoulder to emphasize the contrast of the intrepid, seasoned, front-line veteran with the peaceful population of the rear echelon.

In search for a lookout point, I tried a rise at some distance from the trail. From the treeless top, there was a glorious view of the tranquil hills and swamps, of the glittering water of the distant lake and of the boundless swell of the surrounding land. All of a sudden, I was struck by the pure, sincere beauty of the land, a feeling so intense and overwhelming that the anxiety, sorrow, and fear of death of the past months melted into a great joy. I sat down on a rock, yielding to the spell of the moment and wanting to embrace it all. Deep inside, I knew that I had come to love this land. Alone, I let the tears roll down my cheeks. In my romantic mind, I even went so far as to think that if I was to die in this war it would be good if it were here in the great tranquility of this land.

Recalling that day in the summer of 1944 and looking for an explanation, I think it's simply that a young soldier found a few minutes of happiness our earth sometimes provides for man, perhaps like the first hunters in North Karelia, some two thousand years ago, may have felt when they roamed this wilderness for game.

Hundreds of swarming mosquitoes awoke me from my exalted state. If I wanted to reach the *Soldatenheim* for lunch, I had to be on my way.

I arrived there in time and immediately dug into a hearty meal of goulash and noodles. It wasn't too often that I could have my fill; seldom were the rations enough for us younger ones. Afterwards, sitting there and smoking, I watched two Red Cross nurses working at the bar and cheerfully talking to the soldiers. Just to see real young women and to hear their soft voices plunged me into an inner turmoil. I hadn't been near any females for a long time out there. I sat in my flecked combat blouse and my not-so-clean trousers. Watching them in their immaculate, light-gray dresses with the white aprons and collars, and amidst the general tidiness of the place, I began to understand what Heinrich had warned me of—I felt out of place. When one of the nurses passed by my seat, so closely that she brushed my face with her dress, I was thrown into complete confusion. I quickly got up and fled into the cinema.

As I watched the newsreel, my overall impression was that things were going badly in the East. There still were impressive images of our *Panzer* units and infantry in action. But for the first time, I was struck by the inherent propaganda; it wasn't so much the pictures that showed real combat scenes, but rather the unnaturally excited voices of the accompanying text.

Contrary to the intention of the propagandists, the impression that registered was one of falseness, of fabrication.

The show went on. Under the title, "It Was an Exuberant Ball Night," the film that followed was about Tchaikovsky and his relationship with Nadezhda Philaretovna. It was conceived as a bitter-sweet romance, accompanied by Tchaikovsky's music. Obviously, I was ill prepared for both, particularly for the music. After months of total musical destitution, I was ready for emotional release. I felt sorry for Peter Ilych, I felt sorry for Nadezhda Philaretovna, and I felt sorry for myself. So, toward the end of the film, Tchaikovsky, already stricken with cholera, was directing his *Pathétique*, and when the last movement, the huge wave of the *adagio lamentoso*, surged up— a tear-jerker even under normal conditions—I felt again a lump in my throat and rescued myself by leaving the theater in a hurry.

Outside in the sun, the morbid scenes soon vanished. I wanted to be back in the real world, back to my mission.

I went to get some food and sweets for my way back. I would take my time, and I would take a long rest up on my look-out and watch the sun go down.

15

SENNOZERO

It was a week after summer solstice when the Russians finally launched their offensive.

At first, we heard the faint rumble of artillery fire up at the North Flank. Then an artillery barrage came down on the positions of SS-Mountain Infantry Regiment 12, our neighbor to the left. It was of such tremendous energy that in the following attack, strong Russian forces actually broke into the regiment's forward positions. They nevertheless were thrown out in the ensuing counterattack. Under the cover of more artillery fire, however, the Ivans managed to dig new positions dangerously close to our front line. We answered with a massive artillery bombardment using all the howitzers and heavy mortars at the division's disposal. In the end, the Russians withdrew.

Even with all the casualties this operation had cost both sides, it was only a harbinger of greater events to come. The thunder on the North Flank continued to worry all of us for the next few days. The first rumors came in: the brave Norwegians of Ski Battalion "Norway" had been overrun and driven from their outpost; other strongpoints seemed to have been abandoned, among them the one from which we had started our mission to the lakes in March. The thought that Mannhard was somehow involved in what was going on added to my uneasiness as I listened to the constant rumble. Had he been with the outposts that had been overrun? Was he still alive? Over the days the thunder had increased rather than lessened. It didn't stop at night, but there were no nights anyway. They said even *Stukas* were employed.* Something big was going on up there.

**Sturzkampfflugzeug* = dive bomber, Junkers Ju 87, "flying artillery." Their angled wings and the dreadful wail from a siren during their almost vertical nosedives on bunkers, tanks, bridges made a daunting impression.

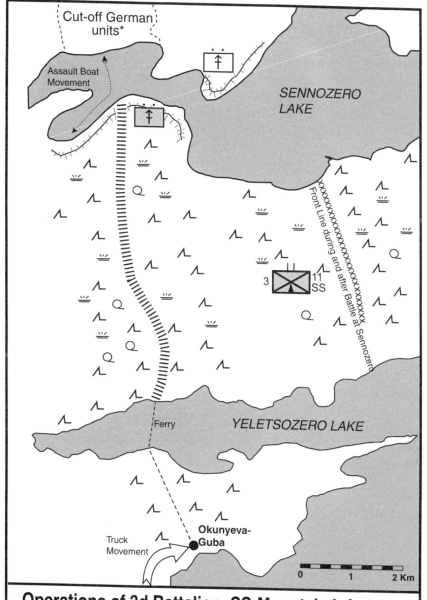

Cut-off German units*

Assault Boat Movement

SENNOZERO LAKE

Front Line during and after Battle at Sennozero

3 ||| 11 SS

Ferry

YELETSOZERO LAKE

Truck Movement

Okunyeva-Guba

0   1   2 Km

Operations of 3d Battalion, SS-Mountain Infantry Regiment 11, vic. Lake Sennozero, July 1944

*Elements of SS-Reconnaissance Battalion 6, SS-Ski Battalion "Norway," SS-Motorized Infantry Battalion 6, and the German Army's 7th Mountain Division

Λ Conifers   ⸌⸌ Swamp   Q Deciduous trees |||||| Corduroy Road

Then, for the first time, we heard the name of Sennozero, the most northern of our strongpoints, another lake, in fact, with a few huts and some hills, a point from whence a flat, impassable region of water, bogs, and thin ribs of land extended over a boundless distance to the north. Here, as we were soon to discover, the Russians had employed a task force of seven battalions, determined to open the way for a thrust into our division's rear area.

We were alerted on one of the first days of July. Schaper rushed into our bunker at seven in the morning. The battalion was to leave its positions within twelve hours, in full combat gear.

In the rear, we found the regimental command post bustling with activity as the battalion assembled. Sergeants major were directing different units here and there. Equipment was being replaced and completed; rations for several days were issued. Finally, our platoon stood in line for an extra item—handed out from a desk standing under some fir trees—a round, tin box of *Schoka-Kola* for each of us.* Such charity was an unmistakable sign that things were getting serious.

I remember clearly the scene I was watching. There, for the first time, I saw the men of our platoon all together, chatting, relaxed, clad in their camouflage blouses, their caps taken off for the light breeze that kept the mostquitoes at bay, their faces tanned from the sunny weather of the recent weeks. I saw Bing, the ever-reliable one, with his machine gun resting on his shoulder; Stricker, with his blond shock of hair; Polzer, the other South Tyrolean of my gun crew, red-cheeked and strong as a mule; Berger, with his good square worker's face; the *Alte* and his men, laughing about one of his jokes; Schmidtchen, the most easy one to entertain; Bäumer; and next to him, Heinrich, with his machine gun on his shoulder, showing a wry smile. I suddenly felt pride and confidence in this unit, in the battalion as a whole which, at that moment, seemed to me invincible.

At some distance, the trucks were waiting for us to embark. Standing tightly packed on the open backs while the convoy slowly turned into the road, we saw a figure standing on the porch of his log cabin seeing us off. That figure was our division commander with silvery oak leaves on his collar patches. He was a small, wiry figure, thoughtfully looking at the second battalion he was sending up to the North Flank in support of the hard-pressed defenders of Sennozero.

---

*In each tin box of *Schoka-Kola* were two disks of dark chocolate, enriched with caffeine. These tin boxes were pure luxury for us.

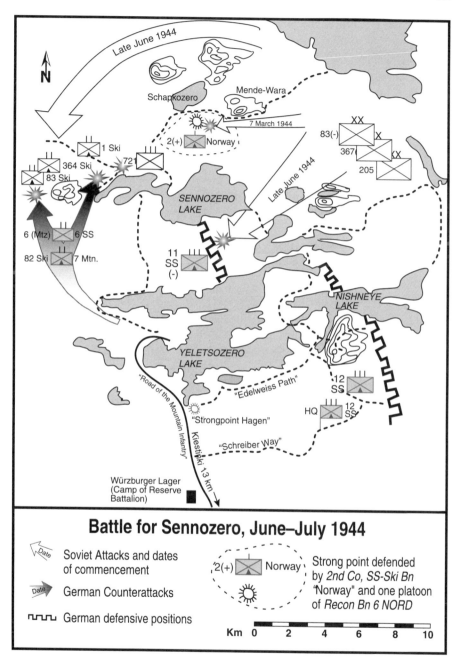

Battle for Sennozero, June–July 1944

↖Date Soviet Attacks and dates
of commencement

Date→ German Counterattacks

ⵑⵑⵑⵑ German defensive positions

2(+) ⊠ Norway Strong point defended
by 2nd Co, SS-Ski Bn
"Norway" and one platoon
of Recon Bn 6 NORD

Km 0   2   4   6   8   10

It was midnight. Ahead of us was the road, that bold, wooden construction leading north. It followed the ups and downs of the terrain as a sailing boat would ride the waves. Whenever we were on top of a hillock and before the vehicles dove down again, we had the strange sight of the road forming a straight row of treeless humps that stretched up to the horizon. And right there in the north, as a huge red disk, the sun was about to rise for another day of combat.

The road ended at Okunyeva Guba, a hamlet, actually only a few huts, on a peninsula between two arms of the Yeletsozero. It was quite near to our own artillery emplacements as we could tell from the incessant noise of their discharges. We started to cross the peninsula on a narrow path further north. It was strenuous work with all the heavy gear on us as we worked our way across the spongy ground. The undergrowth on both sides was thick. The mosquitoes began to torment us again. Our progress was slow. For some reason, again and again, the line came to a halt. Then we would put down our weapons and ammunition boxes and throw ourselves down beside the path for a short break. Suddenly, the distant heavy weapons were silent for a while. Once again we waited for the line to move on, unaware of what was coming toward us.

The first thing we noticed was the snorting of the mules up ahead on the trail, and then their flickering ears above the brushwood. As they emerged they disclosed, one after another, the load that lay across the back of each of them: our dead comrades of SS-Reconnaissance Battalion 6, recovered from the combat zone toward which we were heading. Gently swinging with the pace of the mules, their faces softly touching the flanks of the animals, seemingly unharmed in their camouflage blouses, their limp bodies looked completely exhausted rather than dead. In fact, it was only the unnatural whiteness of their hands dangling from their blouses that unmistakably showed that death was real. It was a long column of twenty-five to thirty animals, with one body draped across each animal.

All of us rose and removed our caps and veils. We let the slow procession pass in utter silence.

Behind the mules, a train of stretcher bearers followed. On their shoulders they carried critically wounded men. The bearers were dripping with sweat, mumbling curses as they once again stumbled or sank deep into the swampy ground. Eventually, the way was cleared. We took up our gear and marched on.

Having reached the edge of the lake, we waited for the ferry to take us to the other side. Heinrich and I were sitting at the foot of a tree, Heinrich chipping a wooden stick with his *puuko*.* The other men of the platoon were scattered around the little landing stage with its small stock of ammunition boxes, fodder for the mules, and gasoline for the boats. We were watching the ferry as it glided towards us. It cut a wide triangle on the smooth surface

*Slightly curved Finnish hunting knife with birch handle and leather sheath, part of our gear.

which reflected the sky with all the fancy colors of this early hour. With the continuing lull in the artillery fire, we could hear the soft hum of the motor. A single figure stood at the stern of the raft-like structure, operating the tiller. It was a scene of absolutely compelling symbolism.

I couldn't help saying to Heinrich, "Look at the ferryman? It's Charon conveying the poor souls across the River Styx. What have we got for an *obolos* to give him when it's our time?" Instantly, I realized that I had missed the light touch I originally intended.*

He forced a smile. "When the hour comes," he said, "we'll have given all we had. Don't worry, he will understand."

When the ferry was moored, it was plain to see that help was needed to bring the cargo ashore: more bodies lay in a row concealed under speckled canvasses. Myth had turned into reality. The mules would soon be back.

On the opposite edge of the lake, there were the boats. They were quite inconspicuous at first, three oblong, flat-bottomed shells of about four meters, lying on the ground upside down, square stern, pointed at the bow, made of light metal and painted green. Next to them were the three motors, two massive cylinder blocks sticking out on both sides of, and mounted on, the upper end of a long drive shaft. The engine had a large handle in front and a propeller on the rear end of the shaft. These were the kind of boats featured in the newsreels with assault teams deeply ducked into the shell, charging some hostile bank in a roaring, rapid sweep across the water and leaving a huge tail wave behind.

We were waiting for the guide to bring us to Sennozero. Meanwhile, we stood around the boats to take a closer look. There was some idle talk, some of us wondering why this valuable equipment was just lying about, when we were interrupted, "Listen everyone!" Schaper was calling from the edge of the wood where he stood next to an engineer sergeant and an officer; both seemed to have come down from the front line. We gathered around them.

"*Untersturmführer* Mannhard of the Reconnaissance Battalion is going to explain to you our next mission," Schaper said and stepped back, leaving it to Mannhard to continue, "Parts of your battalion and ours will mount another breakthrough across the Sennozero at seven this morning; I repeat, seven o'clock. The units will reinforce the battalions that are encircled on the other side of Sennozero, in a bridgehead, in fact. In the same action, our casualties will be brought out. We need your heavy machine guns to reinforce the covering fire from this side of the lake. The breakthrough will be carried out by the three boats we've already got up there and by the three of them still lying here. That means we'll have to bring them to the lake in time. It's

*In Greek mythology, Charon was the ferryman who took the dead across the River Styx that formed the border to the Underworld. For the fare, people would put a coin (*Obolos*) into the mouth of the body being transported.

seven kilometers from here. None of your own equipment will be left behind. We'll need every gun, every ammunition belt, every rifle we've got. It's a difficult stretch, and I know it's going to be rough for all of you, but it can be done as it has been done before." He looked at his watch, "It's high time. Let's get going!"

I looked around. There were only our two platoons assembled on the narrow lake shore. If there were six men for each boat and, say, five men for each engine, there would be only half of our manpower left to carry our normal equipment.

Listening to Mannhard's briefing, I was impressed by his capacity to inspire others with a sense of duty and confidence. This young officer, in his worn battle dress and with his face marked by the strain of the ongoing battle, was undeniably one of us, someone to go through fire and water for.

Somehow, we managed to pick men of equal height for the boats and the sturdier ones, such as Polzer and Berger, for the motors. The extra weapons and ammunition boxes were strapped to the breasts and backs of the rest of the men. We left the shore without delay.

The path wound through a terrain of solid ground, swamps, and brooks, the impassable parts reinforced by corduroy trails and sometimes small bridges. This supply route satisfied the needs of normal movements for mountain infantry and mules, but it was entirely unfit for our task. The boats were much wider than the beaten track and most of the narrow corduroy structures on the ground. Feeling the painful pressure of the gunwale on our shoulders and mostly walking beside the path, we were anxious to avoid any slip which could be disastrous for the team. Crossing the first swamp on the corduroy path, we shifted the load from our inner to our outer shoulders, ducking our heads under the shell of the boat guided only by the two men at the bow. The motor teams were better off as four men each carried the cylinder blocks resting on two poles parallel to the shaft so that two men could walk closely together, a fifth man carrying the rear end. The others walking in line on the trail carried the heaviest loads, their shoulders and knees bent by the weight of the equipment.

After half an hour of balancing our boat along the track, we heard a loud, sharp curse and saw the boat ahead of us crash down to the ground. Instantly, we put down our boat, glad for the interruption. As it turned out, two men had slipped from the poles on the ground and landed knee deep in the bog so that the boat had toppled over. Fortunately, no one was hurt.

Schaper, turning up from the rear and packed with ammo boxes himself, saw that the men were already desperate and near exhaustion. The sun had come up above the treetops and swarms of mosquitoes had been lured by our sweat. It was almost unbearable that we had gone only a small part of our way.

"Come on. Get going. Don't lose contact. We'll take a break soon," Schaper said and helped lift our boats on to our shoulders. The others took up their loads, and the train started to move again.

From now on, swamps and small elevations took turns on our energy and patience. Coming out of a bog, we were glad for once to have solid ground under our feet, but then we had to stumble uphill over rocks and stumps. We took occasional breaks, but it was all the harder to lift our load again and to struggle along. Mannhard, the engineer sergeant, and Schaper spotted those who stumbled and were having trouble struggling to their feet again; they managed to provide for each of them some kind of relief, exchanging one of the men under the gunwales or taking over an ammunition box for a while. This mission was pushing us to the limit. Our hearts pounded like pistons, the carotid arteries sticking out of our necks like rubber tubes gleaming with sweat. The ever-gnawing pain from the gunwales, the poles, and the straps tormented our shoulders. If only our feet could find firm and even ground! Instead, we had to put up with obstacles and spongy sod beside the path and with slipping in the bog. Whenever that happened, all kinds of tempera-ments surfaced: aggression, curses in various dialects and volume (the South Tyrolean for the ears of all others an unintelligible, high pitched rush of words), and then again quiet composure or endurance.

In the end, nothing mattered any longer but our tortured bodies muster-ing their last reserves to overcome our exhaustion, and our wild determina-tion to take the boats to Sennozero on time. We didn't give a damn about the harassing fire of the Russian artillery that kept coming down on us the more we progressed. We had become entirely indifferent to our own combat action lying ahead of us. We had also already forgotten about the column of the dead we had watched earlier that morning. Meanwhile, the boat teams were marching independently of one another, each entirely occupied with manag-ing on its own. The intervals between our breaks became shorter and short-er. Mannhard, like a sheepdog, kept herding the train together, encouraging and, the closer we neared the end of our tour, reassuring us that we had almost made it.

Somehow, indeed, we made it; somehow, after two and a half hours, we reached the landing place behind a rise that stretched along the south edge of Sennozero. Numbed with exhaustion, we delivered the boats and the motors to the engineers, slammed ourselves into a bay that provided cover from the artillery fire, and lay prostrate on the ground, draining our canteens in long gulps.

I was called in for a briefing and looked at my watch. Six o'clock. Still one hour to go. I looked for an opportunity to have a word with Mannhard before he left and before we were emplaced in our firing positions. I found him preparing for his mission. He was going with Hansen, our battalioner who, he said, had been appointed to relieve the wounded commander of the enclosed strongpoint and to take charge of our *Kampfgruppe* in the pocket. The men inside had been suffering for days from massive artillery and mortar fire and holding their ground against continuous enemy attacks. The Russians, Mannhard said, had briefly overrun some outer positions and even advanced to the command post, but had eventually been thrown out in hand-to-hand fighting. As things were, Hansen's new assignment seemed to be a *"Himmelfahrtskommando."** Mannhard said he had to move on, pointing to a group of officers getting ready to embark on boats that were to form the first wave. Hansen was among them, looking just like one of us in his helmet, camouflage blouse, and a submachine gun hanging from his shoulder. Another one of them was our battalion surgeon. "Take care," Mannhard said. I wished him good luck.

My firing position was on the rise overlooking the lake. Right across the water, at a distance of one kilometer, was the hamlet of Sennozero where the men of our two battalions were fighting for their lives. The Russians had managed to block all overland access. Our breakthrough over the lake was to be launched from our landing place at an inlet to our left, concealed from the enemy's sight. Once the boats had come out from behind a rib jutting out into the lake, parallel to the south edge, they would have to cross the open water and be exposed to enemy fire. Our task was to suppress the machine guns across the lake to the right. Dazzled by the sun, I found it impossible, though, to spot them through my binoculars under their camouflage. We would have to wait for their tracers to betray their positions. Stricker rammed his mount into the soft ground on the rise; Bing threw his gun into the traversing and elevating mechanism, and adjusted the sight for the estimated range to the enemy's positions across the lake. We were ready.

⸺⸭⸺

At seven sharp, our artillery and mortars broke loose. From our privileged position, we could see the impacts flashing along a line where we imagined the Russians' eastern positions and gun emplacements to be. In spite of the noise, we could hear the engines of our boats revving up to a deep roar. Soon, they shot out from the inlet, two side by side, then another two, then four, and eventually six, bows rising above the water, light machine guns in front, the men crouched on the bottom, the propellers leaving white, foaming tail waves behind. Only the coxswains stood upright at the stern, both hands on

---

*Literally: Ascension Commando = suicide mission.

their backs in a tight grip on the handles of the driving shafts mounted on row locks on the stern posts of the boats.

As soon as they came out in the open, the coxswains sharply swung the tillers to the right, using the motors to steer and causing the boats to swerve to the left in a wild arc, now heading directly for the opposite shore. A fascinating sight! The boats were very fast; still, they were only boats, presenting fine targets for infantry fire. The Russians remained silent at first, though, a result either of surprise or of the ceaseless covering fire of our heavy weapons. After seemingly endless minutes, the boats shot into an inlet on the opposite shore. The battalioner, Mannhard, and the other men of the first wave had made it safely, so far.

This action was only the beginning of the mission, however. After a while, the first boats appeared back on the lake heading for the rib on our side. Through my binoculars, I saw they were full of wounded. The Ivans seemed to have recovered from their surprise. Bursts of tracers swept over the lake, fired from two machine guns to the right. Now came our job; we knew where they were! Bing sent his tracers over, individual shots at first, then long, sustained bursts. So far I couldn't see an effect. Meanwhile, the boats, widely dispersed, with roaring engines, dashed across the lake in wide swerves to evade the shower of enemy fire we could see either whizzing across them or lashing the water's surface. Heinrich joined in with his gun, rattling through a whole belt. Now it seemed our fire was taking effect; one enemy gun was silent, although the other kept firing. But the boats were getting away from the danger zone. One after another turned into the inlet. They had won again.

By now, though, the Ivan had realized what was at stake. If they let our reinforcements come across the lake, it could mean endangering their whole operation. At any rate, our staging area and our firing positions on the south edge of Sennozero now became the main target of their artillery and mortars. Hell broke loose. Heavy artillery rounds came slamming down on the staging site to our left, mostly shells of the infamous 'Ratsch-Bumm', 76mm high velocity guns, the impact of which arrived faster than the sound of their firing report.

Just when in all that turmoil the second wave of our boats had taken off, their course and our firing positions on the rise came under concentrated Russian *mungo* fire. We hadn't time to dig in, but found some cover between the large rocks cropping out of the terrain. So, when the boats reached the open water and the two machine guns opened fire on them, we blasted away as well as we could. We would count the *mungo* firings and take cover whenever the shells crashed down, and afterwards, we would pop up again and send our bursts over to the Russian machine-gun nests. By then, our fire was much more precise so that temporarily the two machine guns were put out of action.

My full admiration is still with the coxswains of the engineer battalion who, in stoic, upright positions at the stern, kept steering their boats through the hail of machine gun fire and the impacts of the falling mortar shells. They drove through not once, but again and again, always facing another ride through enemy fire once they reached the shore unharmed.

Relentlessly, the Russian artillery kept firing, sending shells into the staging area and dueling with our own guns. Thanks to their closeness to the railway line in their rear, they by far outpaced our own artillery. We waited for the boats to return. Schaper ordered a change of position down to the edge of the lake; on our crest, the *mungo* fire had become too dangerous. I had been looking for a favorable spot, and quickly, between two rounds of the *mungos*, we started down the hill, jumping from cover to cover, toward a rock formation on ground above the lake. Then Berger fell. It was nearly a direct hit by a stray *mungo* round. It got him as he ran down, the last in line and fully packed with his ammunition boxes. I sent one of my men back for help; but he soon came creeping back, his face ashen. Berger was dead.

The boats were back on the lake, evacuating more wounded. This time, the barrage of Russian mortars increased. The boats had no choice. They had given up their zigzag course and were shooting straight through that hail of fire. One of the Russian machine guns was back in action. Its tracers whizzed through the middle of the little fleet. With the concentrated fire of our two guns, we silenced it again, but before we did, one of the coxswains was hit. His craft swerved wildly over the water; someone in the boat took hold of the tiller and eventually brought the boat back to the inlet.

The heavy weapons fire on both sides escalated to a fury, and the outcome was becoming more than doubtful. At this moment, the *Stukas* came. It had been years since they had been in action in this sector. Normally, they operated far off, mainly occupied with the American convoys on the Arctic Ocean. That they were sent to help us could only mean the Army saw the whole front endangered if things went wrong at Sennozero. It was a formation of three, looking like birds of prey with their gull wings, clumsy under-carriage, and camouflage paint. And they acted as such as they swooped down on the Russian artillery emplacements and on the enemy's infantry positions. Their nerve-racking wail, swelling anew with every dive, completed the picture of absolute dominance over their victims; for them, it must have been a nightmare.

The tide turned. Under cover of the *Stukas*, the assault boats shot over the lake unmolested. The next time, they carried only ammunition and supplies. Clouds of smoke rose over the Russian emplacements. Maybe an ammunition dump had been hit. Their artillery and mortar fire had almost stopped for the time being. Now the *Stukas*, guided by flares, turned upon some of the Russian infantry positions, ferociously blasting away with their cannon. At last, they swept once more across the battlefield and then took off. Our opponent had been taken by surprise a second time on this day and his morale was shaken.

Later on, the sun was behind us. The fighting had ebbed. By turns, we took naps. Awakened and instantly recalling the events of the last twelve hours, however, everything appeared strangely unreal. The everlasting daylight, the lack of sleep, and our general exhaustion may have added to that dream-like condition. Behind us, however, up the hill, just where he had been hit, Berger lay under the speckled canvas spread over his body. Thinking back, I recalled our talks in the bunker. With all his plain and unconditional devotion to the *Führer*, his will to live might have been stronger if on this morning there had been for him some kind of choice. There wasn't, though, and so he died with his loyalty untainted.

In the early afternoon, we were called back. Cautiously, we pulled out and leaped up the dangerous forward slope, dragging the canvas with Berger's body along. To our surprise, the Russians left us alone.

On our way back to the assembly area, we went through a hollow where a row of stretchers had been put down with the rest of the casualties who had just been rescued from the pocket. Some of them looked frightfully pale and haggard. I saw the wounded commander who had been relieved; he was obviously unshaven for days and had one arm bandaged up. He was squatting by a young officer who was lying on a stretcher with a waxen face. The commander, seeing us pass by, asked us to move the stretcher out of the sun. He remained with the wounded man, soothingly talking to him and holding him by the hand, "You'll be all right, They'll fix you up in no time." But the young officer was dying, and he knew he was. Just before he lost consciousness, I heard him whisper to his commander, "Do never . . . never forsake the *Führer*."

It is only now that I realize that up there in the wilderness on that day, we saw a dying officer seeking to extend his loyalty even beyond his death.

In spite of all we had been through, we were not meant to enjoy a rest. Some rations, some tea, half an hour of bottomless sleep was all we got and possibly could expect under the circumstances. There was another urgent mission waiting for us, and there were also the wounded who had to be brought back to the field hospital as soon as possible.

What was there to say? Was any unit engaged in this operation better off? And weren't we lucky, so far, in comparison to the casualties that had been sustained by other units? So, stoically, once more we got up to distribute our equipment among ourselves and went over to pick up the wounded. True, this time the load was lighter than the one with which we had arrived, and hadn't we shot a lot of ammunition? As we took up the stretchers and started balancing our moaning burden towards the path we had come up this morning, though, it was hard to believe we could do it again.

We hadn't realized for days the full purpose of our next mission. We figured that the combat group at Sennozero, even with reinforcements, would be unable to break out of the pocket without massive help from the outside. Indeed, we thought our comrades inside would be lucky to escape annihilation. What we didn't know was that a battalion of SS-Mountain Infantry Regiment 12 was working forward through the swamps on the northern edge of the lake to get the Russian attack force from the rear. Our task, as it turned out later, was to search the area south of Sennozero for the left flank of the Russians and launch holding attacks to bind its forces.

After we had delivered the wounded at the landing place, we started back on the trail, but soon left it and turned eastward. From now on, we were moving into a region that was unknown terrain. Up to then, no one had bothered to carry out even reconnaissance patrols in this area between Sennozero and Yeletsozero. It was considered impenetrable for any substantial force. The *Jäger* are said to be a quick-moving unit in difficult terrain; but this terrain beat all we had experienced. The wood was full of all sorts of obstacles: trunks lying all over the terrain, underbrush, rocky barriers, water and bogs which, again and again, posed new problems for our progress. Pillars of old conifers scattered in the green surroundings: completely dried up trunks with their bark long gone and now showing a smooth, silver-gray surface, had been dead for a long time, but were in their stern erectness a symbol of perseverance in the harsh climate of this latitude. Except for the steady rumble of the artillery, the area was eerily still. The continual absence of darkness and the bizarre light of the sun lingering about the horizon for hours and hours added to the awe I think most of us felt as we penetrated this unknown wild.

We were with the 13th Company, first in single line following the trailblazers who had been sent ahead and then in skirmish line, stalking through the more open terrain. We had been walking for hours when we almost ran across a Russian supply route leading to the lake. We attacked instantly and in no time a wild fight with all manner of small arms broke out. As the Ivans' resistance stiffened, we realized we had run into a reinforcement unit which we couldn't defeat. We withdrew and made ourselves invisible by digging in. We found a place for our gun on a rib with a good field of fire amidst the swampy ground.

Improvised as this position was, we were to remain there for the next six weeks.

While the fight for Sennozero went on, we did everything to make life for the Russians' left flank as uncomfortable as possible. During the first weeks, few days passed without attacks by one side or the other at this improvised front line.

Our protection against artillery fire was poor. Because of the constant hostile fire, we couldn't even think of fortifications. Anyone moving in daylight in an upright position immediately took fire. Still, in the short hours of semi-darkness, we managed to cover our hole with a makeshift roof of poles and canvas to protect against the rain that had started, while underneath we constructed a grid to protect us from the water that accumulated in the bottom of our hole. The position remained throughout little more than a patrol post.

Polzer was killed next, the second one of my gun crew to be lost at Sennozero. He went out of our life so quietly that at first we didn't notice. He was on guard duty when an artillery barrage started; the moment the fire stopped, I crawled from my hole and saw him sitting as usual behind our gun. When he didn't answer my call, I thought nothing of it, anxious to check up on the other ones first. It was only when I got on his side to peer over the parapet that I noticed him slumped into a heap, his cheeks ashen, his eyes staring into the void. A small wound at his left temple was the only sign of the shrapnel that had penetrated his skull, just under the brim of his helmet.

By the end of July, the Russians stopped their attacks against our stronghold at Sennozero. Our sister regiment had broken through the encirclement, reinforcements had gone in, and further Russian onslaughts against the bulwark, which had claimed so many lives on the Russian side, appeared fruitless. Our division had prevailed, and we were cited in the High Command's daily bulletin for it. At our front line, the Russians seemed to have vanished from the area. So, after a few days, we started a major reconnaissance patrol into hostile territory which lasted a full day. We advanced in wedge-like formation, stopping time and again, guarding and stalking on—"Indian warfare," we called it. We would search the greenness with binoculars for any distant enemy or conspicuous objects that possibly conceal a foxhole or a gun close by. We looked for a mound strangely out of place, an upright trunk cut off head-high, underbrush that might turn out to be a screen, a piece of birch bark with a rectangular cut-out, particularly hard to notice marks of our opponent's camouflage we had learned to look for. We were lucky on this day and managed to take some prisoners. In the short clash we had with the enemy, however, the *Alte* was wounded; a bullet in the arm smashed his upper arm bone. Heinrich was put in charge of the *Alte*'s gun.

Paradoxically, it was in a setting of great beauty that our mission neared its end. *Ruska* (the color changes associated with autumn) had come to the wilderness between Sennozero and Yeletsozero. It had emerged from the

rains and the chilly nights of the end of August; an explosion of colors turning the green of the birches yellow, the feathery leaves of the mountain ashes
pink, and the dark-green bushes of mulberries and cranberries, covering most
of the ground, flaming red. Now, in the bright sun that had come out again,
even the thick layers of lichen on the rocks and on the trunks in decay were
a rich, copper patina.

At that time, however, we didn't appreciate the glory of the setting. Our
minds were occupied with our primeval environment and grim warfare.
Having stayed there for so many weeks without relief, our life was wretched
and reduced to the bare needs of survival: eating, keeping warm, resting, and
still exercising the vigilance essential for staying alive in this "Indian war."

In particular, we were totally unaware of the greater events afoot at that
time. It was only a few days later that things in Finland were to take an unex-
pected turn.

16

IMPRISONED IN GERMANY

The bugle call of taps is sounding from the tower of our new post. The solemn beauty of the signal, blown in a pure and stable *portato*, invites all the men herded together in this compound, American soldiers and German prisoners alike, to a mood of calmness and melancholy. It is May now, the second year of our captivity.

It's been over two months now since I finished the last chapter, the one about Sennozero. The hospital cage at Romilly had been shut down as the PW camp quickly emptied. They say most of the prisoners have been turned over to the French; others have been discharged, such as the sick and those with some privileged status. Walther's Austrian citizenship, for instance, has miraculously been reinstated, and he has been consequently discharged. Most of us, the staff of the hospital, however, have been picked for service with the US Military Police School that is being set up here in Germany.

Actually, we are some sort of a Royal Household, recruited from the human resources of the Romilly camp: "orderlies" ranging from butlers to footmen; waiters; male nurses; cooks and other kitchen personnel; craftsmen of all sorts; gardeners; musicians (a whole orchestra); coachmen (drivers); janitors, and so on. We are even liveried with neat GI clothes, adorned with a large white "PW" on the back, or dyed totally black.

The new post is a former German Navy barracks, downriver from Bremen. Strangely enough, the Allied bombers left it almost unharmed, while razing the cities both north and south of us; the urban areas were particularly hard hit. Now the barracks' red brick buildings, home-like in comparison with the bleak French barracks, accommodate the US Military Police School since we moved to this place during the first half of this month. We, the prisoners, put

up our tents within a rectangular cage, surrounded by barbed wire and guarded by sentries stationed at the entrance and on two watchtowers—same as
ever.

To be back home but still imprisoned intensifies the feeling of being held
in captivity. When, after so many delays, our train finally left Romilly, it
seemed a promising start. Somehow our future appeared brighter. We were
going home, and that notion alone was sufficient to fill us with anticipation.
The further we rolled into Germany, the more I felt elated. Every hour I felt
I was coming closer to my home. Then, for a while, we could even see the
Harz Mountains emerging from the haze in the east. From then on, rolling on
to the north, however, disappointment grew; the dreadful wounds our country had suffered in the long agony of the last years of the war became more
and more manifest as we passed through the stations, towns, and industrial
sites. But what exactly had we expected? Some kind of miracle? We passed
through Mannheim, Kassel, Hannover, and Bremen. Had we imagined on
our journey back that somehow they would have been resurrected from their
ruins? We faced a grim reality.

Between islands of devastation, the farmland and the villages presented
themselves in the full blossom of May—symbols of hope abounded in every
field, in every cluster of red-tiled roofs and every stand of chestnut trees.
Along the way, something came back to my mind, something from a French
lesson at school in the summer of 1940, the time when France had been
defeated. Our teacher had chosen a quotation from a recent address by
Marshal Pétain, words that had deeply impressed me because, at that time, I
was trying to imagine the feelings of a defeated nation. The text was an
appeal to the French nation for an intellectual and moral recovery. As our
train rolled on, I tried to recall the words the Marshal had used to invoke the
French soil as a last resort, something like this:

*Francais! . . . La terre, elle ne ment pas. Elle demeure notre recours. Elle est la
patrie elle-même. Un champ qui tombe en friche, c'est une portion de France qui
meurt. Un champ de nouveau emblavé, c'est une portion de France qui renaît. . . .**

Words of hope and encouragement. If only *we* were free so we could help
with our country's rebirth. . . .

Freedom and liberty were the subjects of a recent conversation among our
chaplain, Pete, and me. We were standing around after the consecration of
our new chapel (which, of course, is also under canvas) where Pete had

*"Frenchmen! . . . The land does not forsake us. It remains our refuge. It is our country
as such. A field that falls fallow is a portion of France that dies. A field tilled anew is a portion of France that is born again. . . ."

dragged me in. In his sermon, the chaplain had been trying to soothe the general disappointment by invoking faith and hope—faith, he said, that could be practiced in the camp as well as outside; and hope that was like a beam from a lighthouse, as strong and promising as our faith.

Pete expressed how much he had liked the sermon and that he was edified by it. I felt I should say something as well, "I'm sorry, chaplain, I haven't been much of a churchgoer at home, but I can understand that people feel consoled; hope gets stronger if it is shared with others in faith."

"And what about yourself?" he asked smiling, feeling my reservations.

"I'm not blessed with too much hope, I'm afraid; it must be my faith which isn't as strong as it should be. Somehow I feel trapped."

"I'm very sorry for you," he said. "Don't you at least agree with what was said about freedom?"

"I understand your subject was freedom of will and freedom of worship as a last resort in our predicament. It's true. With all due respect, chaplain, our real problem is that we want to get out of here. That's what I think freedom is all about."

"Yes, I understand. Still, I insist. Even outside you won't be as free as you might think. There are always moral obligations or legal requirements or naked *want* that will restrain your freedom. I daresay that in this cage there is more freedom than you have experienced in the last few years as a soldier. Don't you think so? I don't hesitate to go even further: You may even say in our defeat we were liberated."

Although I had heard this view before, I was shocked, "How can you say that? Must I remind you of the bombed-out citizens of Bremen or of the millions of people who were expelled from the East? Do you think they feel liberated? As for me, I volunteered for service."

"That's just what I mean. You were bound by moral obligations, bound by your own will as others are by custom or religion. It's always the spiritual sphere where the most compelling restrictions of freedom originate. And since you are free of your former bondage, you are left with a greater freedom which you can make use of in here."

"As I see it, one bondage of my own choice has been replaced by another bondage which isn't my choice at all."

"The main choice is between a life toward God or away from Him, and in that you are free. The one who really believes will always be free to lead a life that pleases God. That is the message."

"Always? How about life under Bolshevism? Would you say those people are free in your sense? I doubt that; I doubt that very much. Assuming you were right, though, then we could put up with Bolshevism; it wouldn't be that bad after all. Is that your message?"

"My dear friend, it's all a question of faith. If only your faith is strong enough, the message will be true. Faith can move mountains."

I can't find consolation in his belief. Eventually, such a belief ends by submitting to whatever happens to you. It promises peace of mind, like the bugle blowing taps. It lulls us into a state of acquiescence. Hush, it seems to say, don't worry, get it over with; it's not all that bad; someday you'll be released; for the time being get some sleep; believe me, sleep is a great consoler.

Our days in this camp, however, are filled with everyday life rather than with disputes about freedom and captivity. As it turns out, life in the Royal Household is more rewarding than we thought at first, at least in the case of the duties Pete and I must perform. While Pete is assisting a US Army dentist, the kind of work he likes well, my lord and master is an attorney from Chicago.

He's a captain by the name of Herbert, which is his last name in fact. He is in charge of the legal training at this school; as for himself, he lectures on Criminal Law. Handsome, a bit too well fed, about my father's age, his long and sleek hair already going gray, he is, all in all, a man of authority. I'm typing his lectures on Murder, Manslaughter, Robbery, Larceny, and so forth, but also some on Criminal Procedure. In the mornings, he keeps pacing up and down in our office, dictating in his rich voice and rolling his Rs, especially as in "Mu-rr-de-rr," deep in his throat, with great relish.

My typing is poor, but that wasn't the point, as I learned at my first interview with him six weeks ago. What he apparently had difficulties with in finding among the post's military personnel, except for officers, was someone who was able to type his dictation without too many spelling mistakes, in particular when it came to Latin, Norman, or Saxon words or roots. My problem, on the other hand, was avoiding typing errors while trying, with two fingers only, to keep pace with his dictation.

However, things turned out rather well. My work is giving me satisfaction; an entirely new field of knowledge is opening up. Looking at the world from the legal point of view—critically, impartially, factually, analytically, weighing and judging—all that has a certain appeal to me. It even begins to influence my thinking on the Nuremberg Trials. Up to now, I just watched in bewilderment and dismay, unable to approach the subject in a rational way. Now, as I pick up more legal understanding each day, I become curious, which means open to perceiving it also as a legal procedure in which the wording of the Statute, the elements of different crimes, and rules of evidence, become important. My new experience is some kind of legal education, however rudimentary, which interests me in the legal aspects of the trial and may lead to a sounder judgment than the one based on my hitherto strongly emotional attitude.

I had my first lesson when, one night, Captain Herbert returned late to the office to fetch a text he had dictated that morning. He was pleased with the result and was in a jovial mood. Offering me a cigarette, he wanted to know how I liked my work with him. I said I found it interesting and mentioned that it also made me wonder what the basis was of the war criminal procedure. This remark seemed, in turn, to interest him particularly. He sensed my doubts and invited me to put my questions forward quite frankly.

"It's hard for a German to believe in justice at the hands of a tribunal set up by the victors over the defeated," I said.

"Of course, the International Military Tribunal resulted from Germany's defeat," the captain conceded. "Nonetheless, the political idea is not revenge but prevention; it's our determination to get serious about banning future military aggression. Think of all the things our peoples had to go through in World War I and World War II. This must never happen again. Aggressors must be warned. It's a legal procedure all the same, not a mere political action."

"You mean because there is a Statute? Why should the Germans be bound by it? We had no part in it. Isn't it questionable to prosecute defendants under a foreign law brought to their country? I'm afraid people will regard the Statute and the procedure as merely a disguise."

"From the legal point of view, there's nothing wrong with an Allied statute on German war crimes. There's no way around the fact that with the fall of the *Reich*, the Allied Forces have acquired the only state authority there is in this country. No doubt, they were entitled to set up a legal framework for trying war crimes in Germany. The Statute of the IMT is as legal and binding as any law."

"But is it fair and just?" I insisted. "It was set up afterwards, wasn't it? There wasn't any war criminal code in the 1930s. I have read that by proceeding as they are, they are violating an old legal principle, that a defendant may not be punished without being warned by law beforehand. They say this principle has come down to us from the Romans and is established in all civilized legal systems."

"That's a very formal objection. Don't let yourself be confused by it. You can't seriously deny that crimes against humanity, such as murder, rape, deportation, and various other crimes have been well established crimes for centuries, some at least for many decades, among civilized nations."

"Yes, I can see that: Violation of Human Rights," I admitted. "However, the more all parties became involved in an uncompromising, all-out war, in a war for their own survival, the more those well-established rules of mankind began to crumble on all sides. Must I go further into that?"

In general, I agreed that violations of human rights must be prosecuted; not so with the newly established crimes. I said so and continued, "What about the so-called crime of preparing a war of aggression, the main crime, the crime Number One of the trial. That has never been a punishable crime before, or has it?"

"Well, it remains to be seen whether the Court will bring in a verdict of guilty on that point," the captain said, "but at least it has been claimed by distinguished jurists that, after World War I, wars of aggression were regarded as banned within the international community."

I felt encouraged by the captain's quiet way of explaining the legal aspects of the procedure and continued my probe, "There's another question that haunts me since I've read the notification of the IMT in our cage back in France: the provisions on conspiracy and on the criminal character of certain organizations. What really upsets me is the obvious intention of criminalizing even regular combat units, such as the *Waffen-SS*."

On my mentioning the *Waffen-SS*, the captain's jovial manner became somewhat subdued. He continued, however, to play the role of tutor to pupil, "You certainly are aware," he said, "that the criminal character of the *SS* is obvious to most people nowadays, Germans and non-Germans alike, aren't you? Now it's my turn to ask: do I need to go into that further? The court certainly will."

I was on dangerous ground, but to break up our conversation at this point would have left too big a question mark in his mind, so I continued. "Let me explain, sir. A friend of mine was an officer of the *Waffen-SS*, a man of irreproachable character and impeccable war conduct. He was killed in action. From what I have read in the papers, it must be concluded that if the Court should pronounce the *Waffen-SS* guilty, he would become, posthumously, a criminal just by joining that branch of the forces in 1942; all the more, the survivors of these units would be considered criminals, regardless of their personal guilt. What about the principle of personal accountability you speak of in your lectures? How is it embodied in the Statute of the IMT?"

The captain got up and cast me a pensive glance. He went over to the shelf, looking for something special. With a jerk, he drew an old paper from under a heap of material and held in his hands what he wanted: the Statute of the IMT. After some leafing through the document, he quoted from Article 9 and 10 of the Statute:

". . . the Court may in the trial against a single member of a group or an organization, in connection with an action the defendant will be found guilty of, declare the group or organization, of which the defendant was a member, a criminal organization . . . in that case, any of the Four Powers may bring a former member of the organization to trial, and that, in this case, the criminal character of the organization shall not be questioned."

The captain thought about the text for a while, and then continued, "I don't think that personal culpability will be disregarded in the case of members of the organizations. If the Court should find an organization guilty in the sense of Article 9, it will certainly make provisions for groups of members whose guilt may be questionable. On the other hand, if we are determined to bring justice to those who have suffered from the actions of the *SS*, it would be intolerable to allow any defendant to raise anew the question of whether the *SS* was a criminal organization."

I felt Captain Herbert was playing down the charge against the *Waffen-SS*. "Forgive my insisting, sir, but it is a criminal conspiracy those soldiers I mentioned were charged with, conspiracy for the commitment of crimes against peace, of war crimes, and of crimes against humanity. I find it inconceivable even to suggest that hundreds of thousands of soldiers could have joined this part of the German forces to commit crimes. And how can that be proven? There is not even one member of the *Waffen-SS* in the dock."

The captain remained quite composed, almost impassive. For him, the trial seemed to be just another criminal procedure. He thought for a while and then said, "As I said before, there are many who think that the crimes of the *SS* were generally known, so that he who joined one of their organizations must have seen himself as becoming an instrument of crime. Personally, however, I have my doubts that the charge of a conspiracy can be upheld in general. The term as such is a rather disputed one, even in the United States. Maybe the Court won't consider it as part of the law of nations."

I thought it best to leave it at that; our talk had gone far enough. As I think about it, I see there is a point in prosecuting violations of human rights, and maybe there isn't any other authority to do it. To think, however, of those wild assertions, to insist that the crimes of the *SS* had been generally known and, in consequence, to imply the most dishonest motives to the volunteers of the *Waffen-SS*! What a hopeless discrepancy between this construct and reality! I see the mule train with our dead comrades coming down from Sennozero, and I see Berger, who sealed his honest motives by his death, and I think of the young officer who even at his death was not concerned with himself, but with our common cause. They believed in the honesty of the cause and gave all they had in performance of their duty. What a revaluation of values! How suitable is Shakespeare's line, ". . . where foul is fair, and fair is foul. . . ."

A few days later, however, I found on my desk an envelope from the captain. It contained a newspaper report which was a very concise account of the testimony of Rudolf Höss, the former commandant of the Auschwitz death camp.

After reading the details of what, in general, has become known for quite a while, I was left again in a state of bewilderment, and I still am. Three million human beings gassed or starved to death within a twenty-seven month period at one single camp site! It would mean between three and four thousand killings each day, Sundays and holidays included! It's unbelievable! It is an image of utter unreality. It is Höss himself, however, who has confirmed these numbers in his written court confession. How can a human mind, though, confronted with this piece of evidence, possibly imagine the feasibility of such events? How can the facilities and daily operations even be visualized? What about the mental condition of the operators necessary to carry out such a monstrous scheme?

In a vain effort to grasp the enormous horror of the matter, I thought of another event that occurred a long time ago. It must have been in my third year at school when the woods around Gandersheim, a small town where we then lived, were struck with a plague of May bugs; all the schools in town were asked to help implement emergency measures. So one day at dawn, each class started for the woods to shake down the bugs from the trees, stiff and numb as they were from the cold of the night. We then picked up the bugs and dropped them into large sacks, which afterwards were hauled to the school to be burned. I vividly remember my eerie feeling at noon, as I watched the sacks, bulging with the now terrified bugs, being thrown into the roaring fire of the furnace, one sack after another, each causing a horrible hissing sound and more furious flames.

One must put Höss's numbers aside. They are irrelevant to the essence of truth. What matters, obviously, is that mass killings of Jews—helpless men, women, and children, young and old—have taken place for several years in the course of a premeditated, long-term strategy of a higher authority. For the victims, it was an inconceivable disaster. Attempting to understand, I try to imagine that in my own family an ancestor belonging to some newly-designated "inferior race" had been discovered and the police had knocked at our door, rounded him up, and secretly sent him to the gas. As much as I try, even to visualize my own folks among the heaps of skeletons I have seen in the papers, however, the monstrous scheme, although obviously true, remains beyond my comprehension. The other undeniable truth is that the strategy and its execution was the work of the SS, of men who for the most part wore our uniform. Thirty-five thousand men in our uniform were engaged in guarding the camps and operating the extermination machine, Höss said. This constitutes a significant percentage of the *Waffen-SS*.

Thinking back to the bleak morning on the railroad track in 1943, I now realize the sinister truth that loomed behind the scene.

Accepting this truth, the charge of the *Waffen-SS* being a criminal organization becomes plausible, at least for one part. It seems it was our own leaders who, by integrating the concentration camp personnel into the *Waffen-SS*, gave cogency to that charge. It may even have been part of their scheme to have the combat troops appear as accomplices of the killings.

There is another conclusion which, thanks to Höss, I think must be drawn. A regime responsible for such a scheme of mass killings was corrupt to the core and did not deserve to survive. It's a disgrace that we didn't overthrow it, but left it to be eradicated by our enemies.

In these days, during office hours, I overlook the questioning glances of the captain. It's easy to guess what he is thinking, "Whatever you may think of prosecuting criminal organizations and conspiracies," his expression says, "the *Waffen-SS* is nothing to be proud of."

At present I have no answer to that.

I must return to my work of remembrance and carry on with writing down what I have seen. The answer may come when I finish.

17

FINLAND QUITS

One day in early September 1944, the news broke that the Finns and the Soviets had agreed to an armistice. At that time, I wasn't with the battalion but was staying in the field hospital.

The news spread like wildfire through the wards. Soon it became known that the Finns had been negotiating in Moscow for quite a long time behind our backs; the German Lapland Army was to leave Finland by the 15th of September. It came to us as a blow. How could we get out of Finland in less than two weeks? What if we didn't? A few days later, there was more news: the Finnish Army was bound by the terms of the armistice to "expel" the German Army from their territory by that date. To us, it seemed inconceivable that our brothers in arms would turn their weapons against us. Oddly enough, our friendly feelings for the Finns remained almost unchanged and so did our great respect for the brave people who in 1939 preferred to wage war rather than submit to the intimidations of the Soviets as the Baltic States had done. After all, both our peoples were bound by history and geography to stop the Bolsheviks's expansion to the West. Hadn't we fought bravely side by side all these years against our common enemy?

In my ward was an engineer sergeant with a puncture wound on his upper arm, one of the boatmen who had steered the assault boats across Sennozero and had been decorated with the German Cross in Gold, a medal for valor ranking between the Iron Cross 1st class and the Knight's Cross. He thought our prospects of winning the war had become more than doubtful and said so quite frankly. He found it quite reasonable that the Finns would quit as long as there was an opportunity for them to preserve their own national existence. Who were we to blame them? he asked.

Operation *BIRKE* (BIRCH)—The German Withdrawal Through Finland, September–October 1944

— — — —   Finnish/Soviet Border before the Winter War and from July 1941 to 15 September 1944

— · — -   Finnish/Soviet Border until 15 September 1944

— · — -   Finnish/Soviet Border after 15 September 1944

°°°°   Route of Withdrawal of *XXXVI Mountain Corps* (*163rd* and *169th Infantry Divisions and supporting units*)

♦♦♦♦   Route of Withdrawal of *XVIII Mountain Corps* (*6th SS and 7th Mountain Divisions; Division Group Kräutler*, and supporting units)

••••   Route of Withdrawal of *XIX Mountain Corps* (*3rd and 6th Mountain Divisions; 210th Infantry Division; Division Group van der Hoop;* and supporting units)

⊙   Major Finnish towns occupied by Soviets after withdrawal of German forces

In the leisure of hospital life, however, we had a lot of time to speculate on our future. If the inconceivable should happen, wouldn't we be utterly exposed, in particular our division, at the south flank of the German Lapland Army, and dangerously isolated, even from our own troops in the arctic? Weren't we in for a losing battle? Or could we possibly survive somewhere in the vast regions of the woodland, fend for ourselves as individual battalions or regiments? As a *Jäger* regiment we could, perhaps, live on game, mushrooms, and berries like Indians. We knew, however, that the noise of the weapons had driven all game from the woods in recent years. Maybe we could keep cows and sheep, organize some sort of stock farming, and wait in seclusion for the war to end.

Our imaginations knew no bounds, but never in our talks did the thought of surrender enter our minds. We knew that the Finnish option was not for us. For us, it was either victory or unconditional surrender; this choice was the grim truth since the Allies had announced their war aims at Casablanca and thus had rendered the war total. There was no choice but to carry on, one way or another. We soon realized that we couldn't stay in Lapland for long. Somehow, we had to fight our way back home.

In spite of all the uncertainty, I was enjoying my vacation in this clean and smoothly run lake resort. At night, however, lying awake in the dark and thinking of the battalion that soon was to disengage from the enemy, my own "disengagement" from our position out there between the two lakes one week earlier went through my mind.

I had awakened from a wild dream. The night between the Sennozero and Yeletsozero had been clear and chilly. I felt a pain throbbing in my right ankle and rising up my leg. It had become worse overnight, although I had loosened my boots before lying down; I could not remember having them off during the last five weeks. When I started trembling, feeling really silly about it, it slowly dawned on me that I had a high fever. The next thing I found out was that my left side was sodden; the water under the grid of thin poles we had managed to install in our rat hole for two must have risen overnight. Cautiously, I crawled out, not too confident of what I would see when I took off my boot. But as much as I tried, it didn't come off; it was immovably stuck on my foot. Damn! I should have gone to see the medic days ago! But how could I have risked being sent to the rear and leaving my comrades just for a sore foot?

Bing, sitting on guard ten meters away behind our MG, turned round as he heard me swearing to myself. "Anything wrong? How is your foot today?" he asked in the subdued voice we had gotten used to on our standing patrol.

"I'm fine! It's just that my ankle is twice its normal size, the pain is rising up my leg, I'm dizzy as if I was drunk . . . not to mention that I can't walk."

He got the picture right away, "Hey, sounds as if you need some help. Let me get someone to take you to the medic. Come on, take over the gun for a moment; it won't be long." He had come up and helped me crawl over to the gun; walking upright was still dangerous here.

"That doesn't look good. No good at all!" the medic said when he had managed to cut open my boot and had taken a look at my ankle. "If this isn't operated on immediately, I can't guarantee your leg," he added gloomily. "Off to the field hospital, right away!"

From then on, my memory is blurred. I was really ill by now. They put me on a litter and somehow, later on that day, I found myself back at the spot I knew so well, the lakeside where we first had come across the assault boats and where we had brought back the wounded from the lake. There were more litter cases around. The ferry, still in operation, took us across the lake. On the other side, at the small post, I was strapped to a strange Finnish means of transportation, primitive but, as it turned out, highly convenient. A flat rectangular frame of young spruce poles, its top ends sticking out as thills, was harnessed to a mule, while its lower ends rested on and were meant to be dragged along the ground; in the middle of the frame a stretcher was mounted, its reclined position forming an obtuse angle with the frame. I barely noticed the mule getting a slap on its hindquarters when it started off on the trail into the wood, all by itself and obviously quite familiar with its job. So, all alone with the mule, I found myself trailing over the soft ground, the flexible frame gently swinging up and down in a steady motion while I watched the vivid mixture of green conifers and colorful foliage gliding by like a film on Karelian *ruska*.

The later trip on the road in an ambulance was dreadful. The vehicle jolted up and down on the worn wooden planks, intolerably increasing the pain. We reached the field hospital in the evening. The doctor opened up the abscess and removed a great deal of pus.

A field hospital is, in comparison to the front line, a news center. Hardly a week after the news of the Finnish Soviet armistice was released, we learned that a detailed contingency plan had been prepared for the German Lapland Army to withdraw through Finland to the far north, where it borders Norway.

Under this plan, our division would cover the Army's southern flank, which would be open to any conceivable action of the Soviet and Finnish forces, and which in the beginning extended over a range of 300 kilometers from the eastern frontlines to Oulu by the Gulf of Bothnia. In fact, our division was to form the Army's rear guard on its march to the Norwegian border. In doing so, the two mountain infantry regiments, 11 and 12, were to alternately displace, or "leapfrog" past one another along the route. The other units of the division were to be kept at the disposal of the Lapland Army. Of the huge distance to Norway, we had only a vague notion; the distance was some 900 kilometers as we were to learn, step by step, in the coming months.

The large wound at my ankle, once sewn up, healed quickly. The field hospital was already busily preparing for displacement westward to Kuusamo. Before we left, I wanted to look at Berger's grave in our nearby division cemetery. The sergeant went with me. When we got there, we found a detachment occupied with taking down the live runes of birch from the long rows of graves; in one corner, they had already begun to work the place with heavy equipment to remove all signs of its former dedication. In the course of our withdrawal, as in the course of *any* military retrograde operation, it was only natural that we would destroy any of our installations that could be of use to the Russians, particularly lodges, cabins, and bunkers that had enabled us to survive in winter. We knew that. We were not prepared, though, for what we had to see now. They said it was a measure of safeguarding the peace of the dead after all our troops had experienced in the Russia campaign, but watching the scene, our hearts were full of grief and despair, soothed only by the promise to those left unnamed in foreign soil: *You shall never be forgotten.*

When I got back to the battalion, it was already well on the way to Kuusamo. I met my comrades at a small place called Tuhkalla.

18

FROM TUHKALLA TO KUUSAMO

One week after the armistice, the division withdrew from its positions between the northern flank and Kiestinki. Under the cover of darkness, our battalion had slipped out of its bunkers, foxholes, and burrows, unnoticed and unmolested by the enemy.

We were in for trouble when it was our regiment's turn to be the rear guard on the road from Kiestinki to Kuusamo. Somewhere in between was Tuhkalla, a small settlement on a peninsula near the road some 40 kilometers west of Kiestinki. In hot pursuit, the Russians were relentlessly pressuring us from behind. trying to bypass our regiment as we slowly fell back to the west in a long, strung-out column.

As long as the wilderness on both sides of the road receded far enough and the view widened, the men in the columns felt relatively secure. Most of the time, however, when the woods and the thick underbrush closed in, a funny feeling crept over them and stirred their hope the regiment's rear guard wouldn't let itself be bypassed. Nevertheless, as it happened, on the night after I rejoined my squad, the Russians outflanked us and managed to set up two road blocks, west and east of Tuhkalla, respectively. Thus, the regiment was cut off from the division and, as if that wasn't enough, it was split apart.

From my position overlooking a deep ravine with a bridge at the bottom, I had a view of the road winding westward up the opposite slope. Somewhere up in that wooded terrain, the Russians had ensconced themselves in blocking positions on the road. Repeated attacks from our side failed to achieve a breakthrough. Indeed, at that time the regiment was fully occupied with trying to remove the other roadblock east of Tuhkalla to link up with the cut-off rear guard. From the noise of infantry weapons, we imagined it was over there that the real fighting was taking place. The longer it lasted, the more we became aware of how uncertain our chances were of getting out of this precarious situation. Hours passed away. Was our withdrawal already to end here, deep in Russian territory?

Finally, the firing behind us died out. We learned that the rear guard had broken free and that the regiment was reunited. Soon, preparations for cracking the western blockade became visible. Several *Jäger* companies arrived and crossed the bridge to reinforce the units opposite the road block; my gun crew was ordered to strengthen the northern flank of the bridge. On my way down, I spotted two 2-cm quadruple flak wagons rushing westward over the bridge. Meanwhile, it was clear that our attack was directly imminent. Suddenly, I spotted our battalioner in the sidecar of his motorcycle among the general bustle, giving orders, shouting at the men by the road, and organizing the breakout. Although we were in a critical situation, the presence of the battalioner in our midst and his visible, resolute leadership conveyed a feeling of confidence to all of us.

The two 2-cm quadruple anti-aircraft guns opened fire on the Russian positions on the road. At the same time, one *Jäger* company went through the woods on the side and pushed into the Russian flank from the north. At that same moment, the frontal attack began along the road. Three companies stormed forward in a single thrust, the battalioner in front firing from the hip like all his men, sweeping them along until the Russian positions had been overrun and knocked off the road. We followed, immediately securing the flanks against counterattacks by the Russians who had withdrawn into the woods. Meanwhile, the main force of the regiment flowed westwards behind us.

It was a complete success. As we marched out of the pocket, we were received with a standing ovation by a battalion of Regiment 12 that had been rushed back for support and was now resting on both sides of the road. There had been casualties on our side, among them three officers and, most painful of all, two machine gun squads that had been left by the bridge to cover our retreat and had been unable to disengage from the enemy.

It was our last fight with the Russians. We had no further orders to delay the enemy pursuit and therefore reached the Finnish/Russian border unharmed a few days later.

As I recall my time with the battalion on Russian territory, I can't think of any actions which could have tarnished our battalion's honor. It is also my firm belief that this notion is true of the other units. Like all the comrades I knew, I was proud to serve with this division. Was it only good luck? Would we have acted dishonorably if confronted with more difficult situations other than plain combat where friend and foe were clearly distinguished? I don't know. I think our sense of honor wasn't much different from the sense of honor of any normal military unit. Nor did we look down on the Russian soldier; how could we in the face of the battle of Sennozero or, for that matter, the bold encircling maneuver we had just experienced? I think the volunteers' only ambition was to excel as good soldiers. What we probably had on both sides were human beings who didn't want to die young, who loved and were loved, and who were ready to achieve something good in so far as they understood it.

Kuusamo was a place where some of that readiness became apparent.

The battalion reached the village early in the morning after it had held the Mannerheim Line, a string of fortified positions between the border and Kuusamo, for some days. From here, Regiment 12 would take over as the corps' rear guard. It was a short stay. We were to leave the same night, most likely on the road to Rovaniemi. Everywhere in the village, rear parties were busy preparing to leave or removing the rest of the equipment and goods accumulated over the years in the division's main supply base. One could feel the pressure they were under to clear out without delay.

In the late afternoon, I went with Schaper through the village looking for an opportunity to rustle some replacement parts. Passing by the church, we were struck by the sight of some engineers who were working with heavy equipment on the belfry. Slightly puzzled, Schaper turned to an NCO who stood by supervising the works, "Say, what on earth are your men up to?"

"Taking down the bells from the belfry," he said in a matter of fact way without letting his men out of his sight.

"Why is that?" Schaper asked, surprised.

"To rescue them for the time when the war is over," the NCO said. "They'll be buried in the church yard."

"Rescue them from what? From whom?" I curiously cut in. "I thought the war was over for the Finns, that they made their peace with the Soviets."

The engineer gave me a glance that made me feel stupid. "Look around you, man. Are there any Finns left in the village? They're all gone for fear of Russian occupation. They don't believe in peace. People around here got to know the Red Army. Never trusted the Russians anyway.

"If the villagers have left, are you acting on your own?" Schaper wanted to know.

"Yes, we are, on their behalf, of course. Maybe they'd have taken them down themselves if there had been time and the means. The bells are the last thing they would expect to find unharmed once the Russians left—if they were to return anyway."

We walked on, pondering over what we had just seen when, suddenly, a passing motorbike swerved around in a sharp turn and came to an abrupt halt right in front of us. An officer jumped out of the sidecar, and in that moment I recognized Mannhard's features under the *Jäger* cap.

We saluted but he hastened to stretch out his hand to us. It was a real joy to find all of us sound and healthy, and not without reason; we had last seen him going into the Sennozero Pocket, after all, while he said he had heard about the Regiment's escape from Tuhkalla. "Tell him all about it," Schaper said to me before he trudged off to continue his rustling. He let me off for half an hour.

As it turned out, Mannhard was in charge of the rear guard of the Reconnaissance Battalion and was about to leave the village. He was full of admiration for our battalioner Hansen. The Tuhkalla incident had been much talked about in Kuusamo during our stay on the Mannerheim Line. It was only now, listening to Mannhard, that I fully realized how extremely dangerous the situation had been and how much it had depended on Hansen's initiative and skill that the Regiment had been able to extricate itself from the deadly engagement.

I was eager to show him what I had seen in the churchyard, not knowing yet that he had a part in the matter. "I know, I know," he said with a flicker of amusement in his eyes, "I'm not quite uninvolved, it's one of the things that kept me here for another day."

He then told me that when he had seen all the village people clearing out he had thought of a girl he had met there, a *Lotta* from Tampere, during a three days' leave between Christmas and New Year's Day.* They fell in love, quite out of the blue, and had two wonderful days together. They went out for long walks and sat by the fire talking. One afternoon, Mannhard said, they were passing the church and heard a service in progress. The girl dragged him inside. Of the sermon he understood not a single word but he was, he said, touched by the inviting, simple interior, the hewn logs for walls and the brass chandeliers shimmering in the candle light. There was some singing, and when they left, walking by the belfry in the church yard, they enjoyed the glistening snow and the chiming bells. Soon after the girl was posted elsewhere, he hadn't heard of her since; she must have lost his field-mail number.

Now, back in Kuusamo on retreat and revisiting the church, it had struck him that the bells would be irretrievably lost if they weren't taken care of before the Russians came in. The next day, he went to see the commander of the engineers who, fortunately, was understanding, especially after Mannhard had stimulated his professional ambition by suggesting that maybe it was more to ask that he could possibly accomplish.

Lotta Svärd was a Finnish women's organization, wearing light grey uniforms and doing various kinds of service in support of the Finnish Army, not seldom within short distance of the front line. Its members were generally called "*Lottas*."

I said it was a great thing to do and that it said something about why we had been here all these years.

"Don't put too much into it," he replied. "It's one of the few things we can do for the poor people without too much effort. Who knows what we'll be forced to do to them in the future if their army won't let us withdraw in peace."

"Do you really think they'll turn against us, now that the time for our retreat has run out?"

"Well, it won't be long before we'll find out. I'm on my way to Kemi. My battalion is stationed now between Kemi and Oulu."

"How come? It's not the direct way to Norway."

"Yes, but the High Command is worried about the area down there. They think the terrain makes it likely that the Finns will build up a force for a major action against our south flank."

"You seem to be quite well informed. People like me wouldn't know about that," I remarked.

He laughed. "Come on, now! I'm just a humble, front-line officer, not much different from you. It's just a coincidence that the other day I met someone higher up who let me have a glimpse of the overall situation. He had first-hand information about the strong pressure the Russians are putting on the Finnish command to drive us out of the country. I heard some details on our contingency plan as well. It's dubbed '*BIRKE*', by the way, and he told me how important our rear guard mission will be for the southern corps of the Lapland Army"

"So, what's his judgment on the plan. Can it be done?"

"He said it's never been done before in military history, but he is confident. Much depends on how things develop in the Kemi area."

We were back at the church by now. In the meantime, they had managed to haul down the bells, which were lying on their side by the tower in the churchyard. I recall Mannhard saying as he looked up the empty belfry, "I hope I'll return to this place with the girl one day. The two bells, buried in the ground, are my token." When in that instant our eyes met for a short moment, however, both of us saw the fright in each other's eyes and the ambiguity of what he had just said.

His driver pulled up with his motorcycle and we said good-bye.

A few hours later, dusk had fallen on the village. The battalion was formed up in a square. Hansen's husky voice sounded over the place, "*Kameraden!* Tonight we are beginning a long march. It will last for months and will not end until we have reached a seaport by the Arctic Ocean.

"As you know," he continued, "Finland's capitulation has left us without choice. We have to withdraw from a country that we helped defend against Bolshevism, our common enemy. Finland's eastern border stretches over more than a thousand kilometers. It couldn't have been defended without us. Against all odds, dictated by climate and geography and unequal human resources, we have prevailed. And if the Finns are to continue to exist as a free nation, they will do so because of our joint efforts over the past three years. So, although we are withdrawing, we are leaving this country not in disgrace but with pride in what we have accomplished.

"All of you know the Finns are obliged by the armistice to use military force against German troops still on their soil after the 15th of September. We don't know what the Finns will eventually do. I can't imagine our former brothers in arms turning against us in combat, but for precaution's sake, the Army will act is if operating in a hostile country. So, I call on you. If they should decide to attack, they'll find us ready.

"The Army High Command has decided that our two *Jäger* regiments will cover the army's southern flank; at first we'll be with Combat Group East and then, later on and further up, we'll be the Army's sole rear guard. We can be proud of the mission with which we are entrusted. And we are well prepared. With our mountain artillery and our 2-cm anti-aircraft guns, our firepower is enormous. We have had a foretaste of what any delay, by order or by negligence, can mean. I'm determined not to let that happen again. I'm determined to bring us safely back home.

"I know I can rely on you—on your courage and on your tenacity, on your experience as old Karelian hands, on your faith, and on your loyalty. Therefore, I know we can do it."

He saluted and the battalion responded with a thunderous cheer.

As he left, the companies stood at attention, the front ranks of the three blocks meticulously aligned, all ready to march. In the rear, only the mules were stirring and pawing under their load of the wicker baskets and the heavy weapons strapped to their backs. It was almost dark. Only a narrow strip of pale yellow light remained in the sky above the horizon against which the black contours of the surrounding firs stood out. Some sharp commands were given and then, by and by, a picture unfolded that we would see in endless repetition over the next months: the sequence of our companies departing in mountain order, *Jäger* with their light weapons in single file, followed by the mules packed with heavy arms and ammunition, then the train with their equipment loaded on carts and drawn by more pack animals, followed again by another file of *Jäger*, and so forth.

After we had marched for about an hour, I caught up with Heinrich. We hadn't seen much of each other since I had returned from the hospital, and now I was glad to have him to talk to. I was curious to know his opinion about Hansen's speech, "I thought it was a bright spot, uncertain as our prospects were in general. What do you say?"

"A fine speech; but a bright spot? I don't know. Can't see it that way. Have you by chance any idea of the distance to the next port by the Arctic Ocean? Eight or nine hundred kilometers. Or maybe a thousand if detours are necessary. And with every step, we'll be getting further away from where we actually want to go. And what do you think the Finns will do? You really share the battalioner's opinion?"

"How should I know? I would expect them to reckon that the less they disturb our withdrawal, the better for both sides."

"Wishful thinking, I'm afraid. It's rumored that the Finnish units are now being supervised by Russian commissars. So, imagine the Finns, being under that pressure, using their *motti* tactics against us!* For that's what the Russians want them to do. The Finns certainly know their way around better than we do."

I left the implied question unanswered. After a while Heinrich continued, even more gloomy, "It'll be snowing before long. And before you know it, we'll be in heavy frost. Soon, you'll be without a roof over your head, no village as far as we can march in one day, no huts, no nothing in this forlorn country the farther we go north. And the Finns will always be close on our heels."

"Come on, Heinrich! Next you'll fancy them rushing from the woods and cutting down the exhausted remnants of the Lapland Army like the Cossacks who beat up the remnants of Napoleon's Army in the winter of 1813. I don't believe we are in for that sort of thing. We aren't a motley crowd of mercenaries on the run, but a disciplined unit with powerful fighting strength and good leadership. Quite a difference, I'd say."

"We'll see. I wish you were right. At least you won't deny that the test is still ahead of us. And what if we reach the Arctic Ocean? At best we'll embark on one of those troopships. And what then? I'll tell you. We'll have to make another thousand miles, or what have you, across the sea with the British Navy waiting for us where we don't expect them. And the alternative is to walk on the road—I dare not even think of it, with all the fjords and high mountains in the polar night."

"Really, I admire your knowledge of geography. One would think you'd been all around there before."

"Well, I haven't," he said flatly, "but geography always was my favorite subject at school."

"I wonder what comes next," I said, somewhat irritated.

"I'll tell you. Hansen said he'd bring us safely home. Let's cut out the 'safely' for a while; but then, what eventually will 'home' be like? Probably

Motti tactics are encircling the enemy in difficult terrain.

as soon as we'll have arrived there we'll be sent to the Eastern Front. And if we're lucky, it'll be the West. If, on the other hand, neither happens—then it's the worst case, for then the war will be lost before we get home."

"Now, really! Your pessimism comes close to undermining morale. I hope you won't be running around with that kind of talk."

"My dear Johann, I wouldn't think of talking like this to anyone else. But why should I spare you what I think is likely to come? I don't run away from it either. There must be some who are strong enough to face our prospects in less rosy colors so they won't collapse when things turn out the way I said, some who are indispensable for keeping up the troop's morale."

He looked at me, expecting a comment, but I could only offer him a nod. Our talk ended there. Silently, we marched on in the dark. The steady motion of our steps and the muffled noises of the pack animals and their equipment was somehow reassuring. He had taught me a little lesson, and I had seen that there was a hard core in him I had not sensed before. I wasn't too sure I could find the same within myself.

19

KITTILÄ

The battalion reached Kittilä late in October. Four weeks and 250 kilometers of marching were behind us. We had crossed Finland from east to west and were already far beyond the Arctic Circle.

Actually, the small village was nothing but the place of a major break on our march to the north, but in my memory it is a turning point. From then on, my own perception of the war changed. It was there that I was told of Mannhard's death and of the bitter battles between former brothers in arms down by the sea at Tornio and at Kemi earlier that month. Telling of Kittilä, therefore, is telling a tale of sadness and of doom, of broken words and dying hope.

On the day of our arrival, the division's support echelon was just about to move further north. The place was swarming with trucks, ambulances, trains, and, in particular, many wounded and medical personnel. The field hospital should have been displaced days ago, but casualties from the fighting in the south still kept coming in, delaying the hospital's departure. They said that only recently a transport had arrived which had made a detour through Swedish territory—a rumor I couldn't make sense of until later on.

I spotted Herweg, Mannhard's companion in the Reconnaissance Battalion, near the hospital. It was his plastered leg he was briskly swinging between two crutches that first caught my attention. When he passed by there was a moment of uncertainty on both sides before I recognized him and he remembered. He said he had been wounded near Tornio and had arrived with many other casualties a few days earlier when the field hospital had been removed from Rovaniemi to Kittilä. When I asked him about

Mannhard, he evaded all further questions; he had to move on, he said. It was urgent, and couldn't I come to see him in the evening in the hospital?

Since Herweg had so abruptly broken off our encounter, I was left in a state of alarm. Tornio? I remembered that name mentioned some weeks ago. A town right at the Swedish border, linked with the Swedish town of Haparanda by a bridge over the Tornio River that flows into the northern arc of the Gulf of Bothnia. It was a medic who mentioned it when we brought one of our casualties to his dressing station. It was on the day when Russian fighter planes had caught us on the *Eismeerstrasse*, the Artic Sea Road, north-west of Rovaniemi; they left a ghastly scene of wounded and dying men and animals lying in their blood on a site which only moments before had been so idyllic. As we waited for more ambulances, a medic told us that the Finns had captured one of our hospital trains at Tornio, and that fighting was going on there.

Now I recalled this information which then had caused great bitterness among us. To capture a hospital train, cut off from overseas transportation and being about to turn to a new destination in the north was the last thing we would have expected from our former brothers in arms. The action seemed quite unnecessary for any conceivable purpose. Later on, there had been more bits of information, confirming Mannhard's forebodings. Strong Finnish forces had landed at Tornio early in October and more troops were moving up from the south, using brand-new German assault guns, delivered only that summer and thrown into the battle against the Russian offensive in South Karelia. Our supply troops had been forced to abandon the area and combat troops were sent in, the Reconnaissance Battalion among them. The casualties on both sides were said to be heavy.

In our own battalion, all of us by then realized the Finnish troops had become our enemies. It had been only a matter of time before they would attack our units forming the southeastern flank of the German Army in retreat, to destroy at least its rear guard. Yet, instead of withdrawing to the west as fast as possible as we had hoped, our battalion had to suit the Army's time schedule and linger now and then in various temporary positions. Detained there, we would stare through our glasses into the woods and send out patrols to search the surrounding areas. So far, the Finns let our withdrawal remain undisturbed, but we never lost the feeling of being watched. Eventually, at Rovaniemi, we had slipped over the bridge shortly before it was blown up, passed the lines of our sister regiment, glad to leave the terrain behind where a major clash with Finnish forces was most likely to occur. Eventually, it was Regiment 12 that first crossed swords with the Finns, for them an ill-fated venture that delayed the regiment's progress for no more than half a day.

On the road to Kittilä, our battalion had increased the rate of march to gain time. It added to the strain of our daily exercise, 30 kilometers on average. True, we were traveling lightly, carrying only our rifles and submachine guns while the machine guns and the ammunition were handily strapped to the backs of mules, our faithful companions who trotted along among us. The weather had turned bad, however; it rained and we had frost overnight. The winter, however, was late that year. As yet, there was no snow on our way to Kittilä. We saw only a few hilltops wearing white caps.

Herweg was waiting for me at the entrance of the hospital. Signs of dissolution were visible everywhere. We squeezed through a narrow corridor and a small room, poorly lit by some carbide lamps and full of stretchers with wounded; in between, medical personnel, overworked but quietly efficient, were going about their duties. The somber atmosphere matched my apprehension. Herweg led me to a quiet corner to another casualty who turned his back on us and was sitting on a wooden box, reclining against the wall, smoking, his right shoulder and arm in plaster casts. The wounded man turned.

"Hey *Alte*!" What the hell are you doing here?"

"Good to see you," he said, cool as ever. "I knew you'd come; Herweg told me." He stretched out his left hand. "My arm got worse, I'm afraid," he said with a forced smile.

"I thought you were on your way home long ago," I said, sitting down on another box opposite him, while Herweg took a seat beside him.

"Well, I ain't; it's only part of the story you've come here for. I'll tell you later," he said and turned to Herweg.

Herweg took out a pack of cigarettes, offered me one, and fumbled one out for himself, very slowly and awkwardly. There was a pause while he kept staring at the ground and took long draws from his cigarette.

"What happened?" I broke the silence.

"He's dead, Voss. He fell in a raid at Tornio three weeks ago," he said in a low voice, as if trying not to hurt, "I wish I had better news."

It was as if I had known all the time. As we took long draws, our cigarettes glowed in the dark, a darkness much like our own gloom.

"It was his own idea," Herweg continued. "Of course, afterwards it's always the same question: Was it inevitable? Couldn't we have done better? I can only say, it was his way; he wanted to do it. He said to me, let's get them out of there, they are wounded, they can't help themselves. It was the wounded, the transport the Finns had captured, who were his main concern at the end."

"I take it you were with him on the raid?"

"In a way both of us were," the *Alte* cut in. "Herweg was with the patrol, and I was on the transport."

"How is that? You said the transport was captured," I said. "Come on, tell me the whole story, right from the start."

"As you probably know, we, the Reconnaissance Battalion, were stationed between Oulu and Kemi in September," Herweg began. "At the end of the month, a violent storm broke loose that lasted at least two days. Remember? It wasn't quite over yet when the Finns landed at Tornio. Over the next two days, more of them arrived and seized the town. Until then, we still had been on rather friendly terms with the Finns. As far as I know, the local commanders at Kemi arranged to keep the road and the bridges clear for our withdrawal. The fresh troops in Tornio, however, changed the situation entirely. They had already snatched all supply depots and trains and kidnapped that casualty transport of ours; no doubt they were up to a lot more monkey business. Something had to be done."

"It was a hospital train, wasn't it? We've heard about it," I put in.

"No, it wasn't," the *Alte* said. "We had already left the train and were about to start north by a convoy of our own trucks and ambulances."

"So, two days later, as part of an Army combat group, we mounted an attack to regain Tornio," Herweg continued. "It soon became a nasty fight: artillery, direct fire, and *mungos* on both sides. The Finns fiercely resisted by taking advantage of the place and firing from all the barrels they had; we, on the other hand, came down from the hills, blasting our way to the edge of the town, and from there advanced house by house. Our main target was the road to the north that had to be cleared. Slowly, over the day, we managed to take it, but our casualties were terrible.

"Orders came for us to stop, to hold our present positions, and to secure the area to the south. And right then, almost by chance, Mannhard, who was searching the area with his glasses, spotted the casualty convoy. German vehicles, mostly Red Cross, were exposed to our view through a gap in the wooded terrain. He pointed in that direction, and then I, too, saw them through my own glasses. The vehicles, about ten, were assembled in a grove on the peninsula, the Finnish beachhead. 'What do you think?' he said to me, and from that look of his I knew instantly he had already made up his mind. 'Herweg,' he said, 'pick seven men right away. Make sure all have submachine guns. Get one machine gun and some hand grenades; as soon as it's dark, we'll go get them out of there.' The way things had developed, it didn't look as if we were going to throw the Finns out of the beachhead; only a quick and determined raid could do the job of rescuing our wounded. Otherwise, they would be moved out of the area and be lost, ending up imprisoned somewhere in Siberia. 'Speed and resolution,' Mannhard said, 'is our only chance'."

Herweg lit another cigarette before he continued.

"We got permission for our operation and departed as soon as it was dark. We reached the beach unnoticed and then stole along the edge of the wooded terrain on high ground towards the peninsula. Our plan was to eliminate the Finnish sentries and, assuming the convoy was ready for departure, immediately make for the road. We were about 300 meters from the vehicles when we stopped and Mannhard went ahead for close observation. We were to follow on his flashlight signal. I watched him through my glasses, a lonely figure, first stalking, then crouching across a wide, bare stretch that extended towards the edge of the grove. Then it all happened within one or two minutes. Somehow the sentries must have heard a noise or seen him; a flare went up, exposing the dark figure on the light sand; there was some shouting, and then almost instantly they opened fire; he made a last effort, fumbling with his submachine gun when he was riddled by submachine gun bursts at close range."

"Wasn't your machine gun giving him cover?" I asked, exasperated. "That's what you were there for, weren't you?"

"No, we couldn't unless we used the convoy itself for a target." He shook his head in despair. "Really, we couldn't help it. It was only when they came forward from the vehicles and were closing in on him that our machine gun opened fire, but then it was too late."

"Then you left him there? How did you know he was dead?" I asked.

"I can assure you, he was dead right away," the *Alte* cut in. He began his own extraordinary story, "Death must have come instantly," he said. He saw it all from the moment the flare was fired and he peered out from the back of his truck. But Mannhard hadn't died in vain! Using the momentary confusion of the sentries, the *Alte* and the ones who could move about managed to regain their weapons and eliminate the guards. In no time, the transport leader, a medical doctor, had given orders for a quick escape and their vehicles thundered towards the road. From their trucks in front and in the rear— the ambulances with the seriously wounded going in between—they broke all through the general confusion, wildly firing at anyone trying to stop them. To get the transport out of the danger zone as soon as possible, their doctor steered them straight to the bridge across the river, which they managed to reach unharmed. A little later, they were safely in Haparanda on the Swedish side, complete with all their casualties, trucks, and equipment.

"What happened to Mannhard's body? Did you see what became of him?"

"No, we didn't," Herweg replied. "I'm sorry. To recover his body would have meant suicide. I'm certain the Finns gave him a decent burial."

I said that we simply had to believe that and wished Mannhard had known that his mission was fulfilled. The *Alte* continued his account. He and his comrades were received very kindly and treated generously on the other side of the border. Swedish doctors took care of them, looking after the serious cases in an exemplary manner and having them transferred to Norway by rail. The rest of the casualties were allowed to return to their units; they kept their weapons, were supplied with gasoline, and were accompanied by two Swedish doctors on their way to the north along the border. Somewhere at its lower course, they crossed the Muonio River and reached Kittilä only a few days ago.

More than an hour had passed. I had to return to my quarters. I said good-bye and good luck to the *Alte*. Herweg was seeing me out when he was approached by a medic who said that he, Herweg, was to be on the next transport that was to leave in an hour's time. So there was little opportunity for a word I wanted to have with him alone. I just learned that he and the others on the raid returned from their mission at Tornio unhurt and that he had been wounded somewhere between Tornio and Kemi some days later. The Finns, he said, had attacked Kemi with strong forces from the south and at the same time from the islands off the coast. They didn't accomplish what the Russians had wanted them to do, though, which was to cut off and destroy the German combat group in that area. Again, the fighting had been ferocious and caused heavy losses on both sides. Kemi was said to lie in ruins.

When I returned to my quarters, I found my comrades drinking cognac. They were having a great time. For once, they had a roof over their head, and tomorrow was another day of rest. I joined them eagerly, glad to be in their midst and feel their warmth. The cognac soothed my sadness and let a painful notion slowly disappear that had begun to form in my mind, that this war, as probably all wars, was having its own way, paying no heed to high principles, aims, and rules, and even less for those living by them. For this reason the best would die first.

20

MUONIO

Before I write about the events at Muonio, I must come back to Mannhard once more. The subconscious is strange. It makes us do things for some hidden purpose and in the end, lets us discover things that are full of meaning. After I wrote about Mannhard's death, I leafed through a tiny English book of Biblical passages our chaplain, in his concern about my salvation, had given me some days before. I happened to come across the verse of John:

Greater love has no man than this,
that a man lay down his life for his friends.

These words struck me at first for their mere beauty, but then I realized it was an epitaph for Mannhard. If there ever were to be a tomb for him, sometime somewhere on the shore of the Gulf of Bothnia, this verse would be a proper inscription. It would, I think, reveal the true meaning of his life and death. It might even sum up the short lives of all the other volunteers who stayed behind.

Two years earlier, by the end of October 1944, I was far from finding consolation in the words of the Bible. It was perhaps something pagan and romantic with which I tried to ease my grief over what I had heard from Herweg and the *Alte*. As we left Kittilä behind, again, a wide, triangular flight of geese, certainly the rear guard, rushed across the sky, shrill cries announcing their appearance, heading south without heed to borders and to war.

"*...und fahren wir ohne Wiederkehr,*
rauscht uns im Herbst ein Amen."*

* . . . and were we to sail without return,
in fall your rush will be for us an Amen.

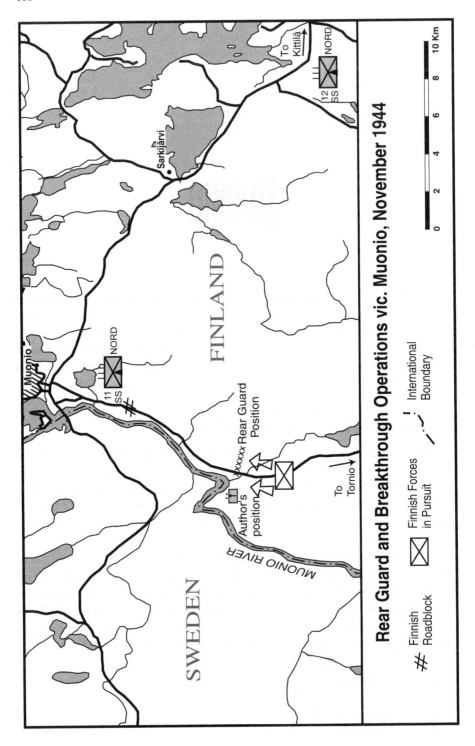

Rear Guard and Breakthrough Operations vic. Muonio, November 1944

The cryptic words of the song lingered in my mind and slowly clarified themselves as we marched on. Yes, I see, it's autumn again, and many of us were not to return from our tour to the North. "Amen!" the wings rushed and whispered, "So be it!" To the the men on the march they said, "Get on with your mission. Follow your call to duty just as we are following the call of nature."

A few days later we were back in combat.

It began some fifteen kilometers south of Muonio where we had arrived after a three-day forced march. The village is right at the Muonio River, which forms the border between Finland and Sweden. Here the road from Rovaniemi/Kittilä meets the road from Tornio, which runs all along the border to the north, from the Gulf up to the Norwegian coast. In those days, this road was our last way out of Finland, and it was full of troops on their way north. For the Finns, the junction was the last opportunity for a major operation against the German forces on their territory. For both sides, the place was of great importance.

At that time, however, I didn't have a clear picture of the general situation, which I have reconstructed only now with the help of a map. As a squad leader, I only knew that Muonio in our rear was not, for whatever reason, to be abandoned before the end of the month and that the place must be held for the few remaining days. Orders were that SS-Mountain Infantry Regiment 12 was to block the road from Kittilä against the east, while our regiment's task was to seal off the road from Tornio against the south.

Throughout the day, we had seen the last units of the combat group coming up from Kemi/Tornio and passing through our line. *Jäger* units marked by the combat stress of the recent weeks wearily marched on and mountain artillery followed with their guns disassembled and carried by mules. Once in a while, even motorized vehicles passed, and then at last a *Jäger* battalion of our own regiment, which we had relieved as rear guard. All of them would continue their march under cover of darkness toward Muonio and beyond. There were hundreds of kilometers to go.

As we built up the defensive line and moved into positions on both sides of the road, our gun crew's mission was to secure the battalion's right flank. "Right limit of fire: the Swedish border," Schaper had said, pointing to the blue line of the river on his map. To reach its bank we only had to go about one kilometer through the forest. It was a reconnaissance patrol, though, for the Finns were thought capable of infiltrating along the sides of the road even at this short a distance. We stalked through the woods in a skirmishing line. The further we advanced, the more we became alarmed. The woods literally smelled of our opponents, who seemed to have been cooking somewhere ahead of us.

Still, we arrived at the bank without enemy contact and found the hut we were looking for. We emplaced the gun there. Searching the hut we saw that someone had been around only recently. There were remains of food and some warm ashes in the fireplace, but we didn't find any traces of troops. Outside there was the river. A few meters down the embankment it murmured over the water-worn stones on its way south, about 300 meters wide and probably not very deep. And then, as we looked over to the opposite bank, an idyllic, peaceful sight presented itself against a wooded background: a small settlement, red-painted cottages with white-lined gables and windows; a few people milled around after work, seemingly unaware of us. As night fell, lights went on and made the water sparkle. "Jesus Maria! It's unbelievable. I had almost forgotten there was anything like it," Stricker said, shaking his head in incredulity.

Both of us remained on guard with the gun and listened sharply for any suspicious noises. Next to me, I saw the outlines of the gun and Stricker's profile, looking over his sight, sharply standing out against the lighter surface of the river. Again and again my eyes wandered over to the other side as the lights went out, one after another. I thought of Peter Paul and his family and of our togetherness at my grandmother's house.

The fighting started behind us. Suddenly, one kilometer behind our line, small arms fire broke out: submachine guns, hand grenades, short bursts by machine guns. At first, during a brief pause, we thought it was a false alarm, but then the shooting continued and grew more intense. So the Finns had managed to bypass us on this side of the road. Listening to the firing, we tried to imagine what the fight was like. It lasted for half an hour, the noise slowly shifting east and eventually dying out. We remained alert the rest of the night.

At dawn, Bing took over the gun. Just as I was about to have a wink of sleep, he saw them and nudged me with his arm. There, in front of us, about 150 meters away where the river formed a bend, a line of soldiers came walking toward us. They were at least a platoon, with perhaps more of them behind, reinforcements for the unit operating in our rear. Obviously, they didn't expect us here on the bank or, at least, not yet.

We lost no time in opening fire, both to keep them at a distance and to alarm the battalion. As our tracers whizzed down the bank, we saw the Finns, only shadows in my field glasses, ducking for cover and then reluctantly returning our fire. Our position was favorable. Under the cover of the hut, we had a good field of fire along the bank. We blasted away at anything we could see moving and kept them at bay. They withdrew. A reconnaissance party from the 12th Company went out, passed by our emplacement and returned half an hour later to report that the Finns had vanished and that the bank was clear.

Our skirmish had aroused the people on the Swedish side from their sleep. They had gathered on the bank, some white-helmeted soldiers with field glasses among them. Full of curiosity, they watched a spectacle which they probably wouldn't see again in a lifetime; the children were chased back to the houses by their mothers. With the enemy behind us, anything could happen now; our situation could well turn into a matter of life and death as it had down at Tornio. With the peaceful land so close by and the people looking on, though, our firefight had a distinctly histrionic touch. I was struck by the thought that since there was this audience, we shouldn't disappoint them if worse came to worst.

Actually, the situation had deteriorated. From the messenger, we learned that the Finns had ambushed our battalion's trains, in which our supplies and wounded were carried; several men and animals had been killed, more were wounded, and a Finnish battalion held a wide stretch of the road between us and Muonio.* As if that wasn't enough, a strong Finnish patrol operating in the rear had come upon our regimental command post during the night; in the ensuing short fight, our regimental commander had been killed by a sub-machine gun. Further in the distance, we could hear the rolling thunder of artillery from the northeast, the direction where we knew our sister regiment was engaged. So it was in a mood of unpleasant and rising uncertainty that we stayed in our position on the bank of the Muoniojoki.

Meanwhile the Swedes on the other side were going about their daily business.

Later that day, we returned to the roadside. Events then began to take place in quick succession. Heinrich was there with his gun squad. Immediately, our two machine guns were ordered up the road, northward to support the 13th Company. Where the road began to bend, we were to report to their company command post. The Finns, they said, had blocked the road right behind. As we were hurrying, we saw that the area on both sides of the road was packed with men from the rifle companies, alert for an assault. We passed mortar emplacements, and—with rising spirits—spotted the 2-cm quadruple flak half-track under camouflage at the edge of the wood. Stricker groaned under the weight of the MG mount on his back, but we hurried on.

We were right near the bend when suddenly, in front, the fireworks erupted. Infantry small arms started first, then Finnish mortars joined in, scattering their shells over the area. In no time, we were in the midst of a deafening battle. A motorcyclist dashed up from behind, passed by at reckless speed, and made for the bend ahead. Only then did we realize that the battalioner had been kneeling in the sidecar, about to take control over a clash that had gone off prematurely. It was a sight all of us needed in these minutes before our attack. "*Ein Mordsker!*"* Bing said admiringly, looking after him as he sped down the road without regard for the mortar shells.

We were still looking for the 13th's CP when the battalioner came rushing back, his motor bike skidding to a halt right beside us, the sidecar sharply swerving about. "Get your guns into position right over there!" he yelled to us, rising in his sidecar and pointing to the ditches on both sides of the road. "And give the quadruple flak cover as soon as she's backed up here."

We hurried over to the bend. No sooner had we mounted our gun in the ditch than the flak wagon came backing up. It moved into position right in the middle of the road. Clearly visible and elevated, it now was utterly exposed to the Finnish MGs, except for the armored shield in front of the crew. In an instant, the wagon was in a hail of tracer bullets. Now we recognized the Finnish positions from their muzzle flashes and the tracers and immediately started hammering away with our gun to keep them down. At the same time, the quadruple cannon burst into life, pouring a gush of 2-centimeter shells directly into the Finnish positions. The gunner, seated in a chair that is part of the gun carriage, easily swiveled the gun at different targets, banging away in short devastating bursts.

In front, we saw the first men of the assault group jumping up and running ahead, keeping close to the edge of the wood, firing from the hip. The battalioner turned up again, racing his motor bike down the road where the men were lying alert on both sides. I heard him yelling, "Boys, we're in for it! Come on now! Let's give them hell!" And then, in a single great thrust, the battalion broke through, the riflemen storming ahead and sweeping away all resistance they met on a stretch of more than a kilometer. We dismounted our gun from the mount, left our ditch, and ran forward with the others. We then moved laterally in support of the parties pursuing the Finns into the forest, firing at random and thus securing the way behind us for the mass of the battalion that was pushing out of its trap.

The Finns had withdrawn into the forest and up the hills to the east, while those on our side, the western side, made it to the river on the Swedish side to get out of danger. When we came to the riverbank, we saw the rest of them swimming and wading through the water. Who could blame them at this stage of the war? We let them go.

On our way toward Muonio, we passed the spot where our trains had been ambushed that morning. It was a mess. Wrecked vehicles and dead mules were still lying about on the side of the road; our wounded had been rescued; our dead had been laid on carts to be taken with us for a decent burial.

*"Daredevil"

We reached Muonio by night.

We couldn't stay there. Finnish artillery had followed up and was shelling the village. We bivouacked outside near the river, passing by our steaming field kitchens, which were waiting for us and preparing to hand out hot pea soup with bacon fat. What a feast!

The next morning we were again assigned as the rear guard and moved into a position before the first houses of the village. We were to hold the line until dark. Heinrich came over for a palaver. He met the messenger and had more news. SS-Mountain Infantry Regiment 12 had had a very similar experience—first, an attack on the regimental command post, and then their rear-guard battalion was encircled. They, too, had shot their way out of it, but their death toll on that road was high.[*]

Before Heinrich left, he said, "Come on, I'll show you something. You simply must have a look." His gun was emplaced by the road next to the village sign. "Here, look!" he said pointing to the post. What I saw were several Finnish medals nailed to the sign, while right above the word "Muonio" the words *"Das war..."* ("That was...") were crudely painted in black letters. Seeing my puzzled face he explained. It was the battalioner who had nailed up his Finnish decorations first, his officers following his example. When he had reached the spot where the Finns had ambushed our trains, he saw the wounded being rescued and the corpses of the dead mule skinners. Most of the latter had been killed with their rifles still slung across their backs, so much were they taken by surprise. The scene had driven him berserk, and now he was thinking of revenge. But what really could he do except destroy the place that was to be set on fire anyway? It ended up with a ceremonial act of revenge, grimly carried out, to soothe the mind of the officer who was deeply hurt by what he had seen and frustrated about his failure to protect his less-seasoned soldiers.

At dusk we departed. Passing through the village, we saw engineers preparing their work of destruction on what was left from the shelling. Now that the Finns had become our enemies, retreat meant also depriving them of all facilities that could serve them as a base for further actions against the rear guard. After we left the village, we didn't walk the road but slipped onto a trail leading through the wood and up the hills that rose east of the road. Rumor had it that Finnish forces of unknown strength were lying in ambush again, somewhere near the road north of us. On our way through the wood, we heard the detonations down in the village. After more climbing, our trail leveled out and we took a break. Standing on a spot high above Muonio, we had a view of the village, which was on fire. When the flames

---

[*]For a full, first-hand account of 3d Battalion, *SS*-Mountain Infantry Regiment 12's battle at Muonio, see Wolf Zoepf's *Seven Days in January*, 48–51.

would eventually go out, only the church and the town sign would be left of the village on the river.

Today, as a prisoner of war, as I recall the scene, I believe that most of us were sad, sad about what happened and sad about the broken word of our former brothers in arms. There was our high regard for Finland and its people, but there also was that breach of loyalty. We rated loyalty very high among the human virtues; it was embossed on our belt buckles: *"Meine Ehre Heisst Treue,"* or "My Honor Is My Loyalty." We also saw, however, that the Finns were caught in a conflict of loyalties. To refuse the conditions of the armistice and to stand by the Germans in loyalty at that stage of the war would have resulted in Finland's destruction as a nation, which in turn would have meant disloyalty to their country. We were untroubled by any such conflict. The unconditional surrender formula left us without an alternative. Moreover, at that time, we didn't know what we know now of the character and extent of the Jewish persecution. Had we known, our loyalty to the *Führer* would likewise have been a gross disloyalty to our country, as it was in fact for the many involved in those dark schemes.

But then, early in November 1944, there was no time for musing. What mattered was evading the next encirclement. We resumed our march to the North. A sudden gust of wind swept over us. It was damp and very cold, and it smelled of snow.

21

March Through the Polar Night

We were fast asleep, Stricker and I, and Heinrich was lying in the middle. When Heinrich stirred and turned over from his right side to his left, it was the signal for us to turn over as well, a ritual carried out several times during this night and many nights before. Despite the extreme cold outside, we felt fairly warm, closely huddled together under three layers of blankets. Each of us had his anorak underneath, its fur lining turned inside out and spread out on a layer of brushwood we had gathered and loaded onto our carts together with a supply of firewood before we left the woodland zone. Our boots were in the middle of the tent around a little stove, which was kept going overnight by the guard.

I had no idea what time it was. It couldn't be long before reveille. I only knew there would be no dawn, at least not before noon. The season for daylight was over, up here in the mountainous north of Lapland in the middle of November. Today the light would creep up the horizon only a little earlier, now that it had stopped snowing and the wind had turned. I was awake by now. Cautiously, I rose from our lair, put on my boots, slipped into my anorak, and went outside.

The cold hit me in the face and instantly caused the mucus in my nose to freeze. The wind from the northeast swept the cold over the land and cleared the sky of snow clouds. Now that the huge sky was spangled with stars of extreme brilliance, it seemed that the cold of the universe was extending its stern rule down to this place on the globe. Our tents, some twenty of them for sixteen men each, were covered with white frost. We had put them up the night before in pits that we had dug in the snow.

From the field kitchen came the clanking of utensils, a sound immediately swallowed by the snow. A man was building a fire to make coffee. I went over to him, curious about the temperature. It's 36 dgrees below zero, Celsius, he said. If he was right, this was the absolute record we had experienced to date. Farther back, I saw a head-high mass that somehow struck me as being alive. I suddenly became aware it was our mules who had been standing there all night under their white, frozen blankets, tightly huddled together in a concise circle, heads in the middle and backs exposed to the cold—motionless, not a flicker of their ears betraying that they were alive, patiently holding out in the cold darkness with endless endurance. I felt warm affection for them. Without them, we would be lost up here. They were right in calling our pack animals "Comrade Mule."

At the edge of our little camp, the dim figures of the guards could be made out against the snow covered ground, sentinels not so much against our pursuers but against the hostile wilderness. It had been nearly two weeks since we had lost contact with the Finns; in this treeless, empty vastness, they had no chance against us, and they seemed to have given up. Now the arctic winter had become the enemy both of us had to fight. It was something of a wonder that warm human bodies could be sound asleep under the thin canvas of our tents.

That night, we finished packing up all our things and loaded them on to our carts and the mules. We departed in good spirits. Ahead of us was the last stretch of our march out of Finland, some 30 kilometers. We were scheduled to pass through a new fortified position after three quarters of that distance, a barrier said to belong to the future front line of the German Army in Norway. We knew we were the last battalion on this route along the Swedish border. The mass of the division was already far ahead, perhaps, as we liked to think, already on the high seas sailing home. Only a few more days, and we, too, would reach the coast where we hoped a ship would be waiting for us. The magic word was Skibotn, a little town and seaport at the Lyngen Fjord where the road ended.

Yet, before this night was over, some greater magic was in store for us. At first, it was only an occasional flicker across the sky. But then, as we were marching on and the hours passed by, it became a yellowish light that, while growing stronger and stronger, was set in erratic motion and became more and more mixed with waves and cascades of blue and green and red. Again and again we glanced up to the sky where this dramatic spectacle was being staged overhead. It lasted for a long time. Then our column came to a halt and we had a rest. There was tea from the field kitchen and *Zwieback* (biscuit rusk). And while we were standing around the kitchen wagon sipping our tea and smoking cigarettes, we saw the lights slowly fading away and unveiling the Milky Way, Orion, the Great Bear, the brilliant cluster of the Pleiades, and all the other constellations in the dome above. Bäumer took out his harmonica and played an old folk song, one that everybody knew:

Stehn zwei Stern' am hohen Himmel, leuchten heller als der Mond,
leuchten so hell, leuchten so hell,
leuchten heller als der Mond.
Ach was wird mein Schätzel denken,
weil ich bin so weit von ihr,
weil ich bin, weil ich bin,
weil ich bin so weit von ihr.
Gerne wollt ich zu ihr gehen,
wenn der Weg so weit nicht wär,
wenn der Weg, wenn der Weg,
wenn der Weg so weit nicht wär.*

At first, we only hummed the melody, but then we sang all the verses. In that moment, our thoughts were back home. At the same time, however, we were saying farewell to that country which so many of us had grown to love and which we had defended as if it were our own, a land where we left our dead and where, perhaps, pieces of our hearts remained.

As usual, a grimmer reality soon caught up with us. We were marching along the road the way we used to, in small groups trotting in single file, our mountain caps drawn deep onto our faces, which were protected further against the icy wind by woolen scarves. In between trotted our mules with our heavier equipment and supplies carried on their backs or drawn in carts. The snow on the road had been trampled in recent days by the hundreds of boots, hooves, and wheels of the units which had already passed through, leaving the snow sometimes crumbled, sometimes hard and icy, depending on the exposure of the respective stretches to the wind. As it happened, we

*Two stars standing in the heavens,
Shining brighter than the moon,
Shining so bright, shining so bright,
Shining brighter than the moon.
Oh, what may my love be thinking,
'Cause I am so far from her,
'Cause I am, 'cause I am,
'Cause I am so far from her.
How I'd like to go to her,
If the way were not so far,
If the way, if the way,
If the way were not so far.

were in sight of the field kitchen drawn by two mules ahead of us. Now the road went into an open bend traversing a slope that rose moderately to the right and dropped steeply to the left, ending in the river. Here the road surface had turned into pure ice and inclined to the left as a result of the snowdrifts. The two kitchen wagon mules hesitated going further round the bend, but the driver, either out of negligence or certainly at the risk of his life, drove them along. Then we saw it happen: the iron-rimmed wheels began to slip on the ice, first the rear wheels, then the whole of the heavy metal body moved to the left, tearing man, mule, and cart down the slope with increasing speed, overturning and crashing down on the ice of the river, splintering and shattering to pieces. Arriving at the edge of the river we found the driver dead under the cauldron; the mules had to be shot; we rescued what was left of the rations; the rest was abandoned. We had to move on.

Nonetheless, we reached the new front line that reclined against steep mountain walls one hour ahead of schedule. We had seen the towering white range slowly emerging from the darkness as we approached from the foothills. The battalion halted across a wide expanse. Nobody seemed to know why. In the grim cold, we kept moving around in place, wondering again and again why the battalion didn't go on. After a while, word got out that the Army guards were under orders not to let us pass before twelve o'clock sharp. So, what should have been a jubilant moment resulted in an encounter with military bureaucracy that didn't care about the last battalion spending another hour waiting out there in the cold. Hadn't our battalioner driven ahead? Had he been with us, he would have forced his way through.

Thus ended our battalion's engagement in Finland.

What then began was the long march we finished two and a half months later, adding some 700 kilometers to the nearly 900 kilometers that we had walked from our positions at Sennozero. From now on we would be marching 30 to 40 kilometers each night in darkness, with only a few days of rest in between, a route paved with hardships, with hunger, with mental and physical exhaustion, with disappointments, and sometimes with despair. How did we make it? I really don't know. Of course, our youth was responsible for winning half the battle, and the awareness of being on our way home contributed to our endurance as well. In the end, I think it was our spirit, that sense of duty that allowed no weakness, and our conviction that we were doing the right thing.

Only fragments of that march have survived in my memory.

It began with our realization that there was no ship waiting for us when we came down the Skibotn valley and reached the Lyngen Fjord. Without delay we were dispatched to march on and were filtered in to the stream of troops that came from the Murmansk front, the northern sector of the Lapland

Army, and which now was flowing back on Reichsstrasse 50, the road built during the war and that, more or less, lines the northern Norwegian coast. We were to cover every single kilometer of this road from Skibotn in the north to Mo i Rana, the terminus of the railway from the south.

If it hadn't been winter at that time, otherwise magnificent scenery would have been our constant companion. It wasn't the season for sightseeing or for discovering Hamsun's *"Town of Segelvoss."* It was the time when in that region the long night was about to begin, the night that would last for one or two months, depending on the latitude. We learned, however, to distinguish between different shades of darkness, and it was usually in the twilight at noon that we got some faint idea of the place we had reached. Sometimes it would be a village we would see, a few red-painted houses by the sea, now and then some villagers, fishermen, their hands deep in their pockets, seemingly dawdling away their time and showing no interest in us intruders. Occasionally, one would come out of his house, grab some fish he had dropped days or weeks earlier on the snow nearby, and disappear behind the door. Sometimes in the evening, when we started another of our daily 30-kilometer marches and were passing by the last houses of some modest settlement, we would catch a glimpse of a family sitting behind blue-checkered curtains around their table for some modest meal, a picture we had almost forgotten and which seemed to us like paradise.

When we marched along the shore of a fjord and the weather was clear and a Navy vessel would be gliding out of the harbor, we would indulge in imaginative thoughts about life on a warship, cabins under deck that were brightly lit with warm and cozy bunks, and sailors who were clean and tidy after their daily showers. Then we would long for the town of Narvik, which we believed to be the final destination of our march and where we were sure we would embark on a ship bound for home.

Most of the time, however, there was fog and snow and frost in addition to the darkness. The road didn't always skirt along the coast, either. I think it was between Balsfjord and Narvik that we traversed a mountain range for three days. The weather was bad, and when we started on our second day it got worse. We had entered the long valley the day before. Our destination for this night was a camp on the pass. It was snowing from the outset and within an hour or two we were in the middle of a blizzard. The road wound uphill and would have been a strain even in fine weather; but now we had to make it against the white squalls, where it was even hard to see the men in front of you. The mules, though, were a solace and relief, relentlessly pulling through the flurry, trotting uphill with their heads eagerly nodding with every pace while we would, from time to time, grab their manes for guidance and support, which they didn't mind.

As the hours of that night went by, our stops became more frequent as more and more snowdrifts kept blocking the road and had to be removed with shovels. Once, we had to stop to wait for a group in the rear to close up; casualties had to be looked after and needed transportation. Meanwhile, more and more squalls swept over the battalion as it struggled uphill. The road couldn't be seen anymore; the only things we could use to orient ourselves were tall poles standing up by the road and marking the route towards the pass. It was even difficult for the men in front to make out the next pole once they had reached the last.

Eventually, we became stuck in a huge bank of snow that required hours to remove by hand. It was clear to everyone by now that we were in a dangerous situation. We tried to keep warm as well as we could, waiting for orders to make camp or whatever. We were lucky, though. In all that turmoil, we heard the muffled noise of a heavy motor vehicle ahead of us. The Army post at the pass had sent out a bulldozer to meet us. Before long, the road was cleared and the battalion passed through, while the drivers in the cabs of their huge vehicles mildly responded to our grateful waves.

The station on the pass was desolate. If we had thought there would be a warm reception with steaming field kitchens, a hearty meal, and warm accommodations, we would have been utterly disappointed. What we got were straw mattresses on the cold floors of metal Nissen huts. The inner walls were thickly coated with ice. There was no opportunity to dry our clothes. The food service was negligible. We lay down cold and hungry, but lucky to have been rescued from the trap in the valley, safe from the snow and the wind howling around the hut.

After we had passed Narvik, again there was no ship in sight to take us home. The long *Jäger* columns walked the endless road as if in a trance, night after night enveloped in constant darkness, ice and snow, many of them more or less asleep, keeping track only by holding on to the mane of a mule. Some of the more unfortunate would miss a road bend and wake up in a ditch. Heinrich, for instance, was a master of the art of sleeping on the march, and more than once my somnambulist companion was guided around an obstacle by a mule or by one of us. On these nights of general numbness, nothing mattered but the one daily object: conquering the next distance lying ahead of us. Even physical pain, blisters for instance, which on departure had seemed to make further walking impossible, went unnoticed after ten kilometers.

Rations were always insufficient. Our main course at noon was mostly *"Drahtverhau"*-soup.* What could we expect, though, being mere transit guests with different Army units every different day? Somewhere between

---

*Literally: "tangled wire," a soup from dehydrated vegetables.

Narvik and Mo, we had a day of rest. Stricker and I lingered about the village where we were allured by the sweet scent of freshly baked bread from an Army bakery. Absolutely fascinated, we watched hundreds of fresh loaves loaded on to a truck closely backed up to the building. After peering into the gap of the door and conquering his pride, Stricker approached the beefy staff sergeant in charge, "Need some help?"

"All right, you paupers. Get yourself in the line over there," he said with grumpy condescendence.

Squeezing ourselves through the gap and surrounded by all those loaves of bread, we felt as though we were in *Schlaraffenland*.* Loading the truck was easy work. Half an hour later, we walked away with one whole loaf each. First we just wanted to sample it, to cut off a slice with our *puukos*, then another one and then, as it is with paupers, we didn't know how to stop and devoured the two loaves on the spot.

On me the feast had adverse effects. We moved on the same night. There was severe frost. After some hours of walking, I began to feel queasy and bowel weary. Since we formed the rear I fell behind when I had to relieve myself. I barely managed to close up when I had to relieve myself further; the distance to the rear of my march unit grew greater and greater. The night was clear, and there was no risk of getting lost. Shivering and dizzy, I eventually became too weak to catch up with our group and found myself quite alone in that forlorn stretch of land. I suddenly realized that if I didn't move on, I would probably die. So, more or less subconsciously, I walked on, tottering and shivering and constantly bullying myself, "Come on, you Arschloch, get moving! And for God's sake, don't stop!" In the end, I reached our camp with my last ounce of strength, literally on all fours.

"Where have you been? You look ghastly," Stricker said when I had found our tent and dropped on the straw.

Aside from our exhaustion, it was the general war situation that made this arctic winter even darker. The disappointment we felt when it turned out there would be no embarkation at Narvik was soon surpassed by the bad news from the fronts on the continent, by the arriving letters about the seemingly indiscriminate and unchecked bombing of our cities, and by the general scarcity of supplies. Heinrich's comments became gloomier:

"You see, it's obvious. Shipping troops down the Norwegian coast is no longer possible. Insufficient tonnage, insufficient protection. That's why we have to make it on foot. And look at our stupid running every silly kilometer around the fjords! They don't even have a little ferry to bring us across. So

---

*Schlaraffenland is a fairytale land of milk and honey, where even roasted pigeons used to fly into the open mouths of idlers.

we slouch on and on, only to find ourselves within reach of the place across the water where we started two days ago."

"Now, come on, Heinrich," I would say, "it's not that bad. First, we're mountain infantry, not the Navy. It's our job to march. It's nearly a wonder we've come so far. Remember the day we started from Kuusamo? Remember your own forebodings? I think we're quite a success."

"What do you mean, success? It's a retreat! A full-blown retreat; that's what we've accomplished. It's the same wherever you look. Look at the overall situation. Can you see anything else but retreat? You must be hallucinating," he said angrily.

"There's nothing so bad as to be without merit," I replied. "At least our front lines will be getting much shorter. That will improve our combat power. The more our fronts close in the better."

"Brilliant! Now I see! Once we are back on the continent, things will take a turn for the better. What do you think the Lapland Army can do in the circumstances? *Jäger* against panzers? It's like going for a machine gun with a crossbow."

"Ever heard of *Panzerfaust*? It's said to be a very efficient weapon for the infantry, mountain infantry included. Anyhow, cheer up! Let our leaders do the worrying. In a month's time, things may look much brighter."

This discussion was in consonance with the pattern of many a talk we had together. Actually, I didn't see things much differently, and I felt drawn to this austere, unromantic character with the long, somber face. As our trek dragged on, all of us went through a process of mental attrition. I believe it was in that December of that year that I, too, lost my illusions about the outcome of the war.

Still, our proud battalion hadn't become a gaggle of demoralized of wretches. Sometimes on our march we would even sing, though it was out of defiance rather than for the fun of it. One night, we finally made it across the Arctic Circle, this time heading south. Clear weather and the moon had set the stage for the occasion. We were in the mountains again. On both sides of the road, white peaks of the *fjells* formed the horizon.* While the first groups were passing the signpost indicating the Arctic Circle, someone in front started singing:

Jetzt kommen die lustigen Tage!
Schätzel ade, ade.
Und dass ich es Dir auch gleich sage,
es tut ja gar nicht weh.
Denn im Sommer da blüht der rote, rote Mohn,

Fjells is Norwegian for "mountains."

und ein lustiges Blut kommt überall davon.
Schätzel ade, ade.
Schätzel ade!*

The song has three verses, but it was the first one, with the merry days to come, that was repeated as often as it took the long line of the battalion to march past the sign. When our squad approached it, we recognized the battalioner standing by the post, somewhat remote, not, as we used to know him, leaning on his stick, but very erect this time, his Knight's Cross gleaming, now and then lifting his hand for a salute. Coming closer, I saw he had tears in his eyes; it may have been the cold wind that was blowing through the valley.

Two days later we reached Mo.

---

*Now then begin the merry days!
Sweetheart farewell, farewell.
And let me tell you right away,
I shan't be feeling pain.
For red, red poppies in summer bloom,
And a merry blood comes of it soon.
Sweetheart farewell, farewell.
Sweetheart farewell!

22

INTERLUDE IN DENMARK

My bunk in the hold of the troopship was the lowest of four. The space up to the next was so narrow I had to squeeze myself in to lie down. All of the bunks, rows of them, were occupied mostly by men of our battalion. Somewhere, a ventilation fan was noisily at work, competing with the chugging engine that kept everything vibrating. We were three decks down on the passage from Oslo to Denmark. It was Christmas Eve 1944.

I was chewing on an extra portion of dry bread, a gift from Heinrich, who was lying in the bunk across the aisle. Handing it over, he managed a forced smile, murmured some felicitations, and then turned away, closing his eyes. He was seasick. His emaciated face had a greenish tint that made me think of him on his deathbed.

It had been four days since the train departed from Mo to bring us down south. We were the last battalion of the division to be transported. We had been in Oslo for one day. From the train, we went directly to the delousing station and the shower baths; there, we received new underwear, haircuts, a fairly decent meal, and then we were off to the docks for embarkation. By then, the brief hours of daylight had been over. Of the city we had seen only the blackout.

In the baths, we heard that the bulk of our division had passed through two weeks before. They probably were already on leave, just in time for Christmas! We needed some luck if we were to spend the holiday in Denmark. We also learned that the Norwegian volunteers had gone home for good. There had been a military ceremony for their formal discharge. Their engagement had been restricted, from the outset, to the front in Finland.

"For Finland and the Honor of Norway" was their maxim. Their mission was fulfilled. Good luck to them. They were great comrades and deserved the ceremony.

While we were putting on our things, those of us thinking about what we had heard realized how unlimited our own commitment had been in comparison to the Norwegians. There were some sarcastic remarks: 'Yeah, the delousing station, isn't that something?' 'There's a ceremony for you!' 'How could we expect anything else?' My own feelings were confused: There certainly was some envy of our Norwegian comrades involved, but then, hadn't we had a ceremony of our own on that night at the Arctic Circle the week before which suited us better than anything? That Karelian chapter, though, was closed.

Our thoughts were not about Christmas that night aboard the ship. Our main concern was to make it safely to Denmark, for which there was no guarantee at all. If that giant sardine box of a ship were hit by a torpedo, we saw no chance of getting out on deck. To think of the panic! By the way, why were the sailors with the submachine guns posted up there around the hatches and the stairs, the black figures with their turned up collars and watch caps we had seen when we boarded the ship? They looked rather sinister.

The next morning, the weather was clear and frosty. The day promised to be fine. Happy about our safe arrival and full of anticipation, we watched our equipment being unloaded on the docks of the Danish seaport. Even the ship had a friendly look, lying there in the morning sun, as if she wanted to say, "See? I made it!" It was fun watching our mules, one after another, hanging down from a derrick, their legs sticking out from a wide-meshed net, being swung over the bulwark and nimbly eased down on the wharf. We then had to sort out our equipment, saddle the mules, and load them with our guns and ammunition, fasten the cinches and prepare for departure. This activity took us almost until noon.

Then began our march began through the town to the barracks.

We walked in single file—some 25 squads of *Jäger*, pack animals, carts, wagons, field kitchens, ambulances, and so on, but no motor vehicles. It was all performed at a route step, only the resultant irregular clatter of mountain boots and hooves sounded on the pavement. Soon we were passing a church. The bells were chiming and churchgoers were coming out—parents with their children; young blond girls; boys with ties; elderly people; ladies proudly in furs; gentlemen in black, fur-lined overcoats and bowlers. The long line of emaciated young veterans in worn-out combat gear, walking through their town, openly carrying their light and heavy weapons, led by their highly decorated commander on horseback, and looking in awe from under the peaks of their battered mountain caps at the people's immaculate appearance and the tidy peaceful surroundings must have been an awkward sight on a Christmas morning.

The contrast between us seemed to have an offensive effect on the Danes; for they averted their eyes, just as we, becoming aware of their reaction, avoided looking at them in return. So we walked on with our eyes straight ahead, trying to look indifferent to the unfamiliar surroundings. I think, on that extraordinary march, many of us recalled the battalion's combat actions of the past and were trying to maintain the pride we needed so badly in these surroundings and that we felt was so justified. Hadn't we also fought—together with other European volunteers—for Europe's freedom to celebrate Christmas? Wasn't that feast long since swept from the Soviet territories and wasn't it likely to be swept from the rest of the continent if the Bolsheviks succeeded in carrying their revolution into Germany, as they had tried before and as the Comintern hadn't stopped proclaiming ever since?

We also came through a residential area where I caught sight of a maid in black dress and white apron, taking the family dog for a walk. How long ago had it been that I had belonged to that world! In our still untarnished thinking at that time, that we were involved in a secular clash of two irreconcilable worlds, I thought this town, as it appeared to us on that morning, was a fine example of the civilized world we were defending. Yet, at the same time, it occurred to me that in the process of that struggle, aside from the sacrifices of the dead, we ourselves had become savages.

Right after Christmas, we went over to the Isle of Fyn for some rest. To us it was a veritable Garden of Eden! Under the clear sky, a lovely, even countryside under a thin cover of snow stretched as far as the eye could see, adorned by snug, red-tiled farmhouses, white fences, and occasionally a small village with a church steeple. We had all the freedom we wanted to roam the neighborhood, as long as we went in pairs and kept our weapons with us. Stricker was my companion in these days. We had discovered a farm where, on the first day, we were given cow-warm milk and thickly buttered slices of bread for which the farmer declined our offer to pay. There were two girls, both very fair, one buxom and lively, the other skinny, meek and endowed with large and gentle blue eyes; her name was Anja. Stricker, coming from a farm, eagerly offered to help with the work in the stables, quite obviously to be with the buxom girl. We spent three days there, arriving in the morning as soon as we were free and leaving in the evening. When we left on the third day, Anja and I kissed in the back of the barn; not much of a kiss, rather a shy one, perhaps something to build on the next day, which was New Year's Eve. That was the end of it, though, as on that day we were confined to our quarters while new equipment was issued—including the new MG 42 in exchange for our good old MG 34—and preparations were made for our departure.

It wasn't girls I was after during that time. I was anxious only to divert myself from a deep sadness that had been lurking in the back of my mind since we had come to that island. The mail, which we had not seen since arriving in Narvik, had been awaiting us upon our arrival. There were two letters for me. One was from Christina, who wrote about her work as a nurse in a hospital at Hannover. It was a brave letter, but the little she wrote about the air raids left me wondering whether we weren't better off in combat than our nurses were in the cities. The second letter was from my mother, a heartwarming letter in her elaborate, lively style.

At the end, she wrote that Philipp had been killed in action two months ago. His parents had been informed that he fell during his division's breakout from the encirclement at Cherkassy. The news came as a blow to me. Deep inside, I felt that Mannhard and Philipp had been my two paragons of our post-war elite and our post-war leadership. Now that they were gone, I could no longer conjure an image of a future to look forward to. It is, perhaps, only now, in recalling these days, that I realize the full meaning of this loss. It best explains, however, the void I felt and the sadness that ensued.

On New Year's Eve, I wanted to forget it all and became slightly drunk with Stricker and Heinrich. I remember us singing more and more loudly, and that at midnight Bing fired a whole box of tracer ammunition in the air with the new MG 42 he had mounted in an anti-aircraft position. We switched off the radio when we heard some Party bigshot speechifying. We wanted none of that.

The next day, we sailed for the mainland, and on 2 January we left by train for our next mission: Operation *NORDWIND*.

23

REIPERTSWEILER

The train rumbled very slowly over the bridge across the Rhine on its approach to the main station in Cologne. Despite the cold outside, Schmidtchen, our sunny comrade from that city, had opened the door of the wagon a bit to catch a glimpse of the river. In the moonless night and total blackout, however, no lights along the river banks were visible and no sparkling reflection on the water marked its course. We were staring into complete darkness. I didn't care. The river had never stirred the patriotic feelings in me that it did in others, nor could I understand its much celebrated romance. My first impression from a rail trip along the river years before had been a scenery of hills that in the monotony of their endless vineyards seemed deprived of their natural beauty. There was another crossing of the Rhine that came back to my mind—December 1939, the war being in a lull, our family was on the way to see my father over Christmas at his station near the Belgian border. This was the same setting, the same thick air of foreboding. In these first days of 1945 on the way to the Western Front, though, it was the river's historical significance that prevailed in my mind. The river had been a symbol of Germany's assertion of her western territory from the days of ancient Rome to the Napoleonic Wars and even to the present. Now the front was getting closer and the battle for the *Reich* had begun.

"Germany's 'River of Fate'," I said to Heinrich; "it prefers to stay in hiding. Just the way we are kept in the dark about our next mission."

"Well, at least we know by now that it'll be the Western Front and not the East," Heinrich said.

"That's right, and aren't we lucky? I hated the idea of being back in the East. Still, where are we going?"

"Whatever, to me, it's all the same. The East or the West, what difference does it make anyway?" Heinrich said ruefully. "We won't hold them up."

The train had now come to a halt in the main station. With the door still slightly open, we could see people hurrying about, if only in the short moments of their crossing one of the dim circles thrown on the ground from the darkened lamps above.

"Listening to you," I said, "one could think of throwing away our arms just as well. Don't you think that with one more great effort, maybe this front can be stabilized or even pushed back? Wouldn't things look quite different then?"

"Yeah, sure, just the way we stopped them on their way down from Normandy. My dear Johann, if you had taken some time to read a paper instead of ogling that Danish girl, you'd know better. This great effort of yours took place only a month ago in the Ardennes. It didn't get us far."

"Sure, I know, but the Ardennes is woodland, ill-suited for a panzer army, and there's more woodland down south. Now if all the mountain divisions coming from the North were employed in the woods, thrown into another real big thrust, it could work, don't you think so?"

"I envy your optimism," Heinrich said, ending our talk.

The train moved on and was going now slowly through the city of Cologne. Schmidtchen stood at the door. We heard him groan in his funny Cologne dialect, "Oh my God! Look! See that? I didn't know it was as bad as that!"

I went to the door and looked out. I remembered towering rear walls of the business and housing districts on both sides of the thoroughfare, but there was total emptiness now. Sometimes a ragged structure glared out from the dark flat, expanse. The city of Cologne was gone. Even in the dark we could see that much. Schmidtchen was shocked beyond words at what he saw. We stood there, not knowing what to say. As the train slowly took up speed, Schmidtchen jerked the door shut.

Some days later, we were back in combat again. Our area of operations was the Low Vosges.

We stood in a small circle, the men of my gun and Heinrich with a few of his men. We were freezing, our hands shoved deeply in the pockets of our anoraks, caps and shoulders under the hoods of our canvas sheets for protection from the sleet that swept through the forest. As always, we had dug in, but it was too cold to remain in our foxholes. We shifted and stomped our feet to keep warm. Other groups stood around, scattered over the area, the wood full of them. All three Jäger battalions of our regiment were assembled, waiting for the attack to begin early next morning. Our objective was to retake the hills that were lost by some infantry division only one day after they had moved into the positions we had held before—two hills near the village of Reipertsweiler.*

The hours in the assembly area before an attack are among the most miserable moments in a soldier's life. The thought of one's own death cannot be chased away, nor can the nagging certainty that one's own luck cannot be permanent. This waiting, I think, is the most somber experience of being up front in a war which seems endless; sooner or later, it is bound to be my turn. Death is no shared or communal experience; it is utterly individual. In those moments, one is quite alone in the middle of his comrades. No one talked, our faces were concealed in the dark; only now and then a face under the peak of a mountain cap would light up from the red glow of a cigarette.

American artillery had already claimed casualties in our ranks during the days before. In the afternoon, heavy artillery fire fell on our assembly area. It seemed as if our new enemy's resources in barrels and ammunition were without limit. From the day we disembarked from the train, the Americans kept hammering our supply and approach routes without surcease. On our march up to the front, we had seen the results: dead horses, destroyed carts, and a dead mule skinner spread-eagled in the middle of the road. Again and again, we sought shelter from bursting shells. We observed a gruesome sight when we walked a forest trail and passed a bunker: a Red Cross flag sticking out and a heap of dead bodies next to it, piled up like firewood. We'd get to know the special way of the Americans with their artillery even more cruelly during the months to come.

The Americans would not send their infantry forward until they had done their absolute utmost to destroy their enemies with awesome displays of artillery firepower, which often lasted for hours. This was a luxury which we, unfortunately, could not even hope for at this stage of the war.

Our SS-Mountain Infantry Regiment 12 had been part of Operation NORDWIND from its start on New Year's Eve. When we reached the area, the rumor was that the regiment had suffered heavy casualties in their first action at Wingen. There were wild stories of the regiment breaking through the American lines, of a great number of prisoners taken and of a deep penetration into Alsace—good news, good for our morale. The bad news, however, was that only a few days later they had had to withdraw because, somehow, the units on both flanks had lagged behind. Our sister regiment had lost too many dead, missing, and wounded. One of them had his testicles shot off, they said. It was hard to shake off all that misery as we gathered on that night

---

*The French version of this town's name—which will be found on all post-WWII maps—is "Reipertswiller." Like so many towns in Alsace and Lorraine, there are both German and French toponyms for many towns.

in the assembly area for our first encounter with the *Amis*, as we referred to the Americans.*

I had seen our new opponents only through my binoculars. On our first day in the line, we repelled a probe they had started, inflicting casualties on them. Their action hadn't ended yet when they sent their medics and an ambulance right onto the battlefield to rescue their wounded. I couldn't believe my eyes. What kind of a war was this? Nothing like that would have happened at the Eastern Front, but here, some of the rules of war seemed still to be in force, valid for both sides. In the background, I saw their officers racing around in their compact little cars—as if we were on maneuvers! This first encounter seemed to support our general feeling that these Amis couldn't be regarded as mortal enemies.

Yet, our first real clash with them was to result in one of the great ordeals we were destined to go through.

"Goddamn!" Heinrich suddenly burst out. "Why are we standing around here the whole goddamned night doing nothing, getting soaked and stiff in the knees? Come on, let's put up a tent, keep the wet out, and try to get some sleep?"

Bing and Stricker went for some brushwood to lie on while Heinrich and I buttoned four triangular canvas sheets together. Others didn't bother that much and just pitched a square sheet for two. A little later, the four of us lay down in our tent, huddling together. The comfort we gained from it was imaginary rather than real. Shivering all over, I felt the sleet trickling down from the canvas upon the moss right beside my head.

I must have slept for quite a while because it was only at dawn that I noticed that the sleet had turned to snow. Outside the woods, the white-covered terrain shimmered through the tree trunks. We removed the tent, took up our gear, and put on our white-covered helmets, ready to go. We then hung around for hours. For some reason the attack was postponed until noon.

When our artillery preparatory fire began, we rushed out and swept in a skirmishing line down the slope that lay between us and the hills beyond. The resistance was feeble; the few advanced posts were soon eliminated or overrun. The *Amis'* main force was on the wooded slopes of the hills. As soon as we arrived at the foot of one hill, the American mortars and howitzers began firing. The rifle companies continued to advance uphill and disappeared into the wood where they now met stiff resistance. All over the steep terrain more and more duels of infantry weapons flared up. Our attack grew into a fierce, uphill fight.

*For a full account of *SS*-Mountain Infantry Regiment 12's action in *NORDWIND*, see Zoepf's *Seven Days in January*. Of the 725 *SS-Gebirgsjäger* who began the mission on 1 January, just over 200 returned seven days later.

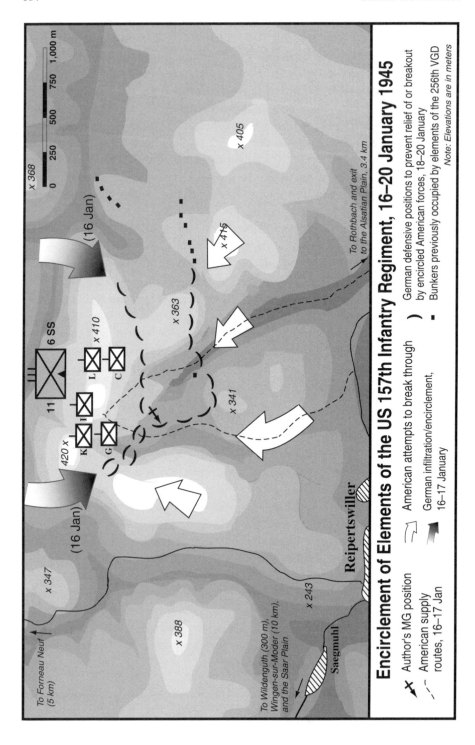

Encirclement of Elements of the US 157th Infantry Regiment, 16–20 January 1945

↗ Author's MG position

⇨ American attempts to break through

⇒ German infiltration/encirclement, 16–17 January

﹉﹉ American supply routes, 16–17 Jan

) German defensive positions to prevent relief of or breakout by encircled American forces, 18–20 January

▪ Bunkers previously occupied by elements of the 256th VGD

Note: Elevations are in meters

Reipertswiller

Saegmuhl

To Forneau Neuf (5 km)

To Wildenguth (300 m), Wingen-sur-Moder (10 km), and the Saar Plain

To Rothbach and exit to the Alsatian Plain, 3.4 km

x 347

x 388

x 243

x 420

x 410

x 363

x 341

x 405

x 415

x 368

(16 Jan)

(16 Jan)

6 SS

11

K   G   L   C

0   250   500   750   1,000 m

My squad dug in at the foot of the hill, ready for action, while Heinrich's gun was already up there on the slope. The American artillery fire was precise and brutal; the shells bursting around us tore up the white cover of snow, leaving behind large craters of brown dirt. Our comrades in the rifle companies further up in the wood bore the brunt. During pauses in the artillery firing, we listened, trying to discern their progress. In the late afternoon, it seemed our men were stuck near the hilltop. We wondered how long they could hold on up there under the continuous mortar and small arms fire from the American positions located on higher ground.

It was a relief when, finally, our artillery sent some rounds over to the enemy's positions on the hilltop; our *Nebelwerfer** joined in, their rounds whizzing overhead with a terrible hiss and rapid rate of fire. We were in a full-scale battle.

The weather worsened. The temperature fell below zero; a light blizzard slowly enveloped the battle in a muffled and weird atmosphere. Then it was our turn. We were assigned to another rifle company and climbed diagonally up the wooded hill. As it turned out, our destination was the enemy's rear. Their present front line was unknown, but it was evident that the mass of them had withdrawn towards the hilltops. So we sneaked round the combat noise while the battle raged on. It was impossible to make out whether our original assault was being continued or whether the Amis had started a counterattack and our *Jäger* were fighting it off. There was no doubt, however, that the enemy was determined to hold his ground.

Only by great luck were we spared becoming victims of our own maneuver, which was to encircle the American position on the hilltop. We were just around the hill, already stalking downward across a wide glade, when we were barely missed by one of our own *Nebelwerfer* rounds. Sent down flat into the snow by the horrible noise of the rockets, we lay there scared to death for a few seconds when the rapid sequence of rockets detonated in the glade no more than 30 meters from us.

Eventually, under cover of darkness and unnoticed by the enemy, we reached the rear of the American force—a reinforced infantry battalion as we learned later. My gun's position was on a steep forward slope, a clearing which fell down toward a trail on the bottom of a ravine leading up to a saddle between two hilltops, one of which we had passed. We emplaced our gun under a rocky outcropping and, without delay, started digging into the frozen ground.

At dawn, it stopped snowing and the temperature dropped further. For a short time, there was a lull all over the battleground. Surveying the terrain, it

*Rockets launched by five-barrelled 210mm launchers or six-barrelled 150mm launchers.

became evident to me that our slope was dominating what must be a vital supply route line to the American battalion on the hill. I searched the ravine with my binoculars. Down to the left was a small bridge; somewhere up along the trail, a detachment of our anti-tank gunners were said to be lying in ambush with *Panzerfäusten*, but I could not see them. We, it seemed, were an inconspicuous part of the snow cover spread over the hillside overnight.

Suddenly, further up the saddle, we heard the engine of a vehicle coming down fast. A dark-green tracked vehicle came into our sight as it was rumbling down from the upper end of the ravine. A big gun stuck out from a turret. Bing opened fire right away. The tracer bullets whizzed home, but they didn't do too much harm to the tank's armor. A minute or two and the thing would be right in front of us, but this wasn't to be. Some distance further up, fate caught up with it. *Whamm!* A fireball! The tank stopped cold and jerked off the road. A *Panzerfaust*, fired from the whiteness, had knocked it out. The crew piled out and our men, emerging from the snow, captured them, and that was that. We, up on the slope, were jubilant for a moment. Never before had we "Indians" seen a tank being destroyed. We also realized, however, how much we were exposed to more tanks once they managed to force their way up the ravine and were not intercepted by our anti-tank gunners in time. It wasn't long before the Americans launched their first massive action to rescue their battalion on the hilltops. They started with an artillery barrage. It was the worst I ever endured. It lasted for at least an hour and a half. Shells rained upon us like hail in a thunderstorm. There must have been tens of thousands of shells scattered over our regiment's positions. How on earth could the Americans mass such artillery in such a small sector? On our slope, we were to some extent protected by the rocks above our position, but the fire was so dense that we thought it unlikely that we would come out of there alive.

I don't know what was going on elsewhere; I only witnessed what happened within my sight. When the barrage ended, the Americans moved two anti-tank guns in. One of them appeared down at the bend of the trail, took up position, and started blasting away, apparently unharmed by our small arms fire farther down. Eventually, under the cover of gun fire, the first American infantrymen came forward round the bend, leapfrogging between the trees along the trail. We opened fire on them at a fairly great distance, more or less at random, but they forged ahead until they came under our more precise fire and were stopped not far from the bridge. There they disappeared in a hollow, seeking shelter from the fire.

After the shelling, a messenger arrived to learn about the situation. It seemed all our men on the slope had remained unhurt, certainly because we formed only a thin skirmish line, widely spread over the terrain, and because we knew how to take advantage of the cover available in a woodland like this. The messenger told us the casualties among the rifle companies were heavy, and Schaper had fallen, he said, up there at the hilltop, a direct hit, tearing him to pieces. It was only later that I felt the loss of an NCO to whom I had grown close. His good-natured features and his rolling gait as he trudged through our position at the Kiestinki front had been one of the human aspects which made me feel at home with our battalion.

Down the ravine, the American guns kept firing, and more of their infantry came forward. If this assault didn't stop, our thin circle would break and the ravine would be open for the rescue of the American battalion. Finally, some rounds of our *Nebelwerfer* came hissing and screaming right over our heads. The first clearly missed its target, the second and third must have totally knocked out the two guns and their crews. The attack collapsed soon thereafter, at least as far as we could see. The forward American squad remained invisible somewhere near the bridge, afraid to come out into the open, trapped in their shelter. We figured they had some wounded among them.

<hr/>

Behind us the battle raged on. The worst area was on the summit of the hill, where, according to a messenger, the now-encircled American battalion was being pressed back into an ever-smaller perimeter. It was obvious they were desperate to find an exit, supported by their howitzers somewhere outside which did not stop firing round after round on our positions in a fierce attempt to crush the besiegers. Listening to the continuous bursting of shells up there, I thought of Heinrich being in the midst of it. We dared not imagine the casualties among our comrades. We never had experienced such massive shelling in the North.

Sometime later on, the inferno burned out and silence descended on this tormented piece of earth. It seemed, and we direly hoped, that we had held the ground around the hills. With the tension easing off, we began to feel our exhaustion. The total lack of food, of sleep, and of protection from the cold for the last thirty hours was written all over our faces. What brought back some life into our worn-out limbs during those lulls—aside from the hope that this matter would soon be over—were the cigarettes which lasted far longer than our food. Nonetheless, there were still duties; we had to keep an eye on the trapped squad down by the bridge and, whether we liked it or not, we had to improve, deepen, and camouflage our foxholes, and fortify our gun emplacement with rocks and timber. Somehow, though, we managed brief moments of relaxation, ordinarily remaining upright in our foxholes and dropping off into a ten-second sleep.

In the afternoon, the Americans made another attempt to get through to the hilltop. It was only a matter of half an hour, but the attack told us something about our new opponents. This time, we saw them dashing up the road with two tanks, their roaring engines announcing their approach long before they appeared round the bend. The gunner of the lead tank continuously banged away with his machine gun. We had expected something like that. If they could pass the bridge unharmed, we, up on the bare slope, only had a slim chance in a duel with them. Our bullets would only scratch their armor while, in turn, they would have us at point-blank range as soon as we started firing.

The trail, however, was steep, especially downward towards the bridge, and the ground was frozen. So, as they rumbled up to the bridge the first tank spun on the ground, slid sideways and offered her right flank to our men in ambush by the bridge. The next moment, the tank was hit. Smoke poured out. The turret opened and the crew climbed out, obviously wounded, and sought cover behind the second tank. The second tank was blocked by the lead tank, and so, in turn, were our men with their *Panzerfausten*. There was a brief moment of hesitation on both sides. Then, suddenly, the turret of the second tank opened and out jumped a single man. Watching through my binoculars, I thought him to be an officer. Ignoring the danger he was exposing himself to, he hurried over to the hollow where the infantry squad was trapped, helped some wounded men to reach the tank and loaded them on the deck, one after the other. Stunned, we followed this extraordinary rescue action without firing a single shot. The officer jumped back into the tank, spun around on his tracks, and dashed back to the rear. Those of us witnessing the scene, whether nearby or more distant, instinctively felt there was no honor to be won by firing upon this death-defying act of comradeship.*

At nightfall, we still were without provisions. Hunger isn't good for morale. There was a growing grumbling among my men. Stricker pointed his chin to the trail below. "What's on your mind," I asked, being sure I was reading his thoughts.

"I think I'll have a closer look at that tank down there," he said.

"Alright, go ahead. I'll give you half an hour. Make sure you don't get shot at by our own people." Cautiously, he made his way down the hill toward the tank that had come down the day before.

*Editor's note: The officer was then-Lieutenant Colonel Felix L. Sparks, Commanding Officer of the 3d Battalion, 157th Infantry Regiment, in command of the American unit opposing the author's. Sparks (later a Brigadier General in the Colorado National Guard) was recommended by his regimental commander, Colonel Walter P. O'Brien, for the Distinguished Service Cross for this action, but was ultimately awarded the Silver Star.

He was back in time and brought a few C-Rations, cookies, and cigarettes; the first provisions we appropriated from the enemy.

My memory of the next two days is blurred, probably the result of the continuing frost, hunger, lack of sleep, and the nagging doubt all of us had about coming out of there alive. Nature, or rather the weather conditions, as well as our physical and mental state, became our primary enemy during the rest of our time on the slope. The weather worsened and the battle raged on. The Americans didn't attempt another breakthrough at our ravine, but again and again, there were nerve-racking exchanges of small-arms fire in our neighborhood, indicating assaults from inside and outside the perimeter. Meanwhile, the American artillery continued firing on our positions around the hill as, in turn, our howitzers kept shelling the summit. Snow had started to fall again, and when the wind sprang up, it turned into a blizzard that swept in gusts over the snow-bound hills. I see myself standing in the foxhole next to our emplacement—in the bottom, frozen water around my feet as I wake up with a start from a short spell of abysmal sleep—and I see Bing's and Stricker's profiles next to me, hard and grim under the rim of their helmets, their hoods on top and their anoraks covered with snow.

I'll never forget my own secret thoughts during the nights. They were about dying and surviving, promises that if I ever got out of there I would never in my life complain about anything on earth as long as there was shelter and warmth and a regular meal. I thought of becoming a farmer, which seemed to guarantee such vital needs—something which never before had entered my mind.

The American battalion gave up on the fifth day after our regiment's attack had begun. That morning, they had made a last attempt to break through, only to suffer more casualties. On that day, efforts from outside had already ceased. They surrendered in the late afternoon at the request of our regimental commander and our battalioner, who had led the fighting around the hilltop. Their losses were terrible. Of the original five companies, only about 450 went into captivity, most of them casualties. They left their positions toward our rear echelon so that, much to our regret, we had no opportunity to have a look at our gallant opponents; I am sure, though, that our comrades behind the hill were forming something of a guard of honor watching the captured GIs passing through their lines. Their officers, some twenty-five of them, were received with all honors at our regimental headquarters.* Rumor had it that all of the men were handed a box of *Schoka-Kola*

---

*Editor's Note: This was, in fact, how the Germans treated the American survivors. After interviewing over 100 participants from both sides (primarily Americans), Lieutenant Colonel Hugh Foster, US Army (Retired) has documented the extraordinary circumstances of the surrender by the American defenders and the conduct of the Gebirgsjäger of SS-Mountain Infantry Regiment 11 upon their capitulation. Not only did many of the each, a fine gesture by our commander, although I heard some grumbling that there weren't any boxes left for us.

At daylight, we had a closer look at each other. We couldn't help laughing at the five-day-old beards on our pale, emaciated faces. For me, it was a mild shock to see my comrades' utter exhaustion. How long, I asked myself, could this go on? To return, we took the shortcut over the hilltop. We walked across the center of the stage, and saw the bodies still lying about in the devastated woodland, most of them separately, some already laid in rows by their comrades; they made peculiar bundles, easily recognized even under the snow.

Battalion headquarters was just around the last bend on the road north. We passed our mule station set up in a small stand of spruce. As we trudged by, the mule skinners watched us as if we had just risen from the dead. In the rear, they said our own casualties were lower than the enemy's, but they were still heavy. Much to my relief, I found Heinrich safe and sound. His number two gunner had fallen, though, shot in the neck when they brought an American attack to a stop thirty meters from their holes, the bullet ripping up the gunner's carotid artery and killing him instantly. One of his South Tyroleans had also been killed. Moreover, I learned that another platoon leader of the 12th Company had also been killed. Later in the day, I had our medic take a look at my feet; he said I had two frostbitten toes; I was lucky.

The regiment had pushed the door wide open. The Americans were in retreat.

The very next day, we began our pursuit south, which meant stalking in skirmish lines through the hilly woodland and mopping up the area. For us, it was quite a new experience. The region had not been evacuated and we were bringing the war back to the people living there in their bleak settlements. They closed their window shutters at our approach, their faces speaking volumes. Certainly, we weren't welcome here.

In a small hamlet on our way, we met some resistance from American troops, but it was quickly broken. We found their remnants, signs of abundance as it seemed to us: cigarettes and candies. It was then that my squad picked up an American heavy machine gun, complete with tripod, cart, and

German attackers actually congratulate the stunned and exhausted Americans as they entered captivity, but they also invited them to pass through their mess line and partake of their rations. Later, the American officers were separately personally praised by Generalmajor Gerhard Franz, Commanding General of the 256th Volks-Grenadier Division (to which the author's unit had been temporarily attached during this action), and many of the prisoners—of all ranks—were praised by the same officer, standing in his staff car, as they began their march to the rear as prisoners of war. The entire battle, including its ferocious conduct and its highly unusual outcome, is being covered in great detail in a forthcoming Aberjona Press book by Colonel Foster.

ammunition. We reckoned that sooner or later the enemy would start a massive counterattack, and that we would need all the fire power we could get. So we took the "extra" equipment. Stricker was "promoted" to this gun's number two gunner.

We reached the village at the foot of the hillside by nightfall. Our advance platoon discovered that the *Amis* hadn't yet withdrawn; at least they had left a rear party there. It was a short fight. Bypassing the village lying in a deep valley, we blocked their withdrawal, seized the place, and picked up the rear party together with their equipment. There were short bursts of submachine guns from our men swarming in from all sides, vehicles with roaring engines stopped in their wild flight. No casualties on either side were reported. Loot was seized, PX goods and lots and lots of oranges—luxuries we hadn't enjoyed for years. All that greatly contributed to our rising spirits.

Mopping up the village took us another hour or so, then all was quiet again. The American main force showed no inclination to come to their comrades' help, although they couldn't have failed to notice what had happened.

We moved our gun into an emplacement south of the village, right beside our anti-tank gunners. Bing was at the gun. I noticed he had become taciturn. I knew he was Alsatian and that somewhere on the plain extending in front of us was his home.

"You must feel funny, coming home under these circumstances. Where is your home town, anyway?" I asked.

"About twenty-five kilometers from here, half the distance to Strasbourg. It's a small village," he replied quietly.

I tried to cheer him up. "Just the right distance for a bicycle ride on a Sunday afternoon."

He remained silent.

"Maybe, on a clear day, you could see it from these hills?" I prompted.

"Yeah, I guess so," he said curtly.

I saw I had missed the right tone, and I felt my own ignorance about Alsace. I knew it was borderland, taken from us under the Versailles Treaty, and in dispute between France and Germany for hundreds of years. I tried again, "It's still French territory, Alsace, isn't it?"

"That's correct."

"Is your family entirely German or Franco-Allemand?" I asked.

"We're German all right; my mother tongue is German" he confirmed.

"But you speak French fluently, don't you?"

Bing responded, exasperatedly, "You know I do."

I remembered him singing a French song in our bunker east of Kiestinki, with Bäumler accompanying him on his harmonica, something he only descended to on our firm request and when he was drunk:

Pour qu'je finisse	To put an end to
mon service	my service
au Tonquin je suis parti,	I departed for Tonquin,
à quel beau pays, mes dames,	for the beautiful country, my ladies
quel paradis des petite femmes.	what a paradise of little women.
Elles sont belles	They are beautiful
et fidèles,	and faithful,
et je suis d'venu un mari	and I became the husband
d'une petite femme du pays,	of a little women of the land
qui s'appelle Mélaolie.	called Mélaolie.
(Refrain)	
Je suis gobé d'une petite,	I'm husband of a little woman,
c'est une Ana-, c'est une Ana-,	she is an Annamite.
une Anamite	
Elle est vif, elle est charmante . . .	She is vital, she is charming . . .

I had always wondered where he had picked up that song; it was a serviceman's song, after all. After a pause he continued, "At any rate, I didn't join the *Waffen-SS* to prove I'm a German, if that is what you mean."

"No, not at all, don't get me wrong," I protested. "It's just that I'm trying to put myself in your position, fighting to win back your homeland, which actually has remained foreign."

"Foreign or not foreign—I don't think borderlines are that important. I once thought it was about Europe against Bolshevism. Then it went all wrong. Now I find myself in a kind of civil war. It's more and more confusing and drives me crazy!" he confessed, frustrated.

Surprised, I blurted, "Now, come on. Civil war! We're fighting the Americans, aren't we?"

"From my view it's not that much different. Besides, do you know who are our opponents down at Colmar?" he asked, expectantly.

"No, I don't," I confessed.

"I learned it only recently: French troops under the command of General Leclerc."

"So what?" I said, still mystified. "They aren't more than '*une quantité négligeable.*' Nothing to be afraid of."

He didn't reply for a while. When I glanced at him, he was looking over the sight of his gun, his chin resting on the butt, a far-away look in his eyes.

"I thought you knew," he said eventually. "If they got me alive, I would be shot right away for defection."

The issue was never pressed. Bing was killed two months later. He was only one of the European volunteers, the ones who set out to fight Bolshevism and in the end became victims of their idealism, either on the battlefield or in the chauvinistic pitfalls of inter-European borders. I cannot believe that their idealism is dead, their vision of some greater zone where the common interest will prevail and where borders, as Bing said, are not that important anymore.

In the morning, when our gun was relieved, we went down the village street, freezing, worn out, dog-tired, and hungry. We hadn't quite gotten over Reipertsweiler. How long had it been since we had had a solid place to sleep in? Now we were promised one: the village church. The weather was clear and frosty. On our way, we went by the kitchen that had somehow managed to follow us over night. We had coffee, genuine coffee, biscuits, and oranges, all of it part of the loot.

The church stood on a small rise. A flight of steps led to the door. Coming nearer, we saw American prisoners assembled in front. An officer and a sergeant were discussing what to do with them. As our regiment was in full motion, they couldn't be sent to the rear. Neither could they be left out in the cold on the village green after they had been there all night. Actually, the church was reserved for us. A solution of brilliant simplicity was found: both the prisoners and ourselves were to share the room on the floor. We went inside and once we settled down it so happened that the prisoners lay down right between us so that *Jäger* and GIs alternately would sleep next to each other on the wooden boards.

By now, face to face with my first American prisoners, I was wide awake. The one to the left was white and pale, the one to the right slender and of brownish complexion. I asked them questions I now find naive: Why on earth had they come over to this continent to fight us? Shouldn't we, instead, have joined our forces and fight the Russians? Wasn't it in our common interest to keep Bolshevism out? They were very shy and didn't have much to say. My English was terrible, out of practice as I was, but I also had my first awareness that English and American are two different languages.

Bing asked me politely to shut up. Soon all of us were sound asleep, at least all of us *Jäger*. One guard stood by the door, and the sun shone peacefully through the stained glass windows.

24

LAMPADEN

During the last days of February 1945, we pulled out of the sector in the Low Vosges. Our front there had served to block further attempts by the Americans to restore the territory they lost close to the German border. Operation NORDWIND had been called off because the German forces, which had attacked into eastern Lorraine and northern Alsace from the north and east on New Year's Eve, had proved too weak to exploit their initial successes. In the end, the operation had failed to accomplish its principal mission object: to win back Alsace and its capital Strasbourg, and to divide the French from the American armies.

Faced with stiff resistance in this sector and preparing for their grand spring offensive, the Americans nevertheless sought to inflict as many casualties as they could without sustaining many of their own during this static interlude. After their retreat from Reipertsweiler, the front lines had remained at a respectful distance from one another. Reconnaissance patrols operated on both sides, activities in which our patrol consisting of Heinrich, a few others, and me were rather successful, given the number of prisoners we took—Heinrich earned the Iron Cross for it, along with one week's leave. Our command knew from the prisoners that the Americans, for the time being, had no intention of resuming the offensive they had halted in mid-December. Instead, they turned on us with their artillery, intensifying their shelling week by week. Time and again we would hear of heavy casualties, especially in our rear echelon; sometimes, whole squads were wiped out when a bunker was hit by some large-caliber shell, and we would realize with bitter frustration that our own artillery, mainly because of the Allied air supremacy, was unable to strike back effectively. We ground away at our patrol activity with no major operation in sight, our fighting spirit flagging. It was high time for us to pull out.

When we turned over our positions to the unit moving in and spent some days assembling in the rear, it was inevitable that we were confronted with the grim reality of the general war situation. Back from the woods and moving along the roads in the open, we instantly saw that "Fortress Germany," as it was called in our propaganda, was a bastion without a roof, open and exposed to Allied bombers. In daylight, except in bad weather, we lay low lest the American fighter planes fall upon us like hornets. Troop movement had become practically impossible in daylight.

One day, we heard on the radio that something terrible had happened at Dresden, of some terror strike of a level and cruelty unknown until then; no details were given. Worse yet, the Red Army had entered the *Reich* and was already west of the Oder. Here on the western front, but further north, the US Army already held two bridgeheads on the east bank of the Saar and was pushing toward Saarburg.

This stage of the war, increasing in ferocity, appeared all the more frightening as apparently there was nothing we could do about it. In hindsight, one could say that it had been obvious all along how things were bound to go. Until then, though, the general thinking among us had been that our High Command was capable of organizing an effective and lasting defense line along the borders of the *Reich* and that some way to end the war could be worked out. Even if it came to the worst, our leadership would know best when to give up to avoid total disaster and the needless sacrifice of human lives. As we listened to the radio, however, we heard little more than the call on the German people to persevere, and the invocations of Providence, for that matter. Oddly enough, we weren't deaf to those appeals. Wasn't this the time for the *Waffen-SS* to show its unwavering loyalty? Yet, at the same time, there was a growing sentiment of doom and an end to hope.

It was also at that time that I learned about Christina's death. The letter I had written her from Denmark came back unopened together with a letter from a friend of hers. Christina had been killed in an air raid while on duty at her hospital in Hannover early in January. So, in the gloomy atmosphere of those days, this news came as another blow, a personal one, but, all the same, fitting into the general pattern. It hurt; the pain with all the other pains went deep into my heart.

Heinrich helped me to get over that dark hour. When I had put back the letter into the envelope, I had seen his questioning glance and told him. A while after I had left the shack to be by myself, he had followed me and appeared by my side. "I know how you feel," he said. "I know it hurts. But believe me, it'll pass."

"You know, I'm wondering what in the end will be left that is worth the sacrifices," I said, leaving out my more personal feelings. "I mean, this war isn't for its own sake. It's for keeping something dear to us, people we love, some part of our own life. Am I right? But if all these things are going to be ruined, what is all the suffering for?"

"Yes, I understand," he said sympathetically. "Don't worry, it's only a weak moment. Three weeks ago, I had my own dark hour when I got my week's leave and had no place to go because Königsberg was under siege. And there've been other dark moments before, I can assure you. I still haven't any idea of my parents' whereabouts. But we can't afford that kind of worrying. It won't make you feel better, anyway."

"How can one stop thinking what it is all for?" I protested.

"By facing the truth that things do happen to us, all sorts of things and all the time, and that there's little we can do about it." He continued, musing, "You see, in general there isn't too much you can do about the course of your life. Most things just happen to you. Having volunteered for our unit was just an exception. But the next moment you were part of the system, no more choices. So you have to put up with things as they happen and play your role, play it as well as you can. No use worrying about what you can't change."

"But you can't stop thinking."

"I didn't say you should. On the contrary, you must think to draw conclusions. If you can't change the course of events, you've got to take it."

"I don't think I can live with that."

"Oh yes, you can."

"I don't know if I want to."

"It'll make you stronger. Once you come to that conclusion, your mind will be free for more important things than worrying."

"Such as?"

"Your duty."

"Point is, I can't help thinking about what our duty is in this state of the war."

"Well, call it loyalty if you have to call it something. Have we fought in Lapland, at the Volga, and in Africa to throw away our arms the moment the enemy enters the *Reich*?"

He had spoken in a low and composed voice. What he said was another invitation to his world of stoicism in which I knew he felt at home. Besides, he was right. Hadn't we sworn to be the most faithful of the faithful? This moment was his hour. There was an air of serenity about him. Hope was no longer needed to outweigh the fear of loss.

A few nights later, we left for a new sector to the north and west. It turned out only later that the division, acting on special orders from the *Führer*'s headquarters, was to launch an attack across the Ruwer River, south of Trier. At first, our transport by truck appeared to be an aimless drive about the region rather than part of a planned operation. Driving by night and resting during the day in obscure places we, the plain soldiers, lost all orientation. We went along winding roads through wooded hill country, sometimes passing through vineyards on steep slopes high above deep river valleys, the Moselle or the Saar perhaps; we didn't know. Somehow the journey seemed to be a blunder. The forlorn villages in the hills, still inhabited, seemed to turn their backs on the troops rushing through the night, as if seeking cover against the war closing in. At last, our tour ended in a little town called Hermeskeil. From there we marched west.

The attack was set for 0400 on 7 March. We prepared as if going on a raid. We didn't take all our MGs with us and left all our heavy equipment behind. Heinrich's gun and my own were combined in one squad, Heinrich acting as gunner. Waiting for our departure time, we stood around in silence and tried to keep warm. For several days, the temperature had dropped below freezing again. A thin cover of snow was spread over the country. The night was pitch dark. You couldn't see the man next to you except for the glow of his cigarette. Suddenly, there was a stir. An officer passed near by, some words in a soft deep voice to the men he brushed with his greatcoat; there was the faint gleam of a Knight's Cross. The battalioner was on a last tour of inspection before we moved. It was good to know that he would be with us behind the American lines. For that was where we were going to operate: in the rear of the enemy's front line, south of the city of Trier.

We started in single file, clambered quickly over a footbridge our engineers had built, and then set off cross-country. I had no idea where our position was to be, nor how we were to get there. Someone somewhere ahead was supposed to know. To not to get lost in the total darkness, each one in the line was tied to the man in front of him by a rope.

First, the path ran parallel to the valley and then upwards toward our main objective: a road which ran along the ridge of the hills from north to south, a main supply route for the US Army. We walked for about one and a half hours, with many interruptions for orientation. About halfway up we walked parallel to the ridge. Then we halted. So far, we had remained undetected. The night was still. Our platoon leader appeared, groping his way along our line, and ordered us to dig in on the forward slope that fell gently down to a village. However, in our jet-black surroundings, it was impossible to make out a proper spot for our machine gun to be emplaced. We just knew that we were standing in a bare field and that the ground was frozen.

"Listen," I said, "this must be a mistake. You don't really expect us to emplace our MG on this ground? What are we supposed to do here, anyway?"

"Secure our men up on the road against the village down there," the platoon leader said. "By the way, the *Amis* have some tanks in there."

"What do you mean? You think we'll fight the tanks with my MG?"

"Don't blame me. The order is clear. We have to hold this ground until further orders. About the tanks, don't worry. The battalion has positioned an anti-tank platoon by the exit of the village; they'll take care of them with their *Ofenrohre*.* There won't be more than two or three, anyway."

"But we can't even dig in. This field is frozen hard as rock."

"We've still got far more than an hour before dawn. That should be enough. If you can't dig, tell your men to scratch themselves into the ground, no matter how, and for heaven's sake, don't make any noise."

"Why the hell don't we attack as long as it's dark and the tanks aren't out in the open?" I demanded to know, but he had already vanished into the blackness. I was desperate.

"This is going to be a fiasco," Heinrich said, scratching the surface of the ground with his spade. "It's pointless to establish an emplacement here. We should try to get out of here as soon as possible."

I told him what the platoon leader had said.

"Oh, shit! What goddamn shit!" was all he said and carried on working the ground. I went around looking after the others of our squad.

All of us feverishly worked with our spades, heedless of the noise, and managed to excavate flat hollows for cover, Heinrich and I even made a small embrasure, but still had no more than a sham of a machine gun emplacement. In between, I lost my sub-machine gun; working the ground I had laid it aside and then was unable to find it again in the pitch dark. So, in expectation of the enemy, I found myself crouching on all fours and groping for my weapon, cursing and feeling panic rise, until I finally touched the treasured piece of metal. Down in the village there was a constant noise of what must have been the idling engines of the American tanks.

Dawn came an hour later. Suddenly, behind us, some two kilometers up on the hill, there were submachine gun bursts, explosions, more small arms fire. Obviously, the battalion had its first contact with the enemy on the road. Then, at various other places, automatic weapons fire flared up, first on the right, then the left. Our artillery sent over their first rounds for support. In no time, a battle was underway behind the American lines.

On our slope and down in the village nothing moved. All of us felt the rising tension. For a moment, we cherished the hope we would still be ordered to attack the village before it was too late; we were prepared for any desperate action if only we could get off this field. This hope was not fulfilled,

*Literally: "stovepipes," the German answer the US Army bazooka. It fired a larger rocket than a *Panzerfaust*, to greater range.

however. For now, down in the village, we could hear the roar of the tanks' engines being revved up, one after another, each roar soon turning into a dark drone. There were more than two or three of them, perhaps many more. We could hear them moving about and preparing for action. All our hope now rested on the engineers and their *Ofenrohre*.

Then, in the gray light of the early morning, the Shermans slowly appeared from the near edge of our rounded slope. Our anti-tank weapons, on which all our hopes rested, remained silent. What had gone wrong down there? Were they employed elsewhere? Slowly, the tanks rolled upward: two . . . three . . .then more, six, or seven, I forget. First, we saw the lead tank with its turret open and the machine gunner opening fire on our foxholes from further down the field. The tank was still too far away from us to open fire. Then we saw American infantry in a skirmish line, cautiously taking cover behind the metal giants. Our men further down the slope had offered no resistance, or were there any? What could be done, anyway, without anti-tank weapons?

While the lead tank was slowly going on and the gunner kept firing away, Heinrich had him his sight. We couldn't take that any longer. In an act of despair, we opened fire, a couple of bursts only, no tracers. Immediately, the gunner disappeared, the lid slammed down, the machine gun pivoting awkwardly on top. The tank stopped, went on and stopped again, and so did the others. Their infantry hit the dirt. Moving forward in a somewhat oblique direction, the tank's crew now had discovered our conspicuous position. The vehicle jerked around on its tracks and came directly toward us while the others moved on, deploying in a dispersed formation. With turrets closed, the tank crews began their deadly work of eliminating each of the foxholes scattered over the field, slowly and without mercy.

The lead tank rolled ahead another length toward our emplacement, stopped, and aimed its big gun at us. Faced with the black hole of the gun's muzzle, we had just enough time, a fraction of a second, to press ourselves with all our might down into our hollow. Then the first shot was fired. It missed entirely. From that moment, though, we were silenced all the same. Just the incredible noise and concussion of the shot at such close range is something no man can take. Waiting for the second shot, head pressed to the ground, I was eye to eye with Heinrich. His complexion had turned pale white, his eyes were wide open and full of terror, just the way I must have looked to him. The second shot hit the ground right behind us but did no harm either.

A short pause. We remained tightly flattened on the bottom of our insufficient cover, completely still. The other tanks passed by and worked their way up the hill. Bing was hit and we heard his terrible wail, "My leg! My leg!"

Then the third shell went off, again meant as a direct hit. It was another miss! It was unbelievable. Were they playing cat and mouse with us? Was it a prolonged execution? A kind of torture? Whatever, we didn't reckon to get out of there alive. Next time they wouldn't miss.

Then, the Sherman's crew had another try. There was another terrible blast, lifting the ground and making our bodies jump, but this time the shot came too short, exploding directly before our embrasure, hurling our machine gun up in the air and throwing up the dirt of the embrasure down on us. It was the last shot.

All the time, I had been fully conscious of what was happening. The firing came to an end. We heard the excited voices of the infantrymen closing in from behind the Sherman. I realized it was over. Miraculously, we had survived and remained unhurt—thanks to the fidgety nerves of an American tank gunner. Slowly, with our hands up, we rose from our hollow. The infantrymen approached, slowly and nervously, constantly aiming their rifles at us. I heard Bing moaning from his hole behind me and looked back. He lay there still seeking cover, one leg strangely twisted and bleeding profusely. "Get up, Bing!" I shouted. "It's over!" But instead of putting up his hands first he grabbed his rifle with both hands, probably to prop himself up. It was a terrible mistake. The same moment, one of the GIs hurled a hand-grenade over into his hole. We hit the dirt, and the explosion followed instantly.

I was deeply shocked and still on my knees when someone jerked at my helmet, choking me violently with my chin-strap until it came off. It was my first and painful lesson as a prisoner who is not supposed to wear a helmet. Standing upright again, we were quickly searched for weapons. We looked around, and what we saw was the saddest sight we ever faced. Wherever we looked, none of our men remaining on the field was alive. Bing's body was torn apart. Stricker was dead, and so was one of our replacements. In the foxholes farther away, the men were lying motionless in the awkward positions of the dead.

For a while, we kept staring at the ghastly scene, before one of the infantrymen was ordered to take the two of us away. Our artillery had begun firing into the village. From a distance, especially up on the road, we heard the battle raging on as it would do for the next two days. For us it already was a distant affair. Stupefied, we tried to comprehend what had happened. Then they took us down the slope to the village.

When we entered the village, I saw that its name was Lampaden.

25

The Condemned

It is October again. One year has passed since I began to write my account of the volunteers under the Black Edelweiss. I believe that my narrative of their victories and their defeats, of their small joys and of their suffering, of their idealism and of their self-sacrifice, are a true picture of that brief span of their lives which is today the object of damnation and disdain. Now that my narration is finished I feel a great relief; as if, at last, I have done my duty.

Coincidentally, early this month after a ten-month trial, the International Military Tribunal has pronounced its verdict and found the *Waffen-SS*, as part of the *Allgemeine SS*, guilty of being a criminal organization. So they've done it! So, under the law of the victors, the volunteers were a gang of criminals, and their dead have died in disgrace. Even those who were in combat all the time are still held responsible for crimes that happened elsewhere behind the lines, crimes that many survivors of their combat tours find difficult to accept as fact even today. The court, however, has stated that the knowledge of the crimes was general, that the criminal program of the organization was so widely known and implied a slaughter of such a colossal extent that their criminal activities must have been widely known by those who volunteered. Such is the construct of their culpability in the findings of the IMT.

The verdict is meant to rob us of our honor, the very last value of which a defeated enemy can be deprived. "*Ehre verloren, alles verloren.*" ("Honor lost, all lost.") Unconditional surrender was not enough; humiliation had to be added to make their victory complete.

In my life as a prisoner, I am still working with Captain Herbert, and I see him daily. He hasn't commented on the tribunal's verdict up to now. I can feel his sympathy, and I am grateful for it, but I have no desire to reopen our former discussion—a discussion of no avail except for having someone listen to one's lament. I can't expect him to dispute the tribunal's judgment. For him it must be *Roma locuta, causa finita.* ("Rome has spoken, the case is closed.")

Moreover, there are, even without the captain's help, my own, if quite different, doubts that warn me against all self-righteousness. Since those mass killings and other crimes against humanity seem to be true, and since they were organized by criminals wearing our uniform, who is to be blamed first, the organization or the court? Is it, then, any wonder that the silver runes are now regarded as a symbol of all wickedness? And who can be surprised that this symbol's power proved to be the overriding force, and that an acquittal, if only for the combat troops, simply could not happen? Wasn't there a great betrayal in the first place, committed by the little man with his thick round spectacles who used to masquerade in field gray but couldn't hope ever to enjoy the respect of the combat troops? Isn't it evident by now that part of his scheme was to associate the soldiers with the vile bequest of his racial fanaticism?

Was ist aus uns geworden? ("What has become of us?")*

Have we been poisoned by the racial fanaticism of our leadership and become an active instrument of the monstrous regime? Judging by what I read in the new German papers, the public response to the verdict is approval, if not satisfaction. And what has become of our people in general? Listening to my fellow prisoners' talk, it seems that only their own individual concerns and future matter; there is at best the indifference that results from a general weariness with all the horrible revelations during months of the trial. Defeating Bolshevism, defending the Fatherland and the *Reich*— these objects of innumerable sacrifices—seem to be of no interest anymore. Was all of that only a creation of propaganda without real bearing for the common people?

Even in terms of territory, I don't know what has become of us. East Prussia, Silesia, Pomerania, and the Sudeten are provinces lost, after our fellow countrymen have been expelled from their soil, apparently forever. They are no longer even considered part of Germany. From there to the west, the Soviet reign extends far into the heartland of our country, all the way to the Harz Mountains—the homeland of the first emperors of the Holy Roman Empire—including Blessheim and much of the land of Brunswick. Is this occupation another dismemberment in the long run? What actually did the Reich mean? Was it just an episode in Germany's history as a German paper editorialized the other day? What is left after the fall of the Reich upon which

---

*From Walter Flex's *Wildgänse rauschen durch die Nacht;* see Chapt. 6, 53, and Chapt. 12, 92.

to build our common future? In the course of this war, Germany had subjected many old countries to her rule and let most of them retain their territorial identities. Is there a country left that can still be called "Germany?" I
do not know.

Our world has perished. A new world dawns, one in which our values are
utterly discredited, and we will be met with hatred or distinct reserve for our
past. Come on, I say, it's not without reason, let's face it! What counts is our
future and what we are going to do with it. That is the territory where we will
have to prove what we were really like, the territory of another probation. I
only hope we will not be denied that opportunity.

Yet there can be no release from our loyalty to our dead, from our duty to
stand up for them and to ensure that their remembrance and their honor will
remain untarnished. They, like all the others fallen in the war or murdered
through racial fanaticism, must be remembered as a solemn warning never to
let it all happen again. There is more in it that must be clarified and maintained, however. The cause for which they died may have been corrupt and
the symbols under which they fought may have been vile, but their profound
selflessness, their loyalty to their country, and their final sacrifice possess a
value of their own; it is the spirit of youth without which a nation cannot live.

Epilogue

The battle at Lampaden raged on for two more days with heavy casualties on both sides. Then the two regiments, or rather, what was left of them, fought their way back to the German lines.

Ten days later at the village of Pfaffenheck, not too far from Bitburg, on the hills between the Rhine and the Moselle, the battalion, together with most of SS-Mountain Infantry Regiment 11, perished. Tired and exhausted, devoid of heavy equipment that had run out of fuel and had to be left behind, they launched a last, desperate attack against the enemy at a bridgehead east of the Moselle. Under murderous artillery fire they withdrew uphill and dug in near the village. The next morning they were attacked from the rear. An all-around defense was organized. The American artillery relentlessly fired into their positions. Their casualties increased hour by hour. In this fight, the commander was killed, in the midst of his men.

The battle of Pfaffenheck was the regiment's last stand, a ferocious fight in which casualties on both sides were heavy. The Americans lost five tanks there and later said it was the worst they had seen in the campaign. And yet, the American Army's rush into the Reich was not stopped for longer than three days. The Regiment could not recover their dead, which amounted to nearly two hundred. The villagers buried them and later created a cemetery in a stand of birch and spruce where also the commander of our battalion was laid to rest.

The terrain in which the battle of Reipertsweiler took place and where so many soldiers found their death, now lies in a *Zone de Silence*. Its existence is a great comfort to us veterans, whatever the reasons for the zoning may have been.

The bells of Kuusamo were unearthed fifteen years later with the help of engineers who had taken part in the rescue. The village, temporarily occupied by the Russians, had been found burned to the ground on the villagers' return. The bells now serve the new church that was built after the war. The old brass chandeliers have been salvaged and are still in use.

Uncle Peter Paul went back to Sweden after the war to work in Swedish industry. He and his family became Swedish citizens, forming today's Swedish branch of the Voss family. Aunt Eda spent one and a half years in a British detention camp from where she returned undaunted rather than purified. Heinrich was turned over to the French in 1945 where he spent three years as a farm worker. He is now living in Berlin. Pete, the medic, became a doctor and left Germany to live in the United States. He met a German girl, and both founded a family of six who all became American citizens. He died some years ago.

As for myself, I was released just before Christmas 1946. On my return to Hardenberg, I found my family stranded there; my mother and my sister had left Blenheim with only a few belongings when it became known that the British were going to move out of that region and turn it over to the Russians. My father had been released from a prisoner-of-war camp in Italy. Nick had come back from hospital after having been wounded early in 1945, and my younger brother had returned, too. My grandmother had also accommodated relatives from Silesia, a refugee family of twelve, driven from their estates now taken in the possession of Poles. Together with my grandmother and my aunts, the house was crammed to the roof. I found shelter in the pavilion. Food and fuel were at a minimum; we lived on beets from the fields and chicken feed, and we stole firewood from the forest. There were no complaints in our family, neither by my parents nor by us younger ones who were full of hope and had seen worse. I strongly felt the underserved luck of having reached the age of twenty-one, and that feeling has never left me since.

I decided to continue my education, despite the four years' interruption. All provisory school-departure certificates, issued during the late war years, were declared null and void so that, for the age groups concerned, it was necessary to repeat the last year of school to qualify for university. At the Hardenberg school I wasn't welcome, though; the headmaster, who was said to have suffered under the previous regime, opined quite frankly that my release as a former member of the *Waffen-SS* was by far premature. I went there all the same, graduated and met a girl in my class, a refugee from the Baltic-Sea coast, to whom I am still happily married.

Every November on Memorial Day, veterans of the division, together with the villagers, assemble at the cemetery of Pfaffenheck to pay their respect for their fallen comrades. Detachments of the *Bundeswehr* and, sometimes, officers and veterans of the US Army attended. With the rise of the peace movement, press harassment and disturbances of the gatherings began and over the years gained momentum. Even the commanding general of the region was eager to keep up with the times, and one day declared he would no longer send his young recruits to a commemoration where *Waffen-SS* veterans were present. The general rose to higher vocations, the *Bundeswehr* eventually returned, and the media went on to other topics.

All this is looked upon by the veterans with a calm and unwavering mind.

Other Titles by The Aberjona Press

Victory Was Beyond Their Grasp: With the 272nd Volks-Grenadier Division from the Hürtgen Forest to the Heart of the Reich *by Douglas E. Nash* "While small-unit histories of World War Two's Allied forces abound, there are few counterparts that tell the story from the German side. The *Wehrmacht's* long retreat and the utter destruction of so many combat units erased the history of its fighting forces. Using a trove of recently discovered materials, Douglas Nash has pulled together the remarkable story of one German unit that was almost continuously engaged in a futile effort to stop the Allied advance across western Europe. Here is the war we rarely see—close combat from the German side. Nash has done a great service to general readers and future historians."—Ed Ruggero, author of *The First Men In: US Paratroopers and the Fight to Save D-Day* 410 pages. 25 Original Maps. 93 Photos and Drawings. Paperbound. ISBN 13: 978-0-9777563-2-2. $24.95 plus shipping

Victims, Victors: From Nazi Occupation to the Conquest of Germany as Seen by a Red Army Soldier *by Roman Kravchenko-Berezhnoy; foreword by David M. Glantz* "A remarkable document, casting light on events little understood. . . . Required reading for students of World War II and modern Russian history." —Walter Dunn, *Journal of Military History* 310 pages. 6 Maps. 22 Photos. Paperbound. ISBN 13: 978-0-9717650-6-1. $19.95 plus shipping

Sledgehammers: Strengths and Flaws of Tiger Tank Battalions in World War II *by Christopher Wilbeck* "This detailed, yet readable study, enhanced by fascinating photographs and superb maps deserves to be on every tank warfare devotee's bookshelf."—*WWII History* magazine 272 pages. 35 Original Maps. 42 Photos. Paperbound. ISBN 13: 978-0-9717650-2-3. $19.95 plus shipping

Slaughterhouse: The Handbook of the Eastern Front *by David Glantz et al.* "A virtual treasure trove of information and lore for all those who can't get enough of the personalities, equipment, unit histories, and orders of battle related to the war in which Hitler fought Stalin. . . . *Slaughterhouse* is a 'must have'." —*Armchair General* magazine 520 pages. 9 Maps. 88 Photos. Extensive 16-page bibliography. Paperbound. ISBN 13: 978-0-9717650-9-2. $29.95 plus shipping

Waffen-SS Encyclopedia *by Marc J. Rikmenspoel* "Few units arouse such intense interest as the *Waffen-SS:* love them or hate them, the *Waffen-SS* has had more books printed about them then probably any other unit. Unfortunately, some of them are more about the '*SS* cult fetish' then tangible information. Thankfully, Marc Rikmenspoel has supplied us with a one-stop reference tool worth its spot on the bookshelf."— *Broadsword Military Magazine* 300 pages. 82 Photos. Extensive 20-page bibliography. Paperbound. ISBN 13: 978-0-9717650-8-5. $19.95 plus shipping

Seven Days in January: With the 6th SS-Mountain Division in Operation NORDWIND *by Wolf T. Zoepf* "The balanced, integrated account of American and German experiences is exemplary. . . . The evolving German perception of their American foe is fascinating. . . . The maps are perfect. . . . Anyone with any interest in the European campaign will find this a compelling, valuable read."—*World War II* magazine 312 pages. Maps. Photos. Index. Paperbound. ISBN 13: 978-0-9666389-6-7. $12.95 plus shipping

Odyssey of a Philippine Scout: Fighting, Escaping, and Evading the Japanese, 1941–1944 *by Arthur Kendal Whitehead* 304 pages. 6 Maps. 20 Photos. Paperbound. ISBN 13: 978-0-9717650-4-7. $19.95 plus shipping

For more information about all our titles, including all the maps that appear in the books, please visit our website at www.aberjonapress.com

The Final Crisis: Combat in Northern Alsace, January 1945
by *Richard Engler*
"Quite remarkable. . . . Superbly researched and well written. . . . What emerges is a clear sense of just how important the individual American soldier was in winning the war in Europe and just how effectively he generally performed in combat."
—*Military Heritage* magazine
368 pages. 25 Maps. 20 pen-and-ink drawings. Index. Paperbound. ISBN 13: 978-0-9666389-1-2.
$29.95 plus shipping

The Good Soldier: From Austrian Social Democracy to Communist Captivity with a Soldier of Panzer-Grenadier Division "Grossdeutschland"
by *Alfred Novotny*
"[Novotny's] wartime experiences . . . come vividly to life. . . . [His] sharply etched memories . . . are compelling in their detail."
—*The Peoria Journal-Star*
160 pages. 62 Photos.
Paperbound. ISBN 13: 978-0-9666389-9-8.
$14.95 plus shipping

Audio CD, 6-disc set, 6.5 hours
ISBN 13: 978-0-9777563-0-8.
$29.95 plus shipping

Into the Mountains Dark: A WWII Odyssey from Harvard Crimson to Infantry Blue by *Frank Gurley*
"Yet another Aberjona Press classic. . . . A profound coming of age story of a young man's transition to manhood. Emotionally charged, meticulously edited, and expertly packaged, *Into the Mountains Dark* is a wonderful WWII memoir."
—*Military Heritage* magazine
256 pages. 7 Maps and diagrams. 40 Photos. Paperbound. ISBN 13: 978-0-9666389-4-3.
$14.95 plus shipping

Five Years, Four Fronts: The War Years of Georg Grossjohann, Major, German Army (Retired)
by *Georg Grossjohann*
"This is not an *All Quiet on the Western Front* or another *The Forgotten Soldier*. In my opinion, it is a better book."
—*The Journal of Military History*
218 pages. 28 Maps. 30 Photos. Index. Paperbound. ISBN 13: 978-0-9666389-3-6.
$14.95 plus shipping

Forthcoming

Defending Fortress Europe: The War Diary of the German 7th Army, June–August 1944
by *Mark Reardon*

Swedes at War: Willing Warriors of a Neutral Nation, 1914–1945
by *Lars Gyllenhaal and Lennart Westberg*

Shipping

Single Book (Within the US and APOs/FPOs): $4.00 for media rate shippping ($4.50 for Slaughterhouse).
Additional Books (Within the US and APOs/FPOs): $1.00 each ($1.50 each for Slaughterhouse).

For international shipping rates: Please contact us via mail, fax, email.

To order, please contact us in one of the following ways:
Toll-free telephone order line: (866) 265-9063
Fax (available 24 hours) to: (814) 623-8668
E-mail: aegis@bedford.net
Mail: Aegis Consulting Group, Inc., PO Box 629, Bedford, PA 15522

THE ABERJONA PRESS
BEDFORD, PENNSYLVANIA